THE CONTROL
OF URBAN
SCHOOLS

THE CONTROL
OF
URBAN SCHOOLS

Perspective on the Power of
Educational Reformers

JOSEPH M. CRONIN

Foreword by David Rogers

THE FREE PRESS   *New York*
Collier–Macmillan Publishers   *London*

The Free Press
A Division of The Macmillan Company
866 Third Avenue, New York, New York 10022

Collier-Macmillan Canada Ltd., Toronto, Ontario

Library of Congress Catalog Card Number: 72–78608

printing number
1   2   3   4   5   6   7   8   9   10

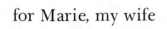

for Marie, my wife

CONTENTS

LIST OF TABLES

FOREWORD

THIS IS AN IMPORTANT BOOK that provides a much needed perspective on the present turmoil over the failures of big-city schools. Taking their governance as the central issue of his study, Cronin has pulled together for the first time an interpretive history, and he has done so for the fourteen biggest cities in the nation, drawing on case materials from previous investigations and from his own field experiences. As Cronin correctly notes, though history does not repeat itself exactly, there is much to be learned about the viability of current reform proposals—community control, for example—by looking at how school systems have evolved historically. The fact that many participants in the educational politics of big cities don't have such a perspective, lack an understanding of those politics, and are often ineffective, indicates the importance of the book.

Indeed it is depressing how little is learned in big-city school systems and other municipal agencies from past experience. Part of the problem is the nature of their situation. The pressures on top policy-makers and administrators are usually so great, and the possibility of building coalitions so limited, that their tenure is sometimes very short. This is particularly true of big-city school superintendents and some of their top staff, who often shuffle from city to city with considerable regularity. In each new job they want to make their own mark, and they often go about reinventing the wheel, disregarding the successes and failures of their predecessors. It is most important, then, that we keep taking stock of past reform efforts, in the hope of benefiting from an analysis of their successes and failures. A history of big-city school systems, accompanied by an analysis of the costs and benefits of their present operations and an assessment of various reform proposals for the future, is one of the best ways to do this. The general outlines of that history are by now well-known to most students of urban politics and are told well in Cronin's book. Big-city school systems were initially organized in the nineteenth century on a decentralized ward basis, with patronage politics determining major educational decisions. Contracts, appointments, and major budgetary decisions were made in a highly particularistic way by functionaries of the political machine. Starting in the late-nineteenth century, the municipal reform movement, led by an upper-middle and upper-class business and civic elite, including some academicians, swept much of that away and helped create centralized and supposedly "professionalized" bureaucracies, with strong superintendents and boards. Based on the ideology that centralization would bring with it many benefits—especially economies of scale, better area-wide planning, more professionalism, freedom from local patronage and parochialism, and more accountability—the development in fact turned big-city school systems into isolated islands of professional power, with New York City leading the way.

Though the pathologies of the New York City school bureaucracy were perhaps more pronounced than those of other big-city school systems (because of its size and because civil service reforms had come so early there and gone so far), some of its characteristics are in fact quite widespread. Burdened with glacier-like accretions of bureaucratic rules, mired in inertia, fragmented into power blocs internally that veto new ideas and prevent the efficient use of resources by failing to coordinate, big-city school bureaucracies like New York's have successfully prevented innovations that would have enabled them to adapt better to changing clienteles and demands. Despite their legally strong boards and superintendents, they are, in fact, quite leaderless, with their top management unable to move the power blocs to effectively implement new programs. They have inadequate auditing, monitoring, or information systems for planning, and to see if policies are in fact carried out; they protect mediocrity through archaic civil service tests that perpetuate inbreeding and often promote former teachers and principals to high administrative and staff positions for "early conformity" to bureaucratic codes, rather than for their qualifications. This situation, in turn, allows protectionist power blocs to develop within the system and solidify their baronies against client demands for change; and it makes big-city school systems and their educators accountable to nobody but themselves.

Power is thus locked up in the hands of the educators inside, who have a monopoly over definitions of professionalism and appropriate educational practice, and who had, until recently at least, the support of many powerful good government groups, especially the old business and civic elite, who gave them their power in the first place. The latter lived under the outmoded mythology that education and educators should be kept insulated from politics, as though they would be immune from developing their own. Hence, the recent interest in community control (to dilute the educators' power), in the voucher system (to break their monopoly and give parents more options), in performance contracting, and in other new proposals to open up the system. It is important to know how and why we got to this point, and Cronin does a thorough job in filling in that story.

He does more than just review that history, however. By synthesizing data on fourteen big cities, he compares the performance of elected as against appointed boards; analyzes how the structure of city government as well as cities' age and size may affect the schools; raises questions about the role of the mayor and the state in school decision-making; differentiates between the old ward politics and community control, a point that needs continued emphasis; and reviews the major reform proposals. He is generally harder on community control and the voucher system than I would have been, expressing a scepticism about their potential benefits that is shared by many educators. My reading of the history Cronin reviews suggests that such radical proposals, for all their imperfections and generality, are worth trying in order to break through the stultifying ritualism and rigidity of many big-city school systems today.

It is, of course, too early to tell which reform strategy or combination of strategies will have the most payoff in terms of improved school performance, since few have been tried. And there is always the question whether any will be implemented on any scale, given past experience. At least for the present, in a period of conservative retrenchment nationally, the educational reform movement seems to be playing itself out. There is now a new emphasis in the education literature, as Michael Katz has noted, on hereditary, genetic factors as critical for school performance, rather than on major shortcomings of the schools themselves.

This does not mean that we should abandon the task of diagnosing the present ills of inner-city schools and, more importantly, of trying to design various solutions, including a political strategy for their implementation. Even if the present political and economic climate are so limiting that such an intellectual exercise is only to indulge in pleasant fantasy, the national mood will eventually change; and we should be ready with ideas on what to do when the resources become available.

Several research questions and reform proposals are worth pursuing in that tooling up process, most of them alluded to in the book. One is the increasing acknowledgment that educational performance is itself a highly normative concept that will require much interpretation and analysis. Many reform advocates often talk past one another, partly because they are asking for different things from the schools and are not always aware of this. In addition to a concern with such traditional measures as reading scores, achievement test results, dropout rates, and the like, many critics are more concerned with such other indicators of performance as the extent of innovation and flexibility in school bureaucracies and programs; parent and student participation; the integration of schools with their communities; informal, open classrooms; competitive school systems; greater involvement of the private sector; and the like. While these other concerns are mentioned only as a means to greater pupil achievement, that aim is not always clear. Thus, arriving at a greater understanding of the goals of educational-reform advocates and taxpayer groups relative to the schools is very important. We may then be in a position to know what kinds of trade-offs among competing goals are possible.

Of particular importance relative to this is the way in which new program planning and budgeting techniques may be adapted for use in education. PPBS (Program, Planning, Budgeting System) has recently lost favor in Washington, as many federal officials found out, often the hard way, that what may have worked for the Defense Department, with its relatively clear and simple goals, does not work nearly so well in health, education, and welfare agencies. There, the goals are much more ambiguous and general, and we know much less about the forces (technology, delivery systems, staffing) that bear on program effectiveness. Nevertheless, public education is in great need of more systematic planning and program development, and efforts to adapt new management techniques to this task should go forward.

Instituting a rational system of performance appraisal should be high on such an agenda of management reforms. I am impressed with the comment of one top New York City school official that education is one of the only big businesses around that successfully blames the customer for its own bad product. Somehow, techniques have to be developed for judging the educators' performance and for basing personnel decisions on such judgment. Changes in governance, such as Cronin discusses, may well be significant, then, but they must be accompanied by major efforts to improve the delivery system of big-city schools; with quality control as an important first step. Indeed, it is difficult to separate the governance from the delivery system issue.

This becomes further evident in an analysis of three of the reform strategies that Cronin takes up, one for increasing the role of the mayor in school policy decisions, accompanied by the elimination of lay boards, such as has been discussed in New York; a second, for increasing the role of the state; and a third, for community control. All may have considerable merit and need not be mutually exclusive, but their rationale, their potential costs, and strategies for their implementation have to be spelled out in some detail.

The current State Board of Regents proposal for New York City to eliminate the lay board of education and replace it with a city commissioner of education selected by the mayor and responsible directly to him has broad national significance and is in many ways an attractive one. It would eliminate the presently divided authority between the superintendent (chancellor) and lay board and even more importantly, between top school officials and the mayor. Ultimately, the performance of the schools is closely related to many other city problems—poverty, segregation, racism, the exodus of the middle class and industry, welfare, and the city's fiscal base. Indeed, the future of the city is dependent on the improved performance of the schools. And in every major school controversy—over desegregation, community control, or collective bargaining—the buck stops at City Hall, where most of the critical negotiations ultimately take place. Since the mayor is the source of much of the schools' finances and is held accountable for their performance, this proposal to increase his presence has much merit.

Moreover, there are considerations beyond that, giving the proposal even greater credibility. In inner cities, especially, where the formal education of students cannot be separated from their many other problems, it is essential to coordinate the delivery of a wide variety of relevant social services—e.g., drug therapy, family and occupational counseling, legal aid— at one site. This site might well be the school. And yet it isn't easy to do that, given the present pattern of inter-agency relations in big cities. Big-city school bureaucracies, as creatures of the state, have often been unproductively insulated from other local agencies. One effective way to break that insularity down is to make the chief education officer a member of the mayor's cabinet, in regular contact with other agency heads. This might then provide a setting much more conducive to delivering a variety of educational and social services to students, and on a decentralized (in school) one-stop basis, than the traditional setting allows.

Mayors, of course, have traditionally shied away from such close involvement in the public schools, and Cronin documents why they will continue to do so as long as the political risks remain high. Moreover, the experience of New York's Mayor Lindsay on the community control issue remains vivid for other big-city mayors. Some even use it as an example of the perils of City Hall involvement. But the mayors' fear of such involvement may itself be functional for educational reform by encouraging them to push for greater school decentralization to put the political heat elsewhere. A reform-minded mayor might also better manage ethnic and racial conflicts around the schools by supporting the position that his city commissioner of education should have a city-wide council of designated local school board members, which would itself have substantial powers to shape school decisions.

Cronin also refers to the states as likely to play a significant role in the future in financing and governing big-city schools. This might be a good thing, especially on the financing side.

What seems required, however, for this to go well, is that state education bureaucracies be substantially upgraded. Improved salaries and a modification of rigid civil service examinations and promotional procedures would probably help a lot. Simply to increase the states' power without moving to improve their capability may not help that much, though of course increased state funds are badly needed.

At the other end of the state—local political spectrum, down at the neighborhood level, Cronin gives us a good comparative and historical perspective on community control. As I have mentioned, he is perhaps harsher on some of the assumed negative features of that movement—for example, its Anti-Semitism in the New York City situation—than I would be. Black Anti-Semitism existed around community control, but it was not nearly as widespread among ghetto blacks as many opponents of community control imply. Instead, it sometimes became a red herring that the teachers' union and supervisory groups used as a political tactic to whip up opposition to community control.

Cronin suggests at the end of the book, in reviewing the community control controversy, that a big issue is maintaining a balance between selecting educators by "merit" versus considerations of race and ethnicity. The broader issue raised in that controversy is one of defining "merit" and "professionalism" in a way that is job relevant. Long before race was an issue, various critiques of the New York City school system's testing procedures made the valid point that there was little relationship between traits and characteristics emphasized by the tests and those required to do an effective job in the classroom or as a supervisor. Given how little we know about what makes for an effective teacher or supervisor, it will be a long time before that task can be done well. But at least it should be defined as a high priority item, and we can begin to get on with it.

One of the things often lacking in the community control movement and in discussions about it is a specific statement of strategy to make it work. Even if big-city schools were under community control in the sense of power being successfully transferred from the educators to elected community boards, new resources, technologies, and curricula would still be needed. The questions of how community boards can get such resources, from whom, with what inducements, and under what organizational and political arrangements must be addressed soon. Securing various city services and more state support, as discussed above, would undoubtedly help.

I would opt strongly, at the same time, to get the resources of the private sector mobilized as well. By that I mean particularly big business, universities, foundations, voluntary associations, and even some labor unions. One need not naively assume that any of these institutions will be activated primarily by appeals to social conscience. But their economic or institutional self-interest is often involved. Large employers, for example, have vital stakes in the school system's workings and are hurt by its poor performance. Their manpower needs are not met, and they bear a big share of the tax burden for the schools. More generally, the resources of all these Establishment institutions must be turned to the task of revitalizing the public schools, and it won't be easy to devise the kinds of incentives required. However, I think it is worth the effort.

Finally, while governance and many of the other things I have mentioned are very important, there are other critical problems that must also be addressed before we can expect major improvements in big-city schools. They include, at a minimum, better teacher and administrator training; improved and more relevant curriculum and instructional methods; upgrading the quality of people going into public education; increasing their empathy for the poor, their capacity to shed ethnocentric, class, and racial perspectives and biases; and, of course, more money.

No single book can ever be expected to deal in any depth with all these complex problems. One of the important contributions this book does make is to provide historical baseline data from which we could begin to understand some of them. For that we owe Cronin a debt of thanks and the hope that he may do further historical work of this nature in the future. In the meantime, this is a valuable source book for all those interested in urban education and politics.

David Rogers
New York University

PREFACE

THIS BOOK BEGAN as an attempt to document the structures and functions of city school boards, especially the way in which they evolved in the late-nineteenth and early-twentieth centuries. What turned up was the revelation that city school boards, which critics today want to decentralize to return "power to the people," actually functioned in a very "un-centralized" fashion prior to the urban school reforms of the late 1800's.

Each city ward selected one or more representatives to run the schools, appoint the teachers and janitor, and solve local problems. Why did it end? First, the upper class and assorted professionals grew upset about the way in which the lower-class immigrant groups controlled and staffed the schools. Journalists spread stories about the patronage abuses and low standards in city schools. Educational "muckrakers" helped forge a coalition of businessmen, university professors, and urban reform groups who decided to take control of the schools away from neighborhood groups. Second, some educators saw in the widespread discontent about city schools the chance to promote the idea of a strong "professional" executive in the form of a superintendent of schools.

Reformers never agree completely and the move to restructure city school boards gave birth to a variety of experiments, including the election of a superintendent of schools and the appointment of a chief executive called director, who would then appoint the superintendent of instruction. Eventually, the superintendent of schools in each city became the

board's chief executive and leader of a central staff bureaucracy.

A popular argument for centralizing the schools and selecting a board of education on a city-wide basis was ostensibly the
removal of urban schools from politics. The issue grew to be a
moral and emotional question as legislatures, themselves heavily
rural, were asked to rescue the schools from ward-based politicians. When mayors appointed their political friends to school
boards or interfered with educational decisions, a second generation of reformers tried to sanitize further the nature of school
politics by restricting the mayor's list of board nominees.

In one sense, the reformers succeeded too well. City schools
became so insulated from politics that in the 1960's they responded with great reluctance to the claims of urban minorities
for quality, integrated education or for a share of the teaching
and administrative jobs. Several cities witnessed turbulent struggles between local community leaders and the city-wide board
and staff employees. The late 1960's and early 1970's were characterized by a swing of the pendulum back toward increased
parent or citizen participation in school decisions. At this time,
a new coalition of minority spokesmen, intellectuals, and liberal-
to-radical political leaders worked hard to re-structure urban
education so as to make it respond to current concerns.

The series of struggles and proposals to reform city school
governance ran parallel to other efforts to manage cities and
city services. Where education differed is in the extent to which
cities agreed on the need for a professional school superintendent,
whereas few cities accepted the city manager as a counterpart
for municipal services. At the same time, public school teaching
never became so fully professionalized or expert a calling as law
or medicine. Teacher unionization in recent years has complicated the discussion of how best to govern city schools. Parents
now find themselves in a new power struggle, as emotional as
the previous rounds, over whether they or their employees
will run the schools and how each other's rights will be respected.

Current proposals for urban school reform are evaluated
in the later chapters of the book along with modest predictions
and proposals for managing resources and conflicts at the appropriate levels of government. This book serves its most useful pur-

pose, however, in lending to students and critics of city schools a full century of perspective on the nature of urban school reform.

J. M. C.
Boston, Mass.

ACKNOWLEDGMENTS

THIS WORK grew out of the Stanford University School Board Studies and "Great Cities" research directed by H. Thomas James during the 1960's. Professor James visited each of the cities discussed in this volume and, struck by the stability of urban school governance forms, asked his staff to find out when and why they changed.

Warren Carson and James Kelly worked on Chicago and New York City and were especially helpful on researching the selection panel or nominating caucus ideas. Chronologies on other cities were prepared by Randall Cognetta, Walter Garms, James Guthrie, David Evans, Chester Kiser, Conrad Potter, H. Gerard Rowe, and Carolyn Wood. I worked on Boston and Cleveland and then reworked the data on all the cities as Assistant Director of School Board Studies at Stanford.

The financial support for this research came largely from the U.S. Office of Education, Cooperative Research Project #2389, a study of "The Determinants of Educational Expenditures in the Great Cities of the United States"; the Carnegie Corporation at the same time supported the study of school board selection patterns. Subsequently, my own work was supported by the Danforth Foundation and by the states of New York and Massachusetts in reviewing school governance in major cities.

Many of my colleagues at Stanford and Harvard read versions of this volume and I am grateful to Norman J. Boyan, Richard E. Gross, Robert Church, Kenneth Prewitt, Herold C. Hunt, Laurence Iannaccone, and David Tyack for their constructive comments. David Rogers offered many useful suggestions. My ideas have also been influenced by numerous discussions with William Greenbaum, Leonard Fein, Jeffrey Raffel, Frank Lutz, Luvern Cunningham, and the Danforth City School Board research teams whose work will be presented in separate volumes. Their ideas were of great assistance but in no way absolve me of my full responsibility for the ideas and interpretations presented here.

I dedicate this book to my wife, Marie, who so successfully organized the life of our large family that I was able to work in at least three states on various versions of this study.

Ward politics is the great bugbear of the city school law-makers, and any amount of inventive genius has been exercised to devise a way of choosing school boards that would make it possible for the ward boss to interfere. Incompetent principals and teachers chosen to 'encourage' the political henchman; contracts corruptly given to fatten the treasuries of partisan organizations; assessments of teachers for campaign funds; unseemly intrigues, strifes and bickering within the schools themselves by adherents of different parties; the son of some local heeler allowed to be habitually unruly . . . because the teacher fears for his position . . . all these evils and more are feared by those who have seen the results when local politics has had undue influence.

JAMES C. BOYKIN

"Organization of City School Boards," *Educational Review*, Vol. XIII (March 1897), p. 234.

The same issues are arising everywhere . . . One cannot help feeling that we are in the grip of a movement against bureaucracy and centralization—particularly where ethnic and racial divisions are involved—that in some way has to be taken into account. Thus, the association of this movement in the United States with the black and the poor . . . may conceal from many of us its real power and seriousness.

NATHAN GLAZER

"For White and Black, Community Control is the Issue," *New York Times Magazine,* April 27, 1969, pp. 345–354.

CHAPTER

* * * * * *I* * * * * *

CITY SCHOOL BOARDS
UNDER FIRE

"WHAT SHALL WE DO with our great cities? What will our great cities do with us? The whole country is affected, if indeed its character is not determined; by the condition of its great cities."

The above questions might have been posed today as the nation wrestles with the problems of urban poverty, congestion, housing, social services, and citizen unrest. Actually, the questions and statement appeared in print in 1891, at the beginning of an earlier period when the problems of the large American city were also placed high on the priority list of those who shaped and made public policy.[1]

One of the most baffling questions has been "What do we do with the schools in the great cities?" The question is not at all new. Urban school reformers of the 1890's thought they found the answer in removing the schools from city politics and streamlining city-wide boards of education.

Of course the question was much broader than one of governance alone. The most vital question in all of education remains the learning process and the adequacy of arrangements for helping children or adults learn. But this question leads to many others: Who shall decide what is worth learning? Who will evaluate learning . . . and the teaching? Who will teach . . . and where . . . for how long . . . at what wages? Who will construct the buildings, hire clerks and custodians, order the fuel and supplies? Far above the fray which is the classroom, legislatures

All footnotes appear at the end of their respective chapters.

struggle with these questions. With amazing unanimity, given the lack of federal direction of education (or even of federal support), state legislatures delegate most of the decisions to local school boards.

For more than 100 years the states have experimented with various types of city school boards, some elected by the people, some chosen by judges or by mayors and councils. Occasionally the states rearrange the format of school boards in large cities, especially when the composition of the city populace changes dramatically. Cubberley, Stanford University Dean of Education, in 1929 wrote that because of the "changing character of our municipal population . . . the great bulk of the problems of school control, which have been before us for discussion and solution during the past fifty years, have been problems relating especially to the city school district." [2] At the head of his list of problems arising from state control of city districts, Cubberley placed that of determining "the best form of organization for the board of control for the city school system; the powers and duties which should be given to such boards." [3]

The issues are as old as the study of government and political theory. Do not school board members try to appear as wise as Plato's "guardians" or philosopher-kings? The questions of "who shall rule" and "how shall they be selected?" remain important —at least to the large numbers of parents and their children who use the schools.

Traditionally, two conflicting answers appear. The first answer calls on democratic theory for the notion that the people themselves shall select the board of education. Many citizens have fought to keep board of education candidates on already long ballots, and thus remain a favorite target for those who prefer elective public governing boards.

Many professional educators remain convinced that city boards should be elected by popular vote on a non-partisan ticket for relatively long, overlapping terms [4] and that "the tendency is clearly away from appointed boards." [5]

A second answer admits to the problem of persuading outstanding citizens to run for school boards in cities and authorizes either a governor, judges, or a mayor and council to select a public school board. Advocates of an appointed board usually insist that elected officials, sometimes in consultation with other sources, must accept responsibility for the quality of school board appointees. Appointed school boards represent no more than 15 percent of all school boards in the nation, but are found in some of the larger cities.[6] Of 4,045 school systems with an enrollment of 1,200 or more that responded to a U.S. Office of Education questionnaire in 1959, 572, or 14.1 percent, have appointive boards.[7]

Of 109 school districts with an enrollment of 25,000 or more, 29, or 26.6 percent, have appointive boards.

Of the nineteen school systems with an enrollment of 100,000 or more, six, or 31.6 percent, have appointive boards.

Of the fourteen large cities to be included in this study, seven boards are appointive and seven are elective.[8]

Of the three largest city school systems—New York, Los Angeles, and Chicago—two boards are appointive and one (Los Angeles) is elective.

The larger the city, the more likely it is that the citizens have considered, adopted, or retained over time a method of appointing school board members as an alternative to popular election.

A third response accepts neither of the first two answers but raises fundamental questions about the system itself. Catholic immigrant parents and their bishops in the 1870's and 1880's objected to Protestant religious practices and viewpoints in public schools. Many cities found a second system of Catholic schools growing up side by side with the public system.[9] In recent years black parents have raised the question of alternative schools, and a number of responsible critics urge that tuition grants be given directly to families so that they may have a choice of schools for their children. Concern over the governing structure of public schools and their unresponsiveness led to the founding of new alternative schools.

But many millions of children continue to try to learn in public schools. Thousands of teachers earn a living as public school teachers. Great numbers work in fourteen city school systems, each of them members of the Great Cities Research Council for School Improvement as of 1964, when a U.S. Office of Education Study was initiated. The statistics (Table 1) underscore the very vastness of urban education.

The cities vary in total population from 500,000 to 7 mil-

Table 1 BASIC STATISTICS ON THE SIZE
OF BIG-CITY SCHOOLS

City	Public School Pupils *	Teachers
Baltimore	190,735	7,871
Boston	97,227	4,652
Buffalo	67,579	3,327
Chicago	572,427	25,403
Cleveland	145,554	5,727
Detroit	282,347	10,533
Houston	231,957	8,897
Los Angeles	648,531	24,239
Milwaukee	132,406	5,140
New York City	1,123,165	57,717
Philadelphia	284,367	13,281
Pittsburgh	68,124	3,382
San Francisco	82,864	5,070
St. Louis	108,549	3,960

* As of October 1971.
These data were obtained from reports of the Research Division of
the National Education Association.

lion, in school population from 67,000 pupils to more than 1 million. Each city operated more than 100 school buildings in the
late 1960's and employed more than 3,000 teachers; the largest
city by the early 1970's hired almost 60,000 professionals other
than teacher aides. These large-city school systems in each instance were governed by a board ranging in size from five to fifteen members. Exactly seven were elected; seven were appointed.

Few observers of the American city have tried either to document or explain this pattern. One student of municipal school
administration in 1902 noted that cities had chosen both "popular election" and "appointment" methods as acceptable, long-run
solutions. He commented that "although this practice seems to
remove direct control from the people at large, it has proven so
satisfactory that no city, so far as the writer can discover, having
adopted it, has returned to popular elections." [10]

Martindale, in a perceptive preface to Max Weber's *The
City,* discusses the breakdown of social and economic structures
due to increased specialization in urban centers and concludes
that "the selection of city officials by popular vote becomes im-

practical under these conditions," [11] at least without assistance from either "political bosses or good-government groups."

The experience of elected boards in large cities in the twentieth century indicated that Martindale's analysis has validity, that good-government groups have on occasion controlled the selection of city board members but that the control of nominations can also be assumed by political party (and/or labor) leaders. Some large cities have preferred an appointive school board and, since 1940, three boards in very large cities, Chicago, New York, and Philadelphia, used a "nominating caucus" technique to strengthen and preserve the appointment method. The experiments do not always satisfy—or even survive. In the case of New York, teachers and their supervisors joined forces in 1969 to oust the existing board and install a board of whom the majority would be elected by boroughs. The Chicago experience, espe cially earlier in the century, raises the question of whether either system really works. This volume examines attempts to make successful one or the other approach to governing urban schools and the parallel movement to shift many critical decision functions away from laymen to professionals.

PAST AND PRESENT CRITICISMS OF CITY SCHOOL BOARDS

City school boards often bear the brunt of criticism from outside observers as well as from employers and clients—the parents of children. George Counts, a critic of city schools in the 1920's, felt that school boards could not help but represent a dominant social class. His tabulation of city school board membership showed that bankers, merchants, and lawyers most often served on boards and that membership rarely included members of the working class. Counts raised the question, "Dare the schools change the social order?" But his hopes for fundamental reform were dimmed by his awareness of school board membership patterns.[12] His charges also triggered a long series of replication studies and a few attempts to show that such boards could muster enough "noblesse oblige" to establish vocational schools and other responses to the needs of the less favored classes.[13]

Public administration scholars have long advocated abolishing school boards and merging school departments with other

city agencies such as health, recreation, and other social services.
Separate status for the schools seems untidy. Rarely have schoolmen listened carefully, let alone agreed, to this principle. One exception was Charles Judd, Chairman of Education at the University of Chicago in the 1930's. The reasons he gave and the
response his stand provoked warrant a more detailed account
later in this volume. May it suffice here to note that many students of government view the separate status of school boards as
anachronistic, as untidy and really quite snobbish, selfish, and
probably unhealthy for the body politic.

During the 1950's, suburban school systems absorbed the
pressures of post-war expansion. Cities seemed relatively quiet;
many older large cities actually shrank in size between 1950 and
1960. But the immigration of southern blacks, Appalachian
Whites, and Puerto Ricans by the 1960's presented major challenges to city school systems whose forte was Americanization
more than urbanization of groups already U.S. citizens.

One set of critics charged that city school boards had allowed themselves to be swamped by the details of big-city school
board operation. A former Chicago Board of Education member,
Joseph Pois, told how an aggressive school superintendent controlled the board agendas.[14] Researchers studying the New York
City Board found "superficial participation" by board members
in some decision areas and failure to achieve policies in other
areas.[15] The Kerner Commission studying civil disorder found
that "ghetto schools often appear to be unresponsive, communication has broken down, and parents are distrustful of officials
responsible for formulating educational policy." [16]

Constructive critics offered competing ideas: parents advisory councils (Kerner Commission), community school boards
(Bundy Panel), borough school boards (Gittell), and other plans
to increase community participation and involvement in school
decisions. Uniting these critics was the notion that the school
bureaucracy was not responsive, that educators must be held accountable for failure, and that parents should have some say in
at least determining the criteria for administrators if not for their
actual selection.

Even the debate over community participation and decentralization was costly. Stephen Bailey vividly portrays the depth

of dissatisfaction with urban education that city school boards face:

> The most difficult issues will continue to emerge in the ghettos of our large cities. What do school boards say to Blacks and Latins who complain, with understandable bitterness, that they are locked by race, language, and/or poverty into residential patterns they cannot easily break; that middle-class teachers with middle-class backgrounds using middle-class materials do not know how to teach poor kids; that teacher attitudes contribute to the psychological insecurity of the child; that the whole school system is set up for the benefit of college-bound middle-class white, and is bureaucratized beyond the point where concerned parents can have any leverage? What do school boards say when the demands for decentralization and community control spread from New York to America's urban hinterland? And what if Mr. Shanker's union or militant NEA counterparts, with their own legitimate concerns, spread at the same rate of speed? The forces let loose can easily consume any central school board that happens to fall into the path of the vortex, as they consumed the New York City Board of Education in 1968–69.[17]

At the same time, other observers proposed metropolitan solutions. Critics of the status quo recognized the growing financial burdens of U.S. cities and the increasing proportion of minority-group students in city schools. Between 1950 and 1970, the minority-group population of the United States increased dramatically. By 1965, approximately one-third of the blacks in the U.S. lived in eleven of the great cities and in Washington, D.C. By the fall of 1970, the public elementary and secondary school enrollment in six of the great cities was over 50 percent black. In nine of the great cities, the proportion of all minority-group students (American Indian, Black, Oriental, and Spanish-surnamed Americans) exceeded 50 percent. In four cities—New York, Houston, San Francisco, and Chicago—Spanish-surnamed Americans made up a significant part of the public school enrollment (see Table 2). The possibility of school integration within cities grew less likely each year as the proportion of minority-group students passed the 50 percent mark.

Peter Schrag, reporting on Boston schools, quotes a 1966 finance commission recommendation urging a metropolitan school district to correct "both the racial imbalance and fiscal imbalance which now plagues Boston and hampers its education

Table 2 PERCENTAGE OF MINORITY-GROUP STUDENTS
IN BIG-CITY SCHOOLS, FALL 1970

District Name	American Indian	Black	Oriental	SSA	Total
Baltimore City	0.0	67.1	0.0	0.0	67.1
St. Louis City	0.0	65.6	0.1	0.2	65.9
Philadelphia City	0.0	60.5	0.0	3.1	63.6
Detroit City	0.1	63.8	0.2	1.4	65.5
Cleveland	0.2	57.6	0.1	1.7	59.7
Chicago City	0.2	54.8	0.7	9.8	65.4
Pittsburgh City	0.0	40.3	0.2	0.1	40.6
Buffalo Public Schools	0.7	38.5	0.1	2.3	41.7
Houston ISD	0.1	35.6	0.4	14.4	50.6
New York City Public Schools	0.1	34.5	1.5	25.7	61.7
Boston	0.1	29.8	1.7	4.2	35.9
San Francisco City Unif.	0.3	28.5	20.8	13.6	63.1
Milwaukee Public Schools	0.5	26.0	0.3	2.9	29.7
Los Angeles Unif.	0.2	24.1	3.5	21.8	49.6

Source: Directory of Public Elementary and Secondary Schools in Selected Districts, Enrollment and Staff by Racial/Ethnic Group, Fall
1970. U.S. Department of Health, Education and Welfare, Office for
Civil Rights.

efforts." [18] Another astute journalist calls city school decentralization "the desperate throwback" and argues for a Toronto style,
or two-tiered structure, of metropolitan school governance. The
concept of "metro" to Robert Bendiner includes accepting as
inevitable the application of federalism and regionalism to the
problems of urban education. Within the U.S. only a handful of
metropolitan areas, mostly in the South—Miami (Dade County)
and Nashville (Davidson County)—accept this approach. Saint
Louis, Cleveland, Philadelphia, and Milwaukee citizens have so
far shown more apprehension than enthusiasm. But Bendiner
views metro as part of "the large and more desperate need to
save our cities" [19] as well as a solution to school problems and the
salvation of school boards.

The Roman deity Janus looked two ways. A few commentators see no conflict in raising revenues on a regional basis while

decentralizing many of the decisions about how to spend the money at or nearer the school level. This raises the central question about what cities and states actually have done to make sense of city school governance.

THE RESPONSE TO PUBLIC DISSATISFACTION

This volume examines in considerable detail the question of what happens to school boards when individuals or groups try to change the way urban school systems are governed. The board itself can be considered not only an object of attack, although it often is, but as a prize to be won or a mechanism to be changed. Participants in school struggles often view the school boards as generals view a beachhead—something to be won as a first step toward a more substantial goal. Such a perception may shock the tender-hearted, those who not only still insist that schools must be removed from politics but who refuse to understand that there is a politics of education. On the other hand, the need to win or change a school board may confirm the worst suspicion of those who consider American society unnecessarily hierarchical and oligarchical with power accruing to a chosen few at the top.

The fourteen cities are treated as "case studies." Despite the uniqueness of each city school system, national trends prevail and school reformers in each city borrow freely from one another. Most of the older cities by 1900 had abolished ward or community school boards and transferred their powers to central boards. When that was not enough, reformers tried to reduce the size of the board and transferred many of the more sensitive duties—teacher nomination, textbook selection, in addition to teacher supervision—to a superintendent. During the twentieth century the superintendents have asserted and won chief executive status by assuming additional responsibilities for school business management. But the trend to delegate more power to professional staff members can be discerned in the last quarter of the nineteenth century.

Why exhume the municipal skeletons of the 1890's? Many readers will be astonished at the familiar nature of the earlier conflicts over how city school boards should be reformed. The nineteenth century school boards reflected neighborhood and community power on a district or ward basis. Laymen ran the

schools the way they wanted to run them, delegating to schoolmen only the more esoteric problems of curriculum and supervision. Most personnel, maintenance, and business matters were
handled by lay boards without professional consultation. The
school superintendency as a role appeared late, grew slowly, and
for most of the nineteenth century bore little resemblance to the
contemporary version.

The network of "uncentralized" neighborhood boards was
denounced and repudiated during the last quarter of the century.
In fact, the abolition of ward boards became a crusade and a
cause as emotionally laden as the call for community control
today. Coalitions of businessmen, college presidents, and reformers combined their talents to centralize the mechanism for urban
school decision-making. Journalists and at least one physician
contributed muckraking accounts of the schools, sensational in
their disclosures of corruption and spoils system politcs. This
coalition, essentially of upper-middle class professionals and businessmen, brought about a drastic reduction in the nember of
people participating in school decisions.

School boards were both centralized and professionalized in
that the reduction in the size of the boards usually signaled a
willingness to transfer some of the functions to school officials—
e.g., teacher recruitment to the superintendent and school purchasing to a school business manager. These changes meant placing a number of significant decisions out of the reach of ward
politicians and into the hands of those who presumably cared
more about pupils than patronage. This strategy backfired on occasion. City bosses in a few cities eagerly sought access to spoils
no longer available at the ward level. Mayors wanted credit for
educational decisions, at least for the popular ones. Superintendents struggled to develop a power base of their own, one based
on professionalism and expertise about educational problems.[20]

One major effect of the reform was to remove power from
the first and second generation of immigrants. The new working-class spokesmen, who found it easy to join and then domi-
nate ward boards, brought with them values quite different from
those of the established settlers. Immigrant leaders wanted jobs
for their followers, friends, and relatives. They also wanted to
preserve the old religious and national identities. This ran di-

rectly counter to native American insistence on naturalization, Anglicization, and civic education for the newcomers.

Native Americans, including rural farmers migrating to the cities, found themselves outnumbered and outmaneuvered by immigrants. *Forum* magazine in 1894 documented "The Irish Conquest of Our Cities" [21] with a large list of cities led by Boston, New York, and Philadelphia governed by Irish mayors and councils. Historian Richard Hofstadter observed that Progressives and Nativists brooded about the future of American democracy and the wisdom of unrestricted immigration.[22]

By the early 1900's, immigrants and their children made up the majority in most cities of the Midwest and Northeast. Their bosses saw in the schools opportunities for contracts and jobs on the one hand, and for the preservation of "old country values" on the other. Thus the priorities of immigrant folk and working-class political leaders clashed with those of Native American businessmen and middle-class professionals. The indigenous groups could not retain control of city schools if they were run by boards elected at the ward level, so they changed the rules. Reform coalitions aimed their public activity and critical reports at the essentially rural legislators, already worried about the mores of the new city people. Thus the states agreed to abolish ward boards in every instance and to reduce the size and power of such boards.

These changes, it will be seen, deliberately took power from the lower or working class. The reformers, in the name of "taking the schools out of politics," substituted their own brand of middle-class politics by canceling the arrangements for school governance at the neighborhood level.

The changes, Altshuler, the M.I.T. political scientist, points out, were made under the banner of democracy.[23] If partisanship led to spoils and corruption, then non-partisanship and a merit system would purify municipal governments. If ward elections encouraged parochial thinking, then at-large elections would inspire a larger view of city issues. Thus a more sanitized and wholesome kind of democracy would presumably be restored.

In the end, Native Americans decided that the problems of big cities and of city government could be solved only by closing the intake valves of immigration. Changes in governance alone would not protect traditional values of capitalism and representative democracy from socialism, syndicalism, and other alien values imported from southern and central Europe.

City school governmental arrangements remained stable for the thirty-year period following 1925. Scholars and critics proposed modest changes but only a handful of cities, usually in the throes of school scandals, tinkered with the pattern.

During the 1950's and 1960's American cities attracted millions of new residents from Appalachia, the black South, and from Puerto Rico. Ironically, the immigration laws could not stem or slow the tide of newcomers this time. Yet those who formed the great new blocs of parents and voters found city school systems unready and often unwilling to adjust to their needs. Furthermore, the system of school governance made it difficult, and sometimes impossible, to change the composition of the school board and top staff, and thus the policies. The political reforms of a previous era had placed school politics on a pedestal for the most part out of reach for the lower class and minorities, new and old.

The 1960's brought an increased interest in community participation in school affairs. Pressures for city school district decentralization appeared even before the War on Poverty. Some of the pressure for increased local autonomy came from teachers and school principals, a demand that can be traced at least as far back as the early 1900's when Chicago Teachers Federation leaders asked that more decisions be made by teachers and principals at the school level.

But the major pressure for greater local participation and control now comes from neighborhood and community groups. Proposals call for additional school boards nearer to the people and closer to the children. Personnel and curriculum decisions would be made by decentralized boards with specified kinds of control over the school and staff. The central school board would retain certain financial functions and whatever else might require centralized coordination.

In many ways the current disputes over city schools reflect two kinds of discontent with structural changes made earlier in the century, or in the closing decades of the preceding century. Critics charge that too many decisions of central importance were removed from the level of the community. The other accusation is that schools try to function independently of other city agencies, especially those with parallel responsibilities for helping urban populations gain decent housing, wages, health, and other basic human rights. The latter is the cry of public administrators. It has been taken up by some big-city mayors.

Mayor John Lindsay of New York City was not the first big-city mayor to get embroiled in politically damaging disputes over school governance. Mayor Edward Dunne of Chicago in 1907 was defeated for re-election in large measure because of his support for the Chicago Teachers Federation and their ideas about making educational decisions at the school level. And another New York City mayor, Fiorello LaGuardia, received sharp criticism from the National Education Association for his attempts to reshape urban education.

Most mayors in the twentieth century refused to challenge seriously the rather unusual phenomenon of separately governed school systems. The urban school board for fifty years enjoyed in many cities a privileged, if not apolitical, status. Until issues of race, community control, and collective bargaining developed and then collided, city school politics were rarely exciting except to the specialist.

The rhetoric of latter-day school reform is summarized by the indictment, "our schools have failed to educate"—especially the children of the poor. Sweeping reforms would include stripping the ineffective central board of its power, which would be redistributed to the people most concerned, the people of a community. Administrative decisions would be made at a decentralized level. Community control of the schools would replace citywide or bureaucratic control. Yet reformers of earlier days, many of them with impressive and genuine progressive credentials, were arguing just the opposite view—that schools must be taken out of "politics," managed by professionals who would report only to a central city-wide school board, and otherwise would be protected from neighborhood (ward) leaders.

Current pressures for decentralization and community control now force city leaders to reconsider their judgments about the value of centralized boards. Political scientist James Q. Wilson calls decentralization "the new slogan of municipal reform." He wryly observes, "The governments of many large cities, already experiencing the greatest difficulty in deciding on—and especially acting on—any policy for handling their problems, are now being told they must hand over control of the schools, police, and other agencies to various neighborhoods—which means, of course, to various neighborhood politicians." He adds, "It was precisely under these circumstances that municipal corruption flourished in the past. Perhaps decentralization is desirable even at the price of more corruption, but no one should suppose the price will not have to be paid." [24]

It seems appropriate to review the development of the earlier reforms. Why were city school boards changed and by whom? What was the extent of disillusionment with school boards at the ward level? How often have cities switched from elective to appointive boards and why? Under what conditions do cities change the way a city school board is selected? Does it make any difference in the functioning of the city school system? What evidence exists to support or discredit the argument that schools need separate boards in the big cities? Who has challenged this function within the profession? What are the options for city school governance in the future?

The next chapter reviews the political and governmental context of city school boards. Succeeding chapters examine the birth of city school boards, the kinds of reorganizations won by urban school reformers, the years of relative peace in city school systems, and the recent turbulence.

It is not exactly true that "those who ignore history are doomed to repeat it." Ward politics will never be the same again. Teacher unions have won power rarely accumulated prior to 1960. And the new masses are native Americans, not the refugees from Europe that flooded U.S. cities in the preceding century. The lessons of the past are more subtle; reforms and changes won at one point of time may bring about unanticipated consequences and indeed themselves require review and reform by later generations.

NOTES

1. The questions were raised by Lyman Abbott in the introduction to *Darkness and Daylight,* Helen Campbell *et al.,* Hartford, 1891, excerpted in A. M. Schlesinger, *The Rise of the City, 1878–1898* (New York: Macmillan, 1933), p. v.

2. Ellwood P. Cubberley, *Public School Administration* (Cambridge, Massachusetts: The Riverside Press, 1929), p. 76.

3. *Ibid.*, p. 80.

4. George D. Strayer, *A Design for the Administration of Public Education* (with particular application to California), Educational Administration Monograph no. 1, Stanford School of Education (Stanford, California: Stanford University Press, 1954), p. 21. However, Herold C. Hunt favors the appointive board of education for all communities with a population of 200,000 or more. He feels that the appointive board is much more able and less subject to, or concerned about, pressures from the "inside."

5. Jesse B. Sears, *City School Administrative Controls* (New York: McGraw-Hill, 1938), pp. 41–42.

6. National Education Association, *Local School Boards: Size and Selection,* Circular no. 2, 1964 (Washington, D.C.: Educational Research Service, N.E.A., February 1964).

7. Alpheus White, *Local School Boards: Organization and Practices,* U.S. Department of Health, Education and Welfare, Office of Education, Bulletin no. 8 (Washington, D.C.: Government Printing Office, 1962), p. 8.

8. The fourteen cities are among the twenty largest school systems but exclude Dallas, Seattle, San Diego, Memphis, and several large Florida and Maryland counties. The State of Hawaii and District of Columbia can be categorized as latter-day city-states, each with unique governmental arrangements.

9. As recently as 1960, non-public schools accounted for as much as 40 percent of the elementary school-age children in such cities as Philadelphia and Pittsburgh, 25 to 30 percent of children in New York, Boston, Chicago, and elsewhere.

10. Frank Rollins, "School Administration in Municipal Government," Ph.D. dissertation (New York: Columbia University, 1902), pp. 22–23.

11. Don Martindale, "The Theory of the City," in Weber (New York: Collier Books, 1962), p. 22.

12. George Counts, *The Social Composition of Boards of Education,* Supplementary Monograph no. 33 (Chicago: The University of Chicago Press, 1927).

13. W. W. Charters, Jr., "Research on School Board Personnel: Critique and Prospectus," *Journal of Educational Research,* vol. XLVII, no. 8 (January 1954), pp. 321–335.

14. *The School Board Crisis: A Chicago Case Study* (Chicago: Educational Methods, 1964).

15. Marilyn Gittell, *Participants and Participation* (New York: Center for Urban Education, 1967).

16. *Report of the National Advisory Commission on Civil Disorders* (New York: Bantam Books, March 1968), pp. 8–9.

17. Stephen K. Bailey, *New Dimensions in School Board Leadership,* a paper prepared for a National School Boards Association Conference, Evanston, Illinois (July 1969), pp. 8–9.

18. *Village School Downtown* (Boston: Beacon Press, 1967), pp. 150–151.

19. Robert Bendiner, *The Politics of Schools* (New York: Harper & Row, 1969), pp. 177–226.

20. Raymond Callahan, "The History of the Fight to Control Policy in Public Education," in Frank W. Lutz and Joseph Azzarelli (eds.), *The Struggle for Power in Education* (New York: Center for Applied Research in Education, 1966).

21. John Paul Bocock, "The Irish Conquest of Our Cities," *Forum,* vol. XVII (April 1894), pp. 186–195.

22. *The Age of Reform* (New York: Knopf, 1963), p. 173.

23. Alan Altshuler, *Community Control* (New York: Pegasus, 1970), especially Chapter Two.

24. "Corruption Is Not Always Scandalous," *The New York Times Magazine* (April 28, 1968), p. 74.

THE POLITICS AND POWERS OF
CITY SCHOOL BOARDS

INTRODUCTION

THE SCHOOLS and the cities are both creatures of the state. Yet opponents of federal aid to education use the slogan "local control" and advocates of autonomy for the major cities generally call for "home rule." Both slogans belie the fact that the state retains the final authority to create and change the form and functions of cities, including city school districts.

What relationships exist between city and state, between city schools and the state, and between the city schools and the city or county? How much influence does the federal government wield over cities? How are city boards of education organized? How are members selected for service on the board? Once organized, what are the major functions assigned to the governing boards? What are the differences between the legally prescribed functions and the political functions found not in the law but in the reality of civic life.

As a preface, it is worth noting the past neglect and present revival of interest in the governmental and political context of education in general, and specifically of urban education.

THE STUDY OF EDUCATIONAL POLITICS

Political scientists have reported encountering an impenetrable phalanx of citizens and schoolmen who for many years have fended off proposals that the governments of schools be merged with other units of local government.[1] Educators with strong support from parent groups and other "friends of public education" so often want to keep the public schools separate from other units of government, fiscally independent, and "out of (or above) politics."

The "politics" which the educators wish to keep out of the schools refers especially to the "old politics" in which large numbers of jobs, including at least some policy-level positions, are awarded to political workers and friends of the victorious party. Politics, to schoolmen, until recently has been synonymous with "spoils system" and with all the overtones of political corruption, graft, favoritism, and machine rule. The generally accepted nostrum has been that education and politics do not mix.[2]

This cleavage has been contributed to by political scientists who, until the 1960's, seldom studied the politics of education and the fundamental interdependence of the two realms. But several developments in the last fifteen years have helped to correct this situation.

First, educators have become fascinated observers of the efforts of the social scientists to identify and define one or more types of community power structure.[3] Professors of educational administration during the 1950's became increasingly oriented toward the behavioral sciences and the possible value of political science in preparing administrators for work in the local school districts.

School administrators now accept as part of their work the inevitability of immersion in school–community conflict over such diverse issues as desegregation of public facilities, the content of the curriculum and of textbooks, the construction of swimming pools in the schools, and collective bargaining with employees[4] School administrators, especially since World War II, have faced taxpayer revolts, sit-ins and other non-violent demonstrations, teacher and student strikes, battles over the passage of bond issues, legal suits, and other forms of political turbulence. It is becoming standard procedure to acquaint prospective practitioners with the array of "interest groups" which they will face as principals and superintendents; simultaneously, professional educators study the relationships between the schools and the polity at several levels in order to understand both the formal and informal networks of control and decision-making in education.[5]

Second, political scientists have resumed an interest in the schools, an interest which has been dormant since the 1930's when Charles Merriam at the University of Chicago directed studies in citizenship education and stimulated research concerning connections between schools and other governments.[6] The increase in conflict has in turn attracted the attention of political scientists, who specialize in studying how resources are allocated under pressure.

During the 1930's, 1940's, and 1950's, much of the productive work on communities and school systems, such as the studies by W. Lloyd Warner and his associates, was done by anthropologists and sociologists. School board and school superintendents in one state were studied in the 1950's by Neal Gross and others at Harvard.[7] In recent years the study of Atlanta by sociologist Floyd Hunter [8] precipitated a number of political studies of several cities, notably New Haven,[9] Chicago,[10] and New York City.[11] The New York City study, for example, included data on the school board and superintendency up to 1960.

The inclusion of data on school decisions in Dahl's *Who Governs?*, the definition of "the politics of education" by Thomas H. Eliot, and the Syracuse University series of monographs on *The Economics and Politics of Education* [12] have demonstrated the renewal of interest by political scientists in the politics of education.

Third, educators themselves have in studies of education decision-making acknowledged the interrelationships of politics and education, government and the schools.[13] Simultaneously, political scientists in discussions of "political socialization" have increasingly recognized the potential force of the schools in identifying and recruiting elites, and in the citizenship training of participants in all sectors of the social system.[14] The total amount of education received by an individual correlates positively with participation in voluntary associations, critical consumption of information presented via the mass media, and other behavior considered useful in sustaining a democratic form of rule.[15]

The city school board can be seen as a political sub-system within the state and, yet, the entire city school organization is a part of the larger political systems of both the local community and the state. In order to better understand the place of the schools in this complex network, it is useful to examine the rela-

tionships between the city schools and government at two levels.
They are:

1. The formal and legal connections of schools to other
   units and levels of government;
2. The city schools as a structure within the larger political
   system.

In the rest of this chapter both levels of relationships will be
summarized as a prelude to examining the city school boards and
the different recruitment methods used to obtain their members.

THE RELATIONSHIP OF STATE GOVERNMENT
TO CITY GOVERNMENT

Historically, the cities are creatures of the state—both in
Great Britain and the United States. While under British rule,
the inhabitants of new communities had to seek charters from
governors representing the crown. After the Revolution, the
states assumed this same power and established conditions under
which towns became municipal corporations.[16] These conditions
were carefully specified by the state, usually in the state constitution, and were supported by legislation and judicial tradition.[17]

If the residents of an area desire city status, they prepare a
petition which state officials review. Then the state authorizes a
local election to see whether the majority of the local residents
wish to see the area incorporated as a city. Even when the state
legislature approves a city charter or extends a large measure of
"home rule" (the power enabling a city to decide its own forms
of self-government), the city remains a unit or sub-division of the
state. Whatever rights or powers the state has granted, such as
the power to levy taxes or select local officials, the state may also
curtail or withdraw.

The fourteen cities in this study all became municipalities
during the nineteenth century, most of them in the years from
1812 to 1850. Most cities periodically revise the city charters
under which the affairs of municipal government are conducted.
The extent to which the cities in this study have enjoyed "home
rule" has varied. For example, Missouri granted home rule to St.
Louis in 1875, but considerable adjudication in the courts was
necessary to determine which of the state laws controls the deci-

sions of a city ostensibly freed to govern itself.[18] Ohio provides for a self-executing form of home rule, which means that cities need not refer new charters to the legislature for review or approval, although the state courts there, too, have had to cope with some of the ambiguities of such a broad grant of power. Michigan's home rule act gives cities considerable power, but cities "generally obtain their powers from legislative action." [19] In Pennsylvania only Philadelphia has a home rule charter and that grant dates only from 1949. Baltimore, Maryland, and most cities in Texas and California, including those in this study, enjoy home rule; only Chicago and Pittsburgh do not have it. however, one political scientist feels that the granting of home rule yields benefits more psychological than substantial because the state remains supreme in determining public policy for all the communities within its boundaries, home rule or not.[20].

Cities, depending on the forms of their charters, may vary widely in the number of elective officials, the kind of and level of municipal services rendered, and the method of organizing the administration of these services (e.g., the power of the mayor vis-à-vis the council, the process for approving budgets, or nominating appointive office holders, etc.). State legislatures can regulate the taxing and borrowing capacities of cities, setting limits on either or both; state courts can review and overrule the decisions of city courts; state bureaus can require reports on municipal activities ranging from the assessment of property to the treatment of sewage; and officers of the state may remove certain city officials or boards in emergencies or when city officials have neglected the performance of their functions. For example, Baltimore and St. Louis police officials remain accountable to the governors of their respective states and Michigan and Pennsylvania state officers have the power to remove a variety of local officials under specified conditions.

States have removed from cities the power to assess or tax certain kinds of property (such as utilities), to hire certain types of employees from other than state civil service lists, or to deviate from state-wide public health and sanitation rules for restaurants, pools, hotels, or other public places. States also, through grants in aid, influence welfare policy, road construction, public health, and other municipal decision-making about many basic functions of local government.[21]

THE MUNICIPAL OR COUNTY GOVERNMENT
AND THE SCHOOLS

New York City embraces five counties, or boroughs. Philadelphia, Baltimore, and San Francisco are coterminous with a county. Boston includes almost all of Suffolk County except for three smaller cities. Chicago, Cleveland, Buffalo, and most other large cities (200,000 population or over) include large portions of the population in a county although the larger portion of the county territory may lie outside the city limits.

In some states the county is in some ways secondary to the city or at least second in the minds of policy-makers. The relegation of the county unit to a place of subsidary importance is evident in two cities, Boston and Philadelphia, where the city councils act in place of a separate county board.[22] The board of education and the superintendent of the San Francisco city schools serve also as the county board and the county superintendent. The county does govern the city schools in the following instances:

1. Detroit, where the county tax board reviews the budget and sets the tax levy;
2. Cleveland and Milwaukee, where county officials help the schools by collecting some of the tax money;
3. Pittsburgh, where the judges who appoint the board of education members are technically county rather than city judges.

However, the struggle for urban "home rule" has usually won for cities the freedom from county supervision. The county retains significance as a unit of school government in many states, but its influence often wanes when an area becomes more urbanized. Except for the functions indicated above, the city school systems in this study are not sub-divisions of county government. (See Table 3 on city, county, and school board relationships.)

The boundaries of a city and the city school district may not coincide. For example, the Los Angeles Unified School District extends outside the Los Angeles city limits to the San Fernando Valley, where approximately one-third of the students in a

Table 3 THE STRUCTURAL RELATIONSHIP
BETWEEN CITY SCHOOLS AND COUNTIES

City and State	County	Relationship of Schools to County
Baltimore, Maryland	Baltimore County surrounds but does not include city	Independent.* The only city in Maryland not governed by a county school board.
Boston, Massachusetts	Suffolk	Independent. No central county school structure in Massachusetts.
Buffalo, New York	Erie	Independent
Chicago, Illinois	Cook	Independent
Cleveland, Ohio	Cuyahoga	Independent. No county coordination of schools. County auditor and tax commission calculate tax levy and rate.
Detroit, Michigan	Wayne	No county school organization. County tax allocation board reviews the budget and sets tax levy.
Houston, Texas	Harris	Independent
Los Angeles, California	Los Angeles	Separate county board and superintendent. Other school districts in the same county are autonomous.
Milwaukee, Wisconsin	Milwaukee	Independent, although some tax funds for schools are collected by county.
New York City, New York	Richmond, Queens, Brooklyn, Bronx, and Manhattan (Kings)	Counties joined for school and other purposes. State aid calculated according to the property wealth of each borough.
Philadelphia, Pennsylvania	Philadelphia	No separate county school organization. City schools serve the county.
Pittsburgh, Pennsylvania	Allegheny	A separate county school board and superintendent. City Schools serve part of the county.

Table 3 THE STRUCTURAL RELATIONSHIP
          BETWEEN CITY SCHOOLS AND COUNTIES

City and State	County	Relationship of Schools to County
St. Louis, Missouri	St. Louis	Independent. The county includes suburban school districts.
San Francisco, California	San Francisco	Same board and superintendent for county and city—coterminous.

* Independent for all cities means no formal or legal tie of the school district to the county (except to judiciary).

750,000 student school district reside. The Houston school board serves some territory outside the city limits but another school district serves some of the territory within the city limits. For such school districts it is impossible to provide a common government for both the schools and the muncipality.

Legally, education is not a municipal function but a function of the state. The courts have held, on numerous occasions, that the schools are agencies of the state, legally and administratively independent of other government.[23] School districts in cities often enjoy a corporate or quasi-corporate status as a special district. It is possible, therefore, for cities and school districts to be geographically coterminous yet separate governmental structures, both of them legal entities whose continuance is dependent on the state legislature, each fiscally and administratively independent of the other.[24]

Does this mean that city school departments exist as entities separate from city hall? Historically, many cities initially placed the schools in a municipal department responsible to the mayor and common council. Currently, the states vary in the actual independence granted to the school boards of a city, sometimes varying the degrees or kinds of relationships of schools to municipal government between cities of different sizes within the same state, or allowing alternative patterns of city school government to continue, as exceptions, for many decades.

City officials may influence school decisions in at least these two ways.

1. The selection of school board members by muncipal authorities. The mayor, city council, or one with the consent of the other, may be authorized to nominate and appoint the school board members.
2. Fiscal dependence, in part or in whole, on the city government for the approval of budgets, for the setting of a tax rate, or for authorization to borrow for school construction purposes. Cities and city school districts may also share responsibilities for the supply of community services such as recreation, public meetings, and health services, some or all of which may be mandated by law. Other kinds of cooperative or informal working relationships range from the use of schools for voter registration or as polling places, to the removal of snow from school yards by city vehicles and the sharing of civil service lists, joint purchase of supplies and equipment, mutual use of data-processing equipment, and other recurring or "ad hoc" relationships.[25]

Even the fiscally independent school districts may share ballots and polling places with the city in the election of officers, or use the same governmental machinery for property assessment and tax collection. Few cities, in return, ignore the city school system, and city schools may even benefit from a working relationship with the city, especially with the park and recreation departments, the police and juvenile court officers, and a variety of social services. Henry and Kerwin in the 1930's found that cities and city schools were in fact cooperating in rendering services to citizens and/or gaining economies by eliminating duplicate services, procedures, and personnel.[26]

The data in Table 4 indicate that in seven of the cities, city officials participate in the selection of city school board members and in seven cities voters elect the members of the city school board. The table also shows that the mayor and/or city council has the power to change the total budget amount in six cities. Participation in the selection of school board members often brings with it the subsequent power to approve school budgets in these cities. Therefore, in theory the cities and schools are separate structures or entities; in practice, the schools of some cities are the equivalent of municipal departments subject to the

Table 4 THE FUNCTIONAL RELATIONSHIP
BETWEEN CITY SCHOOLS
AND CITIES OR COUNTIES

City	*Fiscal Relationship of City Schools to City Government*	*Major Functions Performed by City * or County*
Baltimore	Dependent	Mayor and council appoint board members and, with board of estimate, approve the budget.
Boston	Independent (if under the limit imposed by the state)	Mayor and council approve budget if above a limit set by the state.**
Buffalo	Dependent	Mayor and council appoint board members and approve budget.
Chicago	Dependent	Mayor appoints board members and sets the budget limit. City council approves, but may not change, school budget.
Cleveland	Independent	None. County auditor calculates the levy needed to finance the budget; county budget commission sets levy rate.
Detroit	Independent	None. County tax allocation board approves budget and sets tax levy.
Houston	Independent	None.
Los Angeles	Independent	County board of supervisors legally sets the tax rate— but does not change budget.
Milwaukee	Independent	Common council sets tax levy but may not alter school board budget.***
New York City	Dependent	Mayor, with city council and board of estimate, reviews and approves budget. Each borough president selects one board member.
Philadelphia	Dependent (since 1963)	Mayor appoints members. City council approves budget (since 1963).

City	Fiscal Relationship of City Schools to City Government	Major Functions Performed by City* or County
Pittsburgh	Independent	County judges (Court of Common Pleas) appoint members.
St. Louis	Independent	None. County board must establish tax rate for total approved by the school board.
San Francisco	Independent	Mayor appoints board—subject to confirmation by voters (until 1972).

* The major functions of interest here are fiscal and school board recruitment functions.

** Maximum total set by legislature. Since 1963 the maximum total changes each year according to a formula adopted by the legislature.

*** Maximum rate set by legislature.

mayor, or some other authority, for the selection of board members, the approval of budgets, and the construction of buildings.

However, the state guards carefully the authority which it exerts over all communities in requiring that schools be established and kept open for a minimum number of days each year, that certain courses be included in the curriculm, that teachers meet a minimum standard of training before state certification for classroom service, that money be raised from the community for the general program of instruction, and that the construction and sanitary features of a school building remain above a certain minimum standard of safety and health. The states usually distribute to city schools some portion of the state school revenues according to legislative judgments about the relative wealth and financial requirements of the city schools. The state, whatever the relationship of the school with the city, can visit and inspect the schools, sometimes remove or reinstate a teacher, grant additional or suspend basic funds, and may specify the textbooks or choice of texts available for use. The state legislatures usually preserve the right to alter any of the above policies.

The laws governing education are typically organized in a state education code. The laws are enforced and adjudicated by a state board of education, a body usually appointed by the governor. The board is assisted by a state commissioner of education or superintendent of instruction who is either appointed or elected by the people and who heads one of the administrative departments in the executive branch of the state government.

The New York State commissioner of education, in response to charges of scandal, effected the removal in 1961 of the entire membership of the board of education in New York City, a board then appointed by the mayor.[27]

THE ORGANIZATION
OF CITY SCHOOL SYSTEMS

The board of education serves as the governing body or fiduciary board of the school district or school department. One or more executives may report to the school board as heads of as many major divisions of the staff as may be authorized by state law or board of education by-laws or regulations. For example, the Cleveland board of education until 1964 was served by a superintendent of schools, who headed the education department, and a business manager, who supervised the operation, maintenance, supply, and other support functions of the school system, except for disbursements of funds and financial control, a function which was assigned to a clerk-treasurer with a separate department. Each of the three executives reported directly to the Cleveland board, the clerk-treasurer in a capacity clearly defined in Ohio statutes. St. Louis was authorized in the 1897 charter revision to appoint as many school executives as were deemed necessary, and its city school board has had as many as six executives reporting directly to it. St. Louis had separate superintendents for instruction, school buildings, and supplies, and an attorney, auditor, and secretary-treasurer to the board. In some states, where the legislature has amended the law, certain ambiguities of function remain—e.g., in the rules of the Boston School Committee the superintendent of schools has been made the chief executive officer of the School Committee, but the Business Manager remains the executive officer responsible for business affairs, charged with a specific responsibility for informing the board about mismanagement of funds or possible savings.

In large cities the board and the superintendent presumably oversee the work of instruction in the separate schools. These schools may be grouped by neighborhood, by district, or by borough into administrative sub-units, each presided over by assistant or district superintendents. Other deputy, associate, or assistant superintendents supervise a central office bureaucracy which administers programs of textbook screening, curriculum development, teacher recruitment, coordination of elementary and secondary education, testing and measurement, and a host of other services and special programs.

At the school level, often several echelons removed from the board and superintendent, a principal (of one or a cluster of schools), sometimes assisted by a vice principal, coordinates the work of teachers, aides, and secretaries. The principal also coordinates the school librarians, nurses, and guidance counselors who work directly with children, their problems, and their parents. The organization of the school system may provide for separate schools by age categories, as in the case of elementary, junior high, or senior high schools; day nurseries for pre-kindergarten students; junior colleges; teachers colleges; and sometimes universities (both Houston and Detroit boards have had jurisdiction over city universities). The schools may be specialized by function as in the case of schools for the blind, the deaf, or hard of hearing, or schools for the young scientists, the Latin scholars, the aspirants to apprentice status in a trade or technical vocation, the emotionally disturbed, or the habitually truant.

The external relationships of the city board of education have, on occasion, included jurisdiction over other city structures such as the board of library trustees (in Cleveland appointed by the board of education), or over recreation and other social services. City schools, in practice, work closely with juvenile court officials such as probation officers, with police officials, with city auditors, with the public works department, and other agencies. The Boston School Committee, for example, must use the legal services of the city law department but maintains a separate school health department.

CITY–FEDERAL RELATIONS

City schools still receive a relatively small proportion of their total revenues each year from the federal government, even since the passage of the Elementary and Secondary Education

Act. Much of the federal assistance now available, for the economically or educationally disadvantaged or for vocational education, must meet program specifications of the state departments
of education. Cities have long sought either general aid or large
grants of categorical aids such as might reduce the cost of a
building program.

City schools are eligible for funds under the aegis of urban
renewal when the replacement of obsolete buildings is part of a
neighborhood redevelopment plan. Under Office of Economic
Opportunity regulations, city schools may submit proposals for
funding of programs for disadvantaged groups, especially if the
schools agree to work with or through the various social renewal
agencies or councils which try to coordinate the attack on cultural deprivation and urban poverty.

Federal laws guaranteeing the civil rights of job applicants
apply to the schools, as do minimum wage laws and other legislation concerning employee welfare, unionism, social security, and
other personnel matters. The city schools in the 1960's were very
much involved in school desegregation and integration delibera-
tions. Advisory committees of new agencies, such as the Commission on Civil Rights, held open meetings in some cities to determine the extent of racial imbalance in city schools.[28]

The schools are supervised by the state rather than the
federal government, yet certain federal laws apply with not only
equal but possibly greater relevance to urban schools. The Congress and federal agencies took an interest in urban schools in
1965 that far exceeded the traditional and limited fact-gathering
functions of the U.S. Office of Education.

THE CITY SCHOOL BOARD—
STRUCTURE AND SELECTION

The school board as a legal entity can act only as a whole.
Its members possess no individual powers or authority except in
the role of officers of the board, and then only on behalf of the
board. The modal size of city school boards is seven members
(compared to five for boards of education in all school districts),
but large cities include boards ranging in size from five (Boston)
to fifteen (Milwaukee and Pittsburgh). Although the board
usually makes decisions as a committee of the whole, it may
choose to divide its work into specialized sub-committees which

may discuss detailed questions on budget-making, salaries, textbooks, curriculum, or construction. A board at any time may form an *ad hoc* committee—for example, one to screen candidates for a vacancy in the superintendency. The committees do not, according to law, make the final decisions, but rather report findings and recommendations to the full board for approval.

School boards choose one of their numbers as president or chairman to conduct the meetings the board of education holds. The superintendent is viewed as an advisor to the board and is expected to make recommendations on the annual budget, to nominate teachers for vacancies, or explain proposed changes in the curriculum. If he is an officer of the board, it is usually as secretary or treasurer. He is granted the right to speak at meetings but not to vote, for the city school superintendent is primarily an employee of the board, rather than one of the trustees of the schools. That the superintendent of schools may experience role conflict as leader of the professional staff and simultaneously as the major advisor to the board of education, which decides on salaries and renders other decisions, has been explained by previous researchers of the American school board.[29]

The city school boards are generally selected by one of two methods, election or appointment (see Table 5):

Table 5 CITY SCHOOL BOARDS—METHODS OF SELECTION

	APPOINTMENT		ELECTION
By Mayor	*By Mayor and Council*	*By County Judges*	
Chicago	Baltimore	Pittsburgh	Boston
New York*	Buffalo		Cleveland
Philadelphia			Detroit
San Francisco**			Houston
			Los Angeles
			Milwaukee
			St. Louis

* From a list of names prepared by a selection board, provided for in the 1961 statute which was changed as of 1970 to provide for five elected members and two appointments by the mayor.

** With confirmation by the voters at an election to ratify or reject his nominee(s). San Francisco in November 1971 voted in an elective board plan.

1. The seven elective city school boards in this study are chosen at district wide elections. It is customary to include the school elections on the regular municipal ballot which may be shared by other city, state, or national offices. All the elective city boards in this study were, prior to 1970, elected at large without party identification. The terms are usually overlapping and long enough to guarantee that all board members cannot be replaced at one time; however, all of Boston's board members must run for election every two years.

2. The seven appointive school boards in this study are appointed most often by the mayor, sometimes with the approval of the city common council as in Baltimore and Buffalo. The nominations of the mayor in San Francisco had to be approved at a popular election, but if his nomination were rejected, the mayor could fill the "vacancy" with a selection of his own choosing. The school board of Pittsburgh is selected by the judges of the Court of Common Pleas in Allegheny county. In each of the above cases the appointive authorities have themselves been elected by the people and are, therefore, responsible to the electorate for the appointments they make.

The election and the appointment processes are performed by different structures. The electoral machinery has its component parts—for preparing nomination papers, holding primaries, manning polling places, providing for tabulation, and releasing results and conducting recounts. The appointment procedure is part of the office of the appointing authority and enables that authority to recruit members for another governmental structure, the school board. The appointment process may include the convening of a nominating panel as in Chicago or Philadelphia, or the referral of the nomination to the council for approval, as in Baltimore, or to the electorate, as in San Francisco. The appointment procedures are usually dormant, activated only when vacancies occur and the functions of nomination and appointment need to be performed. What is remarkable is not so much the variation but the fact that so many large cities in separate states agreed on the use of school boards, and continue to use them, whether elective or appointive.

THE FUNCTIONS OF SCHOOL BOARDS
AND SUPERINTENDENTS

Banfield and Wilson argue that any government serves two functions, one is to supply goods and services not supplied by private agencies, the other is to manage "conflicts in matters of political importance." [30] For school boards, the first function refers to supplying a governmental service, education. This is a service also provided by private agencies such as churches or nonsectarian corporations, but nevertheless supported by the state in order that all children might acquire literacy, be trained as citizens, and prepare for roles in society.

The second function of the school board arises from the necessity of resolving conflict. Through the resolution of conflict, the board defines the values and premises on which it makes routine decisions, or the board may be forced to reject these premises and search for more tenable bases for decisions. The school board must also evaluate the treatment received by members of minority groups, the equitable distribution of facilities and services, the effect of policy decisions on property values, and other interests felt by individuals or shared by groups.

The latter assignment really calls for political versatility. Robert Bendiner states the functions more vividly, pointing out that a "school board is really neither legislative nor administrative in function, and only in the most limited way, judicial. Almost entirely outside these normal categories, it has homier and less precise functions, not usually to be found in civics textbooks at all; it is local philosopher; it is watchdog, and it is whipping boy." [31]

The political functions usually include the more formal and governmental, but add that of conflict-resolution. The governmental functions assigned to city school boards are usually found in some detail in the education code of the state statutes.

Assuming that the largest city would include the full spectrum of functions, or at least "representative functions," a close look at New York revealed that twenty-five powers and duties are assigned to the board of education by the legislature. The statute gives the board the power to create or abolish departments or bureaus; to appoint a superintendent of schools and other em-

ployees needed for the "educational, social or recreational work"
and management of the schools; to purchase equipment and
provide textbooks and supplies; to establish and maintain thirteen specified types of schools and others as needed; to establish
and equip libraries, lecture courses, and recreation centers; to authorize courses of study and the textbooks to be used; and to inspect all schools and make such rules and regulations for extra-
class activities, cafeteria or restaurant services, and student
organizations as it deems necessary. The duties, apart from the
above, include those of control and management; prescribing regulations and by-laws necessary for the operation, management,
and "discipline" of the schools; care and safekeeping of property;
providing transportation for certain categories of children; com-
pensating employees for injuries (at its discretion), and appointing trial examiners to help conduct investigations. Other more
specific duties and powers are similarly itemized and qualified in
the statute.[32]

The superintendent of schools in New York City was declared the chief executive officer of the board (until 1970 when
the title became chancellor) and the educational system, with a
seat on the board and having "the right to speak on all matters
before the board, but not to vote." [33] He is charged with the
"power and duties" of enforcing all rules and regulations relating
to the management and activities under the direction of the
board of education and with preparing courses of study and lists
of textbooks which are submitted to the board for approval. He
must supervise the other educators and all other employees. He
handles the transfer and suspension of employees, although he
must report to the board any violations of regulations. He must
organize the staff to evaluate systematically the curriculum and
the work of the pupils and other services, facilities, and activities.
He also handles the issuance of licenses to many categories of employees from school psychiatrists to clerical assistants and "tool
boys." He is aided in some of these duties by either a community
school superintendent or by a board of examiners. Separately
listed in the statutes are the responsibilities of the board of education for preparing and adopting an annual school budget, for
entering into all contracts for services and materials, and for con-
structing buildings.

The statutes recognize and provide for managing internal
conflict arising over the authority to supply services and to make

decisions about the "goods" (textbooks, equipment) needed for the students who will attend the schools. In comparison, little reference to external conflict appears in the education code; [34] internal conflict is covered by references to trial boards, investigations, employee compensation, and other techniques for resolving differences among members of the school system and differences among the members concerning the system itself.

Observers of decision-making by school boards have found ample proof, however, of the existence of the conflict-management function. The city school budgetary process itself usually involves the clash of groups competing for the distribution of scarce resources, money, staff, and facilities.[35] Cunningham observed the debates and decisions of one board of education which was considering the use of public versus private power for the schools, an enormously critical local issue.[36] Other school boards have become embroiled in conflict over the teaching of controversial issues, in protests over the titles of library books available in school libraries, or about the content of specific topics in the curricula, such as teaching evolution in biology classes or studying U.N.E.S.C.O. in the social studies courses.[37] Crain's study found the city school board especially tested by conflict over school desegregation and that boards, not superintendents, set the tone of the integration decision.[38]

The two functions of government cannot be separated. Urban school critics charge that city schools have failed to deliver services to the public, triggering a series of conflicts over whether school integration or decentralization or more money would make a difference. Such conflicts account for the new visibility of urban school boards. Such conflicts may also bring about their demise. At this point the question must be raised about how and when city school boards were organized as mechanisms through which problems might be attacked. It is worth asking whether changes in city school boards made by the end of the nineteenth century strengthened or diminished their ability to resolve school conflicts in the 1970's.

NOTES

1. Nelson B. Henry and Jerome C. Kerwin, *Schools and City Government* (Chicago: The University of Chicago Press, 1938), p. 2.
2. Thomas H. Eliot, "Public School Politics," in Edward C. Banfield

(ed.), *Urban Government* (Glencoe, Illinois: The Free Press, 1961), p. 583. Article originally in *The American Political Science Review*, vol. LII, no. 4 (December 1959).

3. Cf. Luvern Cunningham, "Community Power: Implications for Education," Chapter 2, pp. 27–50, in Robert S. Cahill and Stephen P. Hencley, *The Politics of Education* (Danville, Illinois: Interstate Printers and Publishers, 1964).

4. School conflict is discussed in James Coleman's *Community Conflict* (Glencoe, Illinois: The Free Press, 1957).

5. One of the most comprehensive texts designed to explain these relationships is *The Organization and Control of American Schools* by Roald F. Campbell, Luvern L. Cunningham, and Roderick F. McPhee (Columbus: Merrill, 1965).

6. Cf. Henry and Kerwin, *loc. cit.*, and John A. Vieg, *The Government of Education in Metropolitan Chicago* (Chicago: The University of Chicago Press, 1939.)

7. Neal Gross, *Who Runs Our Schools?* (New York: Wiley, 1958).

8. Floyd Hunter, *Community Power Structure* (Chapel Hill: The University of North Carolina Press, 1953).

9. Robert Dahl, *Who Governs?* (New Haven: Yale University Press, 1961).

10. Edward C. Banfield, *Political Influence* (New York: The Free Press, 1961).

11. Wallace S. Sayre and Herbert Kaufman, *Governing New York City* (New York: Russell Sage Foundation, 1960).

12. Eliot, *loc. cit.*, and see the twelve monographs in *The Economics and Politics of Education* series prepared under the direction of Jessee Burkhead (Syracuse: Syracuse University Press, 1963). A second set of studies led by Alan K. Campbell was published in the late 1960's with several volumes scheduled for the early 1970's. Marilyn Gittell in New York City wrote a series of volumes beginning with *Participants and Participation,* (New York: Praeger, 1967), and including *Six Urban School Districts* with T. Edward Hollander (New York: Praeger, 1968). See also Robert Bendiner's *The Politics of Schools* (New York: Harper & Row, 1969), for a review of city school boards and their response to crises.

13. See studies by H. Thomas James, J. Allan Thomas, and Harold J. Dyck, *Wealth, Expenditure and Decision-Making for Education* (Stanford, California: Stanford School of Education, 1963), and those of R. L. Johns and Ralph Kimbrough. See Ralph Kimbrough, *Political Power and Educational Decision-Making* (Chicago: Rand McNally, 1964).

14. Cf. Robert E. Lane, *Political Life* (Glencoe, Illinois: The Free Press, 1959), and Gabriel A. Almond and Sidney Verba, *The Civic Culture: Political Attitudes and Democracy in Five Nations* (Princeton: Princeton University Press, 1963).

15. Cf. H. Thomas James, "The Schools Are in Politics," *The Nation's Schools,* vol. LXII, no. 4 (October 1958). Vincent A. Ostrom, "Education & Politics," *Social Forces Influencing Education,* The Sixtieth Yearbook, National Society for the Study of Education, Part II (Chicago: The University of Chicago Press, 1961).

16. Arthur W. Bromage, *Introduction to Municipal Government and Administration,* Second Edition (New York: Appleton-Century-Crofts, 1959), p. 108.

17. Dillon's rule, which the courts accept virtually intact from Judge John F. Dillon's *Commentaries on the Law of Municipal Corporations,* 1911.

18. Edward C. Banfield and James Q. Wilson, *City Politics* (Cambridge, Massachusetts: Harvard University Press and M.I.T. Press, 1963), p. 117.

19. *Ibid.,* p. 119.

20. Charles R. Adrian, *Governing Urban America* (New York: McGraw-Hill, 1961).

21. Bromage, *op. cit.,* Chapter 9.

22. John A. Fairlie, *Local Government in Counties, Towns, and Villages* (New York: The Century Co., 1914), p. 83.

23. Newton Edwards, *The Courts and the Public Schools* (Chicago: The University of Chicago Press, 1955).

24. It is not intended here to review the deep sense of injustice felt by many students of government about this sharing not only of territory but of tax base and bonding power, seemingly uncoordinated and sometimes competitive.

25. Bromage, *op. cit.,* p. 19. The present study emphasizes the formal legal link between the city and the city schools and, therefore, the first and second relationships listed above will consume the body of this report and analysis.

26. Henry and Kerwin, *op. cit.* (see Table 2).

27. "The New York Mess," editorial in *The American School Board Journal,* vol. CXLIII (October 1961), p. 36.

28. The Civil Rights Act of 1957 created the U.S. Commission on Civil Rights, an independent federal agency with state advisory committees. The Massachusetts Committee on March 20 and 22, 1964, heard the testimony of expert witnesses on racial imbalance in the Boston public schools, the summary of which is in a report to the U.S. Commission dated January 1965.

29. Neal C. Gross, Ward S. Mason, and Alexander W. McEachern, *Explorations in Role Analysis, Studies of the School Superintendency* (New York: Wiley, 1958).

30. Banfield and Wilson, *op. cit.,* pp. 18 and 22.

31. Bendiner, *op. cit.,* p. 3.

32. Article 52, Chapter 2566, New York Education Law.

33. Article 52, Chapter 2554, New York Education Law.

34. Although the law of contracts, or of tort liability, with certain specified exceptions, is of major concern to school boards and school administrators.

35. H. Thomas James, James A. Kelly, and Walter I. Garms, *Determinants of Educational Expenditures in Large Cities of the United States* (Stanford, California: Stanford University School of Education, 1966).

36. Luvern Cunningham, *A Community Develops Educational Policy: A Case Study*, unpublished Ed.D. dissertation (Eugene, Oregon: University of Oregon, 1958).

37. Coleman, *op. cit.*, p. 10.

38. Robert L. Crain *et al.*, *The Politics of School Desegregation* (Chicago: Aldine, 1968).

THE BEGINNING OF
CENTRALIZATION, 1850–1890

LOCAL SCHOOL government in the United States developed earliest in New England. From this region some of the forms were transplanted to other settlements and states. The early schools in Massachusetts, especially those in Boston, were supervised first by the town meeting and then by the selectmen, who were chosen by the townspeople to manage the "prudential affaires" of the town, including the schools. To perform the necessary tasks of hiring a teacher, building a school house, and inspecting the schools, various groups assisted the selectmen: the ministers, the overseers of the poor, and visiting committees.[1] Eventually each town, and later each city, delegated this work to a school committee or board of education.

This chapter describes the early provision for school boards in each of the fourteen cities, and explains why ward or district representation lost favor later in the century. The chapter concludes with an analysis of the impact of centralizing the school boards and the hiring of central staff officials to hire and supervise the teachers.

THE ORIGINS OF CITY SCHOOL BOARDS

None of the fourteen cities were formally incorporated until the nineteenth century, but most of the early city charters made some provision for a school committee, board of trustees, or subcommittee of the common council for the supervision of the public schools:

1. Baltimore decreed in 1828 that the city council should appoint six school commissioners, one from each district. By 1839, the number of commissioners had risen to thirteen.[2]
2. The Boston "school committee" properly began in 1789, although not until 1822 was the city incorporated. The city charter then provided for a school board which included the mayor and aldermen and twelve school committeemen, one from each ward.
3. In 1818 the village of Buffalo appointed three trustees to handle the affairs of the schools. When Buffalo became a city in 1837, the office of trustee was abolished, the mayor and council became commissioners, and a superintendent of common schools was appointed.
4. Chicago's first school board was authorized in 1835, and in 1837, when Chicago became a city, the common council appointed seven school inspectors and three trustees for each school district.
5. An act incorporating Cleveland in 1837 authorized the city council to appoint a separate board of school managers, one from each of the three districts (wards). In 1859, the board became elective.
6. Detroit developed in 1842 an arrangement by which the mayor chaired a school board composed of himself, a recorder, and two persons from each of the six wards.
7. Houston did not begin its city schools until 1876, when the mayor appointed three persons to a board of trustees.
8. Los Angeles in 1850 began to rely on the common council, which acted as a school board until 1854, at which time the common council appointed three of its members as a sub-committee and board for the schools.
9. In 1846, Milwaukee's mayor and council appointed two commissioners from each of the five wards to govern the free schools.
10. Citizens in New York City, under the leadership of De-Witt Clinton, agitated for a board of education in the 1790's, but without success. After 1842, an elective board of commissioners, two from each ward, governed the schools of Manhattan, and the Common Council of Brooklyn, with district representatives, constituted a board of education for Brooklyn.

11. Philadelphia provided in 1818 a board of nine control-
    lers to establish schools for paupers. After 1838, the boards
    of directors in sub-districts appointed a central board of
    twelve men to manage the common schools.
12. The voter of Pittsburgh elected in 1834 six school direc-
    tors, one from each ward, and each ward was to be a
    school district with educational and taxing authority for
    the establishment of a school.
13. In 1833, after several attempts to establish schools had
    failed, St. Louis elected a six-man board, composed of two
    representatives from each ward.
14. San Francisco appointed in 1848 a board of school trust-
    ees. However, the events surrounding the Gold Rush
    prevented the opening of schools until 1851, when the
    common council made the mayor president of a board on
    which two aldermen and two citizens served.

Between the years 1818 and 1853, thirteen of the fourteen
city schools under study established some form of school board.
Three of the boards included the mayor, eight of them were
either appointed by or included some of the city councilmen (or
aldermen), and one board selected a superintendent whom they
decided should report directly to the council. The members of
eleven boards were first appointed by either the council or
mayor; of the other three, the St. Louis school board was
chosen by ward elections, and two Pennsylvania city school boards
were chosen by and from the elected members of district
boards.

THE RISE OF DISTRICT AND WARD BOARDS

Most of the fourteen cities, for at least some part of the nineteenth century, provided representation from each ward or school
district within the city on the central city school board. Representation by wards was valued highly, whether the board
members were elected or appointed. Records on committees of
inspection for the Boston schools reveal early precedents for sub-
dividing city schools by wards or districts. In 1784, a committee
to take a school census for Boston was organized on a ward
basis.[3] Other city functions in Boston and in the other older

cities had been conducted by wards (tax collection, for example), and during the Revolutionary War many problems required the attention of ward committees.

Martin, the chronicler of Massachusetts education, traced the origin of small school districts back to the middle of the eighteenth century when town schools were often "moving schools" which traveled from neighborhood to neighborhood with a limited stay in each district of a township. A Massachusetts law of 1789 sanctioned the use of committees to manage the schools by districts, a development which had begun to emerge early in that century. Although the 1789 statute gave no financial power to the local school district, in 1880 the power to tax was conferred upon the people of the school districts. "They were authorized to hold meetings, to choose a clerk, to decide upon a site for a schoolhouse, and to raise money by taxation for buying land and building and repairing the house." [4] In 1817, school districts were empowered, as corporations, to sue and be sued and to enforce contracts. In 1827, the towns with districts were required to choose a committeeman within and for each district to supervise the school property and the selection and employment of teachers for each district.

Martin identified 1827 as the year in which the school district became a political institution, "the culmination of a process which has been going on steadily for more than a century. It marks the utmost limit to the subdivision of American sovereignty—the high-water mark of modern democracy, and the low-water mark of the Massachusetts school system." [5] Martin wrote these words in 1894, at a time when educators had become thoroughly disillusioned with the rivalries and feuds surrounding the selection of teachers and textbooks, the problem of identifying school sites satisfactory to all inhabitants in the district, and the bickering which so often marred the district meetings. But a hundred years earlier citizens were disenchanted with central governments generally.

Concern in Massachusetts with the failure of some towns to provide schools and about the poor preparation of teachers and the lack of coordination of education in the state led to the establishment of a state board of education in 1837 and the appointment of Horace Mann as secretary. The district boards, however, were popular, and some legislators were concerned about the fate the districts might suffer at the hands of the state board, whose potential strength they distrusted. Despite a threat in 1839 to abolish the state board and to appoint boards of education in each school district, the followers of Horace Mann, during the 1840's, mobilized support for the repeal of the district system and the reorganization of local schools. A series of statutes authorizing the discontinuance of district units were passed and then repealed during the 1840's and 1860's, until a statute in 1882 re-established the supremacy of the town school committees. This statute marked the close of a prolonged and bitter fight by rural school leaders to retain the district system.[6]

Suzzalo suggests that the ward organization performed for city schools in densely populated sections the functions such as teacher selection and supervision that the district system performed for more remote places where population was scattered.[7] Boston was large enough after 1789 so that, in lieu of previously used visiting committees of up to eighty or ninety men, twelve men were chosen from the wards of the town by the town meeting itself. The Boston committee that studied the need to reorganize the schools and which had recommended the appointment of the school committee, was itself appointed by wards. "The ward unit for recruitment of school board members persisted in Boston for a long period of time." [8]

Although popular in New England, the idea of ward school government gained eloquent advocates in other regions. Support of the ward as a unit for the division of cities and counties (or parishes) and for the supervision of free elementary education was the idea which Thomas Jefferson had proposed without success to the Virginia House of Burgesses as early as 1779. According to Samuel P. Huntington, Jefferson later "expanded his early idea of the ward as an educational unit to the ward as a unit of general government, and from 1810 to the end of his life, the establishment of a general system of public education in Virginia and the subdivision of its counties into wards were his two great objectives." [9] Fearing the corrosive effect of urbanization on republican forms of government, Jefferson strongly advocated, as an antidote to corruption and tyranny, government by "ward" republics. As the populace moved West, so did the district concept. Illinois recognized school districts in 1825, Michigan in 1828.

WARD AND DISTRICT REPRESENTATION
ON EACH CITY BOARD
IN THE NINETEENTH CENTURY

Each of the major cities, except Houston, selected the members of its city boards of education on the basis of ward or district representation for some portion of the nineteenth century. The districts were invariably coterminous with wards; the terminology often changed to coincide with state legislation dealing with the far greater number of rural districts in the state. The popularity of ward and district representation mounted after the 1820's, except in Buffalo, which used only sporadically a separate city school board. Support for ward representation increased as the century went on, showing no sign of waning until the 1860's and the 1870's when several cities began to adopt methods of selection from the city at large. The big cities provided for ward or district representation as follows:

Baltimore

Baltimore created in 1828 a board of commissioners of public schools whose six members were to be appointed annually by the city council, one commissioner from each of six school districts. The membership of the school board was subsequently increased from six to thirteen members at the request of the school board, and in 1849 the city council increased board membership to twenty, one commissioner for each city ward. By 1892 there were twenty-six members. This mode of selection persisted until 1898.[10]

Boston

When Boston became a city in 1822, the mayor and alderman succeeded the selectmen on the school committee, but the provision for twelve committeemen, one from each ward, continued. The composition of the school board in 1835 was changed to include two citizens from each ward, supplemented by the mayor and the president of the common council. A city charter revision in 1854 provided for the election of six citizens from each ward for the committee, in addition to the mayor and council president, seventy-four men in all. Also, the 1854 charter eliminated a separate primary school committee. By 1875, school committee membership, because of the annexation of new territories, totaled 116, at which time it was reduced to twenty-four members, elected at large instead of by wards. The city council president was dropped from board membership. In 1885, the legislature decreed that the mayor would no longer serve as chairman or member, although he could still veto school expenditures.

Buffalo

In 1818, Buffalo organized the entire village as one school district with three trustees. The Buffalo city charter, in 1837, discontinued the office of school district trustee, provided for commissioners of common schools, and directed the mayor and aldermen to be the commissioners and to select a superintendent as the chief executive on the common council for school matters. In 1838, the provision for the election of one trustee for each school district by persons residing in that district was restored. Again, in 1853, the officers of trustees and commissioners of common schools were abolished, and their duties were restored to the common council. Between 1853 and 1916, the office of superintendent was elective rather than appointive, but the mayor appointed a board of examiners to inspect all the schools for the common council.

Chicago

In Chicago, from 1837 to 1854, the common council appointed a seven-man board of school inspectors for the schools and three trustees for each school district. The trustees were eliminated in 1854 on the selection of a superintendent of schools. The number of inspectors grew to fifteen in 1857. From 1864, to 1872, they were selected by the council, one inspector from each of sixteen, and later twenty, wards. The responsibility for appointing school inspectors was transferred in 1872 from the council to the mayor with the approval of the council, and the necessity of appointment by ward was terminated. By 1891, the board had increased to twenty-one members.

Cleveland

The Cleveland city council after 1836 appointed a three-man board of managers of common schools, one for each district, which was authorized to conduct schools for at least six months a year, to employ instructors, certify to the city council the correctness of all accounts, and report on the fiscal and other concerns of the schools. The board of managers became an elective board in 1859, the "qualified electors of each ward" electing "one judicious and competent person who shall at the time be a qualified voter in such ward." The board of education members continued to be elected by wards, one member from each, and between 1873 and 1892 increased in size from eighteen to twenty-six.

Detroit

In 1842, the Michigan legislature passed a bill to provide free public schools and a board of education was formed composed of the mayor of Detroit, a recorder, and two inspectors from each of six wards. An act of 1869 provided for the mayor's appointment of a school board consisting of two inspectors from each ward. The growth of the city by the 1860's was such that, with new wards, membership rose to twenty and by 1876, to twenty-six, with no reduction in size until 1881. At that time the size of the board was reduced to twelve and the mode of selection changed to popular election with candidates nominated at party conventions and elected at large. But in 1889, Detroit adopted ward representation once again.

Houston

Houston once had been deep in Mexican territory and then the center of a spirited, if short-lived, republic. The Texas legislature did not enact a statute to enable cities to operate their own school systems until 1876, at which time Houston's city council provided for the appointment by the mayor of a three-member board of trustees and a three-member board of examiners to certify teachers.

Los Angeles

The Los Angeles city council in 1853 appointed three commissioners to serve as a board of education. The board had the power to examine, employ, and dismiss teachers, and one of its members was to be appointed city school superintendent. After 1866, the school board was elected (as was the superintendent of schools between 1866 and 1870). Not until 1889 were board members elected, one from each of nine wards.

Milwaukee

The charter of 1846 provided for Milwaukee a board of school commissioners consisting of three members from each ward, to be appointed by the mayor and common council. From 1846, the date of the incorporation of the city, until 1897, two commissioners from each ward were appointed by the mayor and council. The school board complained to the common council in the late 1860's about the independence and destructive effects of ward schools, recommending that "the city should be divided into school districts without regard toward ward lines." Although no action was taken at this time and "the struggle to shake school district lines free from ward boundaries continued in the 1860's, 1870's, and 1880's," the board grew in size to forty-two members until the laws of 1897 reduced its size.[11]

New York City

The schools of Brooklyn and New York were governed separately until the consolidation of 1897. Five trustees of the public school society administered some of the schools in New York during the first quarter of the nineteenth century. In 1835, the common council of Brooklyn appointed a board of trustees of three members from each district, three inspectors for the entire city, and three commissioners to serve the city school system as a whole. The legislature passed a law in 1842 establishing for Manhattan a board of education composed of two elected commissioners of common schools for each ward, and two inspectors and five trustees, also for each ward.

The following year the board for Brooklyn schools consisted of a member of the common council and either two or three appointed persons to represent each district, a governing body of twenty-eight. In 1850, the legislature provided for a board of education of thirty-three members to be appointed by the Brooklyn common council. Meanwhile, by 1855 the Brooklyn board had grown to forty-five members because of consolidation with several other districts.

In 1864, the number of trustees for each ward in New York City (Manhattan) was reduced from eleven to five. Twenty-one inspectors, three from each of seven school districts, were nominated by the mayor and confirmed by the board of education.

After an 1869 act prescribing a board of twelve elective members was passed and then repealed (1870), the seven districts were re-established and provision was made for the appointment of twenty-one commissioners for common schools, again by the mayor. These commissioners constituted the central board of education. By 1884 there were twenty-four boards of trustees subordinate to the board of education, and the mayor of New York appointed three inspectors for each district.

Meanwhile, Queens had adopted a five-member board of education, also appointed by the mayor. The Bronx in 1874 was annexed to the city of New York, and the Bronx schools were placed under the control of the New York City board of education.

Philadelphia

An act passed by the Pennsylvania legislature in 1838 established the board of controllers of the public schools in Philadelphia. The members of this central board were appointed by the boards of directors of the sub-districts, who were elected by the people to manage the schools of that section. In 1854, when the city and county were consolidated, the board of controllers grew to twenty-four members. The power of appointment was transferred in 1867 from the boards of directors to the judges of two courts: The Court of Common Pleas and the District Court, but the sub-district boards continued to wield power over fiscal matters and personnel for the ward schools.

Pittsburgh

Delegates from local districts met in the Pittsburgh court house on November 11, 1834, and agreed to establish a school. The voters elected six school directors, one from each ward. From 1834 to 1855 the ward boards had control of the educational and financial interests of their respective schools. Each ward was a school district and, although the act of 1854 established a central board and provided for the abolition of sub-districts, the sub-district continued to appoint teachers, levy local taxes, and to appoint one of its members to a central board (which grew in time from nine members to a total of forty-seven) until the reorganization of 1911.

St. Louis

The St. Louis public schools were founded by a special state law in 1833. Adult white males were eligible for election to the six-man board of directors, two members from each of three wards. In 1837, the board of directors appointed a lay board of school inspectors for the selection and supervision of teachers. Between 1833 and 1887, the city grew so large that the number of wards rose to thirteen, and, therefore, the number of board members to twenty-six. So in 1887 the legislature fixed twenty-one as a maximum size. However, each district retained one representative (fourteen of the twenty-one, seven others were elected at large) until the 1897 charter provided for "at large" elections for all members.

San Francisco

At a town meeting in San Francisco on February 21, 1848, five men were elected to a board of school trustees to open a school. Due to the boom town growth following the Gold Rush, the common council in 1851 passed an ordinance which divided the city into seven school districts with a school in each and provided for the annual selection by the common council of the board of education. The board was to consist of an alderman, two citizens, and the mayor as ex-officio president of the board. After 1856, both the board and superintendent were elected, the board members by district. The board of twelve members was elected "at large" after 1872.

THE FUNCTION AND FATE
OF BOARD REPRESENTATION

That the board of education in many cities performed the function of representing the citizens in each ward is clear from the data in Table 6. All twelve of the city school districts formed before 1850 adopted a method of ward representation, two by the 1820's and nine during the 1830's. San Francisco was among the last to adopt and among the first to abandon the principle of ward representation.

Many of the cities increased the size of the school board to allow for the adequate representation of new schools built to

Table 6 THE RISE AND FALL OF WARD
REPRESENTATION

City	Ward Representation Begins	Terminates
Baltimore	1828	1889
Boston	1789, 1822**	1875
Buffalo	1838	1853 (replaced by appointed board of examiners)
Chicago	1839	1872
Cleveland	1836	1892
Detroit	1838, 1842**	1881 (but later restored, 1889–1916)
Houston*	—	—
Los Angeles	1889 (no board until 1853)	1903
Milwaukee	1836, 1846**	1897
New York City	1835 Brooklyn 1842 Manhattan	1897 (consolidation to borough representation)
Philadelphia	1838	1867 (for central board; sub-district boards remain ward boards until 1911)
Pittsburgh	1834	1911
St. Louis	1833	1897
San Francisco	1848	1872

* City schools, established in 1876, never used ward representation.
** When two dates are included, the second is the date of municipal incorporation but the first marks the adoption of the principle of ward or district representation.

take care of added population and territory. During the middle of the century, several cities shifted the power of appointment from the common council to the mayor. Most of the city boards, except in Pennsylvania, began as appointive boards, but during the nineteenth century the boards in Cleveland, Detroit, and Los Angeles became elective. The citizens of Boston initially elected in their town meeting the aldermen, mayor, and other representatives who served on the Boston school committee. St. Louis citizens chose the school board members of that city by popular election from the start.

Discounting Buffalo, where the city council retained most of the functions otherwise performed by city school boards, the first city to break from the pattern of ward representation was Philadelphia, where judges began to appoint the members of the citywide board. Two vestiges of ward representation remained, however: each of the appointed members retained membership on a sectional (ward) board, and the authority for taxation and selection of district school staff remained in the hands of the sectional boards.

San Francisco and Chicago in 1872 were the two city boards, one elective and the other appointive, which broke most sharply from ward representation. Chicago reduced the total number of representatives, which made even an informal continuation of the practice difficult. Boston reduced its huge central board in 1875, at which time ward representation was also dropped, and Detroit attempted to discard it in 1881 but restored it eight years later. The other cities in this study eliminated the ward boards or ward representation in the 1890's or early in the twentieth century.[12]

The use of ward or district representation was one of the major characteristics of the nineteenth century city board of education. Its decline was attributable in part to the rapid growth of cities due to immigration, an increase in the number of wards, and the consequent growth in the size of the boards. However, district organizations outside the cities were also on the wane, especially toward the end of the century, as illustrated by this statement by former city school superintendent Andrew Sloan Draper in 1900:

While in the first half of the century the general educational purpose seems to have been to make the district system more perfect, the tendency in the latter half has unmistakably been to merge it into a more pretentious organization, covering a larger area, and capable of larger undertakings. Because of this there has been a desire for larger schools taught by teachers better prepared and capable of broader and better work, as well as the purpose to distribute educational advantages more evenly to all the people . . . it is at once seen that the township system is much less democratic and much more centralized than the district system. It has doubtless produced better schools and schools of more uniform excellence.[13]

The abandonment of ward representation on city school boards constituted a shift in emphasis from widespread participation of neighborhood spokesmen in decision-making to centralization and a decrease in the total numbers of city school board members. A factor contributing to the shift was the increase in the number of functions assigned to the city schools. Many cities also added programs for the handicapped, high schools, and normal schools for teacher training.[14] The growth of added functions and additional schools for new territory severely burdened the existing board structures. However, most of the selection structures persisted until it came to the attention of civic leaders that several leadership functions were not or could not be performed in a way that satisfied them.

THE DELEGATION OF FUNCTIONS TO FULL-TIME EXECUTIVES

Before the appointment of school superintendents, school committees and boards of education found it difficult to perform all the functions assigned to them, especially the responsibility for visiting the schools and inspecting the work of the teachers and pupils. As city schools grew in size and numbers, the complex arrangements for managing the schools gradually consumed all the time of at least one member of the board, if not many members.

The Public School Society of New York City, a philanthropic organization which maintained several pauper schools in the early nineteenth century, appointed in 1828 one member of the board of trustees to visit the families of the poor and to persuade them to send their children to school. In 1833, this person was appointed a general business agent for the society. When the schools of the Public School Society were consolidated with the public schools of New York City, he then became the assistant superintendent.[15]

The problems confronting city boards of education, which gave rise to the creation of the office of superintendent, were ill-defined and the post itself so new as to stimulate a variety of expectations toward the first superintendents of schools. Baltimore wanted a person to scrutinize carefully the books which were to be adopted rather than have decisions made by laymen who might succumb to the influence of friends and book agents. In San Francisco, the superintendent was instructed to rent or otherwise obtain an adequate number of buildings for schoolhouses and to prepare them for operation.[16] Other boards simply wanted an agent through whom to communicate with the teachers. In Buffalo, information about the schools was so meager that the first duty of the superintendent was to "ascertain where the schools were situated" and the superintendent was sent out with horse and buggy to make inquiries.[17]

From the vantage point of the twentieth century, it has become possible to trace the emergence of the superintendency as an evolutionary development. However, during the nineteenth century it was by no means clear the superintendent of schools was to become the chief executive of city school systems. On the contrary, late in the century the Department of Superintendence of the National Educational Association endorsed a Cleveland plan to make an elected school director the chief executive who would, in turn, select a superintendent of instruction. The director, however, performed the overall direction and business management of the city schools.[18]

Six of the fourteen city boards in the nineteenth century first hired or used administrators other than a city superintendent of schools (see Table 7). Chicago benefited from the services of the Cook County Commissioner of School Lands, who distributed the state school funds until 1840. Cleveland, at approximately the same time, instituted a position of "acting manager" to perform the business function. The treasurer of the Baltimore school board and the school building inspector for Philadelphia were full-time administrators for eighteen and seventeen years, respectively, before superintendents of schools were appointed for those cities. The mayors of Detroit and Los Angeles became the first school administrators of those cities. County school superintendents preceded the appointment of city superintendents for Brooklyn, New York City, and Pittsburgh.[19]

However, during the 1830's and 1840's all the cities except San Francisco and Houston (whose schools emerged after 1850) experimented with the appointment of a full-time administrator. Even in Philadelphia the school board asked the principal of the high school to assume the "general superintendence" of the schools.[20] The power of the sectional boards in Philadelphia

Table 7   THE CITY SCHOOL SUPERINTENDENCY

City	First Administrator *	First Superintendent	Major Alterations, Additions, or Discontinuity (if any)
Baltimore	1848. Treasurer, became full-time	1866	
Boston		1851	
Buffalo		1837	Elective 1853–1916
Chicago	1831. Commissioner of school lands (Cook County)	1854	
Cleveland	1841. An "acting manager"	1853	1892–1904. An elected school director instead of the school board appointed superintendent
Detroit	1842. Mayor	1855	1875. Separation of secretary's role (business) from superintendency
Houston		1876	
Los Angeles	1853. Chairman of 3 commissioners to be superintendent, mayor, first incumbent	1872. Legal authorization granted to board	1866–1870. Elective 1870–1872; no superintendent
Milwaukee		1859	1871. General secretary to board (for business)
New York	1843–1844. County superintendent	1848 Brooklyn 1851. New York City	
Philadelphia	1866. Building inspector, later superintendent of building & repairs	1883	1840. Principal of high school assigned "general superintendence" of schools; no successor
Pittsburgh	1854. County superintendent	1868	

City	First Administrator*	First Superintendent	Major Alterations, Additions, or Discontinuity (if any)
St. Louis		1839	1887. Three other executives assigned building and business functions
San Francisco		1851	Elective 1856–1923

* First administrator if that person was other than a superintendent of schools.

Source: Reller, Gilland dissertations (see Notes, 2).

was such, however, that the likelihood of assuming control of the district schools was very limited, and no successor was appointed to or assigned to perform that function for forty-three years.

Although Buffalo and Louisville, Kentucky, are normally credited with hiring the first city superintendents of schools in 1837, the new office was quickly adopted by other cities. Within twenty years, nine of the twelve cities which had schools in 1837 adopted the innovation.

The three remaining cities were Baltimore, Los Angeles, and Philadelphia. The Baltimore treasurer was a former teacher and minister who was in the process of becoming the superintendent. Los Angeles was moving from the appointment of the mayor to the superintendency through a succession of other short-term superintendents from 1853 on, until the attainment of legal authorization for the superintendency in 1872. In Philadelphia the school board had at least attempted to assign the duties of a superintendent to one of the principals, albeit unsuccessfully.

The development of the superintendency, Reller concludes, was slow, varied widely from city to city, and occasionally retrogressed in the same city.[21] Although superintendents in many cities came to be designated as the chief executives of the board of education, this neither guaranteed control over the nomination of teachers nor did it mean that other executives were denied direct access to the board of education.

The supervision of instruction was but one of several functions of the city school boards strengthened by the addition of full-time personnel. During the 1870's the boards in Detroit and Milwaukee separated the business functions from the superintendency. St. Louis added executives for auditing and for the supervision of buildings during the 1880's. By the end of the century Chicago had added a business manager for the school board, Boston a schoolhouse agent, and Cleveland a full-time school director.

The popular election of superintendents constituted an alternative to the recruitment structure of selection by the board. Such superintendents were accountable only to the people who elected them, but the evidence is slight that this mode of recruitment added to or strengthened their functioning. The superintendent of San Francisco was elective because all other boards and officials, including the chief of police and superintendents of streets, were also voted on by the electorate.[22] The Buffalo superintendents suffered from very short tenure in office during the 1870's and 1880's, but the last elective superintendent (his term lengthened by statute to four years), enjoyed a twenty-five-year total term in office. For both these cities the practice of electing a superintendent persisted for more than fifty years. Although the fear of rule by politicians was voiced by appointed superintendents elsewhere, a large number of the elected incumbents were former school principals for whom education was the only career. Rapid turnover would seem to have been the major hindrance to the management of the schools in such cities. Clearly, the citizens of San Francisco and Buffalo, and of three or four other cities which used the elective method of selecting superintendents, perceived no overriding dysfunction in this method of selection. The major criticism outsiders could voice was that only insiders stood a chance of being elected and that the city may have been depriving themselves of the potential services of talented and mobile superintendents serving smaller cities elsewhere.

The superintendency had been established before the ward boards lost favor. As the number of ward representatives continued to grow, the chances of a superintendent acquiring responsibility for personnel in the schools did not increase. Only when these functions were centralized would the central board, and its advisor for instruction, the superintendent, become other than an administrator of details and an initiator of suggestions about curriculum. The addition of separate officers for business functions enabled the superintendent to specialize on matters of personnel and instruction yet often divided the attention of the board between two executives, while also dividing the responsibilities for management of the schools.

The superintendency in the nineteenth century was not allowed to develop as a structure capable of sharing or assuming some of the board functions. Observant citizens outside of the board of education, however, perceived that the usefulness of the superintendent was linked to the organizational structure of the board of education, and that the reorganization of the board might lead to the strengthening of the superintendency.[23] Restructuring the board might also lead to strengthening the capability of the school system to respond to demands for more services. Toward the end of the century, spokesmen for the reorganization of school boards began to coordinate their efforts and mobilize support for restructuring the city boards.

THE MEANING OF STRONG CENTRAL BOARDS AND SUPERINTENDENTS

What was the impact of the decline of ward representation? The major change was the gradual loss of power by parents and voters in a neighborhood to select the kind of teachers and principal with whom they could identify. A ward board, or ward representative, could "ask around" and talk with people about vacancies and about the particular problems faced in an individual school building. Such a board could also select a few teachers from a recently arrived ethnic group once their numbers became significant. The ward boards governed geographical areas small enough to enable them to give personal attention to problems and to award jobs on personal or ethnic grounds.

What will be shown in subsequent chapters is that the move from ward-based school boards to central boards also shifted power from the working class (who by the 1880's "captured" many city wards) to the upper class and to more cosmopolitan professionals who claimed to be revolted by disclosures of inefficiency and corruption. Henceforth, the schools would be run by a "guardian" class who because of their own superior education presumably knew what kind of schools should be maintained.

They wanted teachers to be loyal to their elite values rather than those of the ward boss. Thus, the control of the schools passed from the "people" to the tiny minority of owners and college graduates who wanted the schools to preserve and protect their way of life.

The second loss of power involved entering into contracts, whether to furnish the schools, repair the building, or to buy supplies. No longer could neighborhood spokesmen make these judgments on local or particularistic grounds. They would be made centrally and according to generally applied criteria. Businessmen criticized the way in which laymen took part in so many detailed decisions. The Philadelphia Public Education Association made explicit the model its well-born members had in mind (Issel found 75 percent of the officers' names in either the Blue Book or the Social Register):

The Board of Education holds the same relation to the public schools as a Board of Directors holds to a bank or railroad. It would be as reasonable to argue that the Board of Directors of the Pennsylvania should run the road, and dispense with a President, as to argue that the Board of Education should assume the duties of superintendents.[24]

The rationale for a strong central staff thus came into full view. The school system could and should be run like a railroad or any of the newer industrial bureaucracies. It need not be run like a church or a hospital.

Such a view, expressed by civic elites in most of the industrial cities, meant that principals would have less power to select teachers and that teachers would have less autonomy over the curriculum, textbooks, and methods of instruction. This trend, however, was stoutly resisted in many cities, but most conspicuously in Chicago.

Chicago teachers worried individually about the decline in working conditions between 1870 and 1900—the growth of class size, the stability of their salary scale, the loss of say over textbook selection, and the closing of the Chicago Normal School as an economy measure in the 1870's. (New teachers thereafter were recruited directly from the high schools and given a few years' probation on the job.)[25] Margaret Haley, a Chicago teacher and early leader of the Chicago Teachers' Federation, complained bitterly about centralization and predicted that "our city school systems shall become great machines, in which one superintendent 'presses the button' and all the teachers move absolutely as he directs." [26]

The Chicago teachers, under Haley, fought hard for teacher participation in local school decisions and opposed new teacher selection by standardized examination. They opposed the strengthening of the central office and the superintendency. But this was the heyday of the Progressive movement whose leaders wanted to reduce corruption and take power and positions away from politicians. Public systems could then be run by specialists, by experts carefully selected for their skills and knowledge, but removable if inefficient or ineffective. Robert Wiebe suggests that the Progressives believed in a doctrine of "expert responsibility" and in more rational and efficient systems of government than they felt were possible under the ward-based boards.[27]

Thus the growth of stronger central school boards and appointment of superintendents meant the decline of Jeffersonian "small unit" democracy and the rise of a meritocracy of city-wide policy-makers and of highly paid city school administrators.

The superintendents gradually won board acceptance of their recommendations to hire additional supervisors and assistants, to make system-wide rules, and to treat teacher and parent requests objectively and impersonally—in short, to create a bureaucracy.[28] At the same time this development circumscribed and may have impeded the professionalism of teachers. It certainly limited their autonomy, may have reduced their need for much advanced education, and forced teachers to be more loyal to their employers than to their calling. The pay and status remain low to this day, earning for teachers inclusion in a category called the "semi-professions" by the sociologists of work and organization.[29]

These changes began to take place prior to the 1890's but it remains to be shown how the movement began to achieve a dramatic momentum in the last decade of the nineteenth century, a momentum which in some cities did not subside until the 1920's. The movement was progressive, elite, and centralizing; the effects included the decline of lay responsibility for education and the diminished powers of teachers and principals to make decisions about their own work. By the turn of the century the reform of centralization would be accepted by most of the elite business, social, and academic leaders and the working class would lose much of the influence once afforded them by ward boards.

NOTES

1. Henry Suzzalo, *The Rise of Local School Supervision in Massachusetts,* (New York: Teachers College, Columbia University, 1906).

2. Several monographs, dissertations, and special studies on each city were used to document the origins of city school systems. The general studies by Reller and by Gilland on city school superintendencies and boards were especially helpful. See Theodore Reller, *The Development of the City Superintendency of Schools* (Philadelphia: The Author, 1935) and Thomas McDowell Gilland, *The Origin and Development of the Power and Duties of the City School Superintendent* (Chicago: The University of Chicago Press, 1935).

3. Suzzalo, *op. cit.,* p. 99.

4. George H. Martin, *Evolution of the Massachusetts School System* (New York: Appleton-Century-Crofts, 1894), pp. 91–92.

5. *Ibid.,* p. 92.

6. *Ibid.,* pp. 204–205.

7. Suzzalo, *op. cit.,* p. 107.

8. *Ibid.,* p. 107.

9. "The Founding Fathers and the Division of Powers," in Arthur Maas (ed.), *Area and Power* (Glencoe, Illinois: The Free Press, 1959), p. 176.

10. The fourteen cities are here listed in alphabetical order. For other purposes in subsequent sections, the cities will be arranged according to the type of or timing of change in recruitment structure.

11. Superintendent of Schools, Milwaukee, Wisconsin, *Our Roots Grow Deep,* The Eighty-Fourth Annual Report of the Milwaukee Public Schools (Milwaukee: Board of Education, June 1943).

12. Except for Houston, which at no point used ward representation.

13. Andrew S. Draper, "Education Organization and Administration," in Nicholas Murray Butler (ed.), *Education in the United States,* Monograph no. 1, (Albany: J. B. Lyon, 1900), pp. 9–10.

14. A. M. Schlesinger, *The Rise of the City, 1878–1898* (New York: Macmillan, 1933), Chapter VI, "The Education Revival."

15. Reller, *op. cit.,* p. 20.

16. *Ibid.,* p. 55.

17. *Ibid.,* p. 29.

18. N.E.A. Proceedings, *Journal of Proceedings and Addresses, 1894,* of the National Education Association (St. Paul, Minn.: N.E.A., 1895), p. 375.

19. Reller, *op. cit.*, pp. 20–21.

20. John Trevor Curtis, *The Public Schools of Philadelphia* (Philadelphia: Burk and McFetridge, 1897), p. 21.

21. Reller, *op. cit.*, pp. 300–301.

22. Ellwood P. Cubberley, "The School Situation in San Francisco," *Educational Review*, vol. XXI, no. 4 (April 1901), pp. 364–381. Goodnow points out that many cities experimented with the popular election of executive department heads whether or not they also reported to boards. Mayors were generally weak, power fragmented, and Goodnow reports that by 1880 many people agreed that such a board system did not work satisfactorily. See Frank J. Goodnow, *City Government in the United States* (New York: Appleton-Century-Crofts, 1904), pp. 73–79.

23. Raymond Callahan stresses the influence of Dr. Joseph Mayer Rice, whose criticisms of three dozen school systems were published in 1892 and 1893. Rice urged city school boards to give superintendents enough power to improve the schools. See Raymond E. Callahan, "The History of the Fight to Control Policy in Public Education," in Frank W. Lutz and Joseph Azzarelli (eds.), *The Struggle for Power in Education* (New York: Center for Applied Research in Education, 1966), p. 20.

24. Public Education Association of Philadelphia, Annual Report, 1882, pp. 8–9. Quoted in William H. Issel, "Modernization in Philadelphia School Reform, 1882–1905," in *The Pennsylvania Magazine of History and Biography*, vol. XCIV, no. 3 (July 1970), pp. 361–362.

25. The decline of teacher status had other causes, summarized in Cherry Wedgwood Collins' "The Chicago Teachers' Federation: The First Teachers' Union," Doctoral qualifying paper (Cambridge, Massachusetts: Harvard Graduate School of Education, March 1970), p. 9.

26. Margaret Haley quoted in *Current Literature*, vol. XXXVI (June 1904), p. 612.

27. *The Search for Order 1877–1920* (New York: Hill & Wang, 1967), p. 168.

28. For more detail on the bureaucratization, see Michael B. Katz, "The Emergence of Bureaucracy in Urban Education: The Boston Case, 1850–1884," *History of Education Quarterly* (Summer and Fall), 1968.

29. Amitai Etzioni, *The Semi-Professions* (New York: The Free Press, 1969). See especially the chapters on teachers, on women in bureaucracies, and on the limits of professionalization.

THE REORGANIZATION MOVEMENT, 1890–1900

INTRODUCTION

STRONG CAMPAIGNS to reorganize the city school board structures both preceded and followed the 1890's. But few periods in the history of city school systems contain as much political ferment and citizen concern for administrative reorganization as can be found in this decade. The sensational disclosures of Jacob Riis and Joseph Mayer Rice early in the 1890's served to alarm prominent citizens who had been complacent about the education of children and the management of schools. Churchmen, women, and others, already quite willing to take up the cudgel of municipal reform, soon added the problem of the city schools to the list of battles to be fought. When it became evident that adverse publicity about school conditions did not discourage the "grafters" and "boodlers," the *New York Times* suggested that, "The best method of proceeding to reform the schools is by eforming the whole system of their management." [1] What was it that generated such a strong drive for school reform and how did it change the way in which big-city school systems were governed?

THE SOCIAL AND POLITICAL ENVIRONMENT OF THE CITIES IN THE 1890's

While Ward McAllister was describing the "Four Hundred" most socially prominent New Yorkers in 1890, reporter Jacob Riis was discovering and writing about "How the Other Half Lives." [2] During the 1880's immigrants had swarmed into the cities, swelling the still young Chicago from a population of 500,-000 in 1880 to over 1 million in 1890; thus, it passed Philadelphia as the second largest city. The populations of Detroit, Milwaukee, and Cleveland each grew 60 to 80 percent in the same decade. Two older eastern cities passed the million mark, New York in 1880 and Philadelphia by 1890. During the same period, Baltimore and Boston had grown to half a million and Buffalo and Pittsburgh, whose waterways were not traversed by the transport ships and immigrant packets, had reached 250,000. The West had only recently been linked to the rest of the nation via railways, and the South was still recovering from the ravages of war and reconstruction, with Louisville and New Orleans the only cities over 100,000.[3]

With both the influx of country youth from the farm to the city and the waves of immigrants from Europe, the cities grew crowded and living conditions deteriorated. Municipalities found sewage disposal facilities, water supplies, housing for immigrant families, police and fire protection services all inadequate for the expanded populace.[4]

Long after the Revolution, many Americans continued to voice a distrust in the concentration of power in any executive, preferring governmental forms which guaranteed broad citizen participation in civic affairs through such forums as the town meeting and the large elective city council. The twin forces of increased population (which generated a need for more police, school buildings, roads, and prisons) and the addition of costly new services (street cleaning, lighting, paving and parks, and public health facilities) caused local tax rates and indebtedness to rise. Although municipal corruption and inefficiency may have reached an apex around 1870 (exemplified by the activities of the Tweed Ring in New York City) the cities were larger in 1890, and there were more citizens to be governed and served. Therefore, governmental inefficiency and political corruption increasingly attracted the attention of foreign commentators and municipal reformers.

GOVERNMENTAL INEFFICIENCY

The political theory that all municipal officers should be selected at the ballot box may have facilitated corruption in government during the last decades of the nineteenth century. Police graft, bribery in exchange for public franchises, favoritism in the granting of contracts for municipal construction, the friendly underassessment of property, the traffic in "jobs created mainly for patronage purposes," [5] all served to discredit the political system and dissuade the "good citizens" from running for offices except under the banner of reform. Ernest Griffith, a student of comparative municipal government in Britain and America, placed some of the blame for expensive government on the "long ballot" which, as the cities grew, allowed candidates to be nominated whose virtues or vices few would know. He also criticized the "degeneracy" of the post-Civil War political parties, state interference in local self-government, and the perpetuation of provisions to keep the mayor weak and the council strong.[6]

The political bosses, such as New York's Croker, "Blind Boss" Christopher Buckley of San Francisco, or Colonel Ed Butler of St. Louis [7] have received a great measure of the blame, but Griffith explains, if he does not quite exonerate, the men who filled this role:

. . . in the hodgepodge of elected officials in America, in the indefinite relationship between the council and the executive, and between both and the state, and in lack of any sort of statutory budgetary procedure, some dominant coordinating force was needed. In fact some force was inevitable, if the government was to function at all. The boss was almost a necessary evil.[8]

Griffith points out that once the boss established his machine he used it for "personal and extralegal ends," finding it advantageous to resist any major modification of a system which was solving the problem of chaos in the major cities. The lack of centralized legal machinery created a demand for extra-legal coordination; the work of the boss was a response to the need for executive leadership.

POLITICAL CORRUPTION
PROVOKES PROPOSALS FOR REFORM

Lincoln Steffens, whose muckraking specialty was to become city politics in the next fifteen years, was already noticing the link between businessmen and politicians, first in New York City where he and Riis began as police reporters, later in Philadelphia, St. Louis, Chicago, Pittsburgh, and elsewhere. Steffens later denied that "Philadelphia, Corrupt and Contented" was the "worst in the land. It was only *older* than St. Louis and Minneapolis." [9]

While Philadelphia was run by the notorious "gas ring," A. M. Schlesinger recounts how six capitalists pooled their resources to control the street railways of New York, Chicago, Pittsburgh, and dozens of other communities. Businessmen elsewhere specialized in concessions for electric lights or trolleys, or profited from rented property wherein prostitution was overlooked by bribed public officials. Both Steffens and Schlesinger attribute the plight of city government to "this unholy alliance of big business and bad politics." [10]

Lord Bryce in his several visits to America could not refrain from commenting on the extravagance and mismanagement of the cities he visited: "There is no denying that the government of cities is the one conspicuous failure of the United States." He inquired about the causes and learned about the spoils system, the shortcomings of political parties, the interference in city affairs by state governments, and the withdrawal of cultivated citizens from the "vulgarities of practical politics." He was forced to conclude that "in great cities the forces that attack and pervert democratic government are exceptionally numerous, the defensive forces that protect it exceptionally ill-placed for resistance." [11]

Bryce, even before municipal reformers had accomplished their proposals or even joined forces, catalogued proposals for reform such as the use of separate boards of finance to limit the common council's power to spend money, the separation of municipal from state or national elections, the placing of limits on the borrowing power of the city, and the strengthening of "the general control and appointing power of the mayor." [12] He also learned of a proposal and moderate trend toward the election of a city council "or of a school committee, on a general ticket (at large) instead of by wards." [13]

THE CITY SCHOOL AND THE MUCKRAKERS

Some of the corruption spilled over to the schools. Politicians, as long as the sub-district or ward committees had a hand in the selection, appointment, and promotion of teachers, used these powers to place less than competent aspirants in teaching positions in the district schools. Andrew Sloan Draper in 1900, after he had left the Cleveland superintendency, tried to be objective but could not hide his wrath and frustration:

It would not be true to say that the business of the schools has suffered as seriously as municipal business, but it certainly has been managed badly enough. All this has come from the amounts of money that are involved and the number of appointments that are constantly to be made. More than a hundred millions of dollars are paid annually for teachers' wages alone in the United States. People who are needy have sought positions as teachers without much reference to preparation, and the kindly disposed have aided them without any apparent appreciation of the injury they were doing to the highest interests of their neighbors. Men engaged in managing the organizations of the different political parties have undertaken to control appointments in the interests of their party machines. And the downright scoundrels have infested the school organization in some places for the sake of plunder.[14]

Not only politicians but textbook publishers invaded the realm of textbook selection. After Lincoln Steffens had printed a list of Missouri trusts which had been found by the St. Louis attorney, Joseph Folk, to be engaged in corrupt business practices, a textbook trust representative threatened to fight Steffens if he tried to "expose the whole textbook business in politics." "I had not thought of it," Steffens replied, but he wrote later that he had heard everywhere about the activities of textbook publishers, which he felt, "if verified and printed, would make a lovely scandal," one which the Hearst papers did try to uncover sometime later. Steffens "ached to dig into the school book business," to tell how the publishers used not only money but "women to 'get' principals of schools, trustees, and teachers" to adopt a certain line of textbooks under threat of blackmail.[15]

The city schools quite early had their own "muckraker," Dr. Joseph Mayer Rice of Philadelphia, who visited schools and observed classroom teaching in thirty-three cities. Separate articles on the public schools of New York City, Baltimore, Buffalo, Boston, Philadelphia, St. Louis, and Indianapolis, Chicago, and St. Paul appeared in a series of articles published first in the *Forum* magazine during 1892 and 1893 and later collected in a book published in 1893 entitled *The Public School System of the United States*.

For the mechanical and uninspired teaching of children that Rice witnessed, he blamed the meager amount of supervision, the inadequate examination of teachers, appointment by "pull" rather than according to qualifications, and the dependence of school board members for their election on ward politicians. Board after board he called "a purely political organization," whose actions in "some cities" are "governed to a considerable extent by selfish motives." [16] The elected superintendent of Buffalo, he thought, must "almost necessarily be a politician," and he questioned how that one supervisory official could supervise by himself the 700 teachers in that city, a comparatively small number of whom had graduated from normal school. He concluded that the removal of city schools from ward and partisan politics, the strengthening of a corps of supervisors, and the examination of teacher candidates by experts rather than laymen were necessary before the standard of the schools could be raised.

Despite the sharp attack on the performance standards and management of the city schools, the fact that a magazine was willing to finance this investigation reflected a growing public awareness and concern about the work of the schools. The "closing decades of the century," Schlesinger judged, "saw an educational renaissance comparable in many respects to the great days of Horace Mann and Henry Barnard" of which "the cities were the chief beneficiary." [17] Kindergartens had been started in St. Louis and Boston in the early seventies and the idea now spread to other cities. More high schools had to be built. New studies such as the sciences, business education, manual arts, and homemaking were introduced to the curriculum, and the rate of illiteracy continued to decline.[18]

The disclosures of Jacob Riis about the "Children of the Poor," in a sequel to *How the Other Half Lives,* shocked and provoked a number of prominent New Yorkers to launch a drive for more kindergartens and school playgrounds and for the "removal of schools from politics." Demands for less political and more scientific administration of the schools became part of the total Progressive effort to reform the cities in the 1890's. Dismayed at the conditions in which immigrant families lived and children were being raised, alarmed at the return of Irish Catholics to the control of New York despite earlier success at ousting Tweed and his Tammany ranks, aroused by Riis and his grim accounts of slum conditions, the "New York Reformers seized on education and the public schools as the Great Panacea." [19]

Cohen traced the birth of the Public Education Association of New York to the ladies auxiliary of Good Government Club E., one of the more vigorous anti-Tammany groups of the mid-1890's. Supported by Riis, Nicholas Murray Butler, and the press and fanned by the rising Protestant fear of Catholic control of public education and general city government, the ladies helped a Committee of Seventy (with a sub-committee on schools) elect a businessman mayor, William Strong, and fought for major revisions of the New York State School Law. The "school war," as both Butler and Riis called it, was waged for the replacement of the old board of education with a twenty-one-man board to be appointed by the mayor with the simultaneous abolition of lay school inspectors and of ward trustees. [20]

THE EXTENSION OF MUNICIPAL REFORM TO CITY SCHOOL SYSTEMS

Municipal reform, in general, had previously been concerned with city finance, dishonesty in government, and the curtailment of waste, but had been only temporarily effective, in part since the support of reform mayors depended on citizen outrage that subsided soon after elections. The work of the city was so great as to require much "informal government," and the naïvete of good-government leaders about city. management was so disabling that their efforts in office could be easily discredited and the old regime restored.

Structural reforms such as the establishment of bi-partisan boards, the adoption of at least the trappings of civil service for cities, and the strenthening of the mayor's position were remedies popularized during the 1880's. Reformers slowly learned the complexity of politics and government and held an inter-city conference in Philadelphia in January 1894, out of which grew the National Municipal League with sixteen city government reform group affiliates. The sporadic efforts of local reform groups developed into a spirited national movement and the more successful strategies for reform as well as ideas for new city charters began to be shared.

Some of the city school reformers were caught up in the trend toward national affiliation and "confederation." In 1898 the New York Public Educational Association invited the civic leaders of other cities in the East to confer for two days in New York City. Representatives from other public education associations, civic clubs, and school reform associations in Philadelphia, Boston, Buffalo, and New Haven attended the conference, as did Clinton R. Woodruff, the National Municipal League secretary from Philadelphia. The following year the Conference of Eastern Public Education Associations was formally launched at a similar meeting in Philadelphia, and the group then met annually to read and discuss papers on such diverse topics as school sanitation, nature study, and evening schools.[21] Not all school groups cared to learn how to lobby for reform legislation, but the various educational societies and committees of laymen served to articulate the interests of the middle and upper classes, whose concern about city schools and city government had not previously been communicated. The city P.E.A.'s and the Eastern Conference helped to aggregate the interests, spread the more appropriate strategies and techniques of reform, and helped to sustain the morale and energy of reform leaders in several cities. The disclosures of the early muckraking journalists and the sympathetic support from municipal reformers helped set the stage for a series of structural reorganizations of city school boards in the 1890's.

One possible reform could have been the strengthening of the mayor's role in education, or at least in supervising the work of an education department and director. Another reform might have been the extension of more complete control of education by the states, which quite frequently assumed responsibility for selecting city department heads in the last quarter of the century. Goodnow notes the demise of many departmental boards in Brooklyn and New York City in the 1890's; so might city school boards have disappeared to be replaced by stronger executives. Instead, the redistribution of authority was relatively slow, and the strengthening of either the superintendency or a school bureaucracy was a gradual phenomenon often requiring a series of steps over decades. Even the elective superintendencies faded slowly.

THE MAJOR REORGANIZATION EFFORTS
IN THE 1890's

Which of the cities did in fact decide to reorganize in the 1890's the arrangements for governing city schools? What new organizational plans were considered, which were adopted, and which were defeated or deferred until another time?

Six of the fourteen cities in the 1890's reorganized their method of selecting school board members and redefined the functions and relationships of the board and the superintendent. Major changes in the size and functioning of school boards were wrought through charter revisions and statute amendments for New York City, St. Louis, Milwaukee, and Baltimore. The superintendents of Buffalo and Cleveland at a National Education Association meeting in 1894 reported two rather unique arrangements for governing urban schools.

Buffalo

At the meeting the Buffalo spokesman told how his city had grown rapidly in the 1890's and how the rapid turnover of superintendents (virtually every two years a new man was elected) had precluded orderly administration. Therefore, a new charter for Buffalo placed the school business functions under the public works department, provided for a five-man board of examiners to be appointed by the mayor, but kept the elective superintendent responsible for teacher appointments, dismissals, and the preparation of estimates of expenditures on which the city council would pass. These procedures in Buffalo were not entirely novel for that city in that they included a return to a board of examiners plan similar to one in use from 1853 to 1870. Superintendent Emerson told the N.E.A. that he was not completely satisfied with the procedures, and pointed out that his own tenure in office was never predictable. He suggested that an ideal form of organization would be an appointive or elective board of seven to nine members who would then employ a superintendent.[22]

Cleveland

Andrew Sloan Draper explained the Cleveland situation to the NEA. Four businessmen in the 1880's found a board of twenty-six members and three paid executives in control of education, construction, and finance (with as many as twenty-three committees to cope with the administrative detail). The businessmen decided that the organization of the schools had become too unwieldy and proposed a seven-man council and full-time executive director. Both the seven-member "school council" (the legislative branch) and the paid, full-time "school director" (the executive branch) would be elected and then keep certain checks on the other. The council appointed teachers, adopted textbooks, selected sites for new buildings, and prepared estimates for a tax levy for the Cleveland Board of Tax Commissioners. The school director, who attended meetings, but could not vote, was given veto power over council actions. He could appoint the superintendent of instruction and other employees, except teachers and assistants to the superintendent. He was to enforce and adjudicate the rules governing the board of education and to carry on the business functions of purchasing, personnel supervision, and execution of contracts. The city auditor kept the school accounts, however. The salary paid to the director was high enough to secure outstanding candidates, and the first director (1892–1900) in turn selected superintendents who were acknowledged to be outstanding educators.

Cleveland's "Federal Plan," approved by the Ohio legislature in 1892, seemed so plausible a remedy that the N.E.A. Committee on the Reorganization of City School Systems recommended its adoption elsewhere as "the most desirable form of school organization for the large cities." [23] Despite the N.E.A. endorsement of the "Federal Plan" in 1894, none of the nine other cities that reorganized their school boards in the ten-year period from 1895 to 1905 copied the Cleveland model. Many school board members resented the attack on their role.[24] Even some of the superintendents felt that the plan concentrated too much power in the hands of a single individual. The advocates of city school reorganization agreed only to strengthen the board's reliance on a superintendent, and they concentrated on the "abolition of ward trustee boards" and the reduction in size of board membership.

New York City

The effort in New York City to reorganize the school board demonstrates how the advocates of new school programs (such as play centers, kindergartens and manual training classes) found it useful to work closely with the municipal reformers in order to accomplish their objectives. The friends of public education in New York City in general were politically naive, but they obtained expert advice from Jacob Riis and other sophisticated and experienced critics of the status quo. Frank Goodnow, a municipal government professor at Columbia University, who with Nicholas Murray Butler drafted the 1896 legislation to abolish the ward trustees, urged that the management of the schools be reorganized as a first step toward the other changes sought. Their efforts drew support from urban reform groups such as the City Club, the Good Government clubs, the City Vigilance League, and the German American Reform Union. The upstate Republican machine, led by Thomas Platt, angry at the independence of Republican Mayor Strong, joined with the Tammany Democrats and city school teachers in killing an 1895 school reorganization bill. Success at the 1896 legislative session was due, at least in part, to new support from the Public Education Association. Under Butler's tutelage the P.E.A. had become a militant lobby whose lady members attended the Albany hearings and lectured legislators on the urgent need for school reform.[25]

A compromise bill was passed which abolished the ward trustees and enabled Mayor Strong to appoint an entirely new slate of fiteen members to replace the twenty-one-man central board. The new board appointed fifteen assistant superintendents to help the superintendent supervise the teachers and principals. The mayor could then appoint five inspectors to visit the schools in each district, partly as a palliative to some highly respected citizens who wanted to keep the people informed about conditions in the schools.[26]

Some of the "progress" was undone the following year when the two huge school systems of Brooklyn and New York, all of Richmond County, and part of Queens were consolidated under the Greater New York Charter of 1897. To convince the other school boards that their autonomy would not be totally submerged, a complex and unwieldy "borough system" was established. The new superintendent was selected from Brooklyn (after Andrew Sloan Draper and Daniel Coit Gilman declined the position). Despite his great reputation as an administrator, William Maxwell's power was limited, since borough superintendents retained considerable authority for the period from 1898 to

1902. The central board of education was composed of forty-six "delegates" from the borough boards. However, the Butler group was satisfied for the moment to have gained Maxwell and to have kept the board appointed by Strong.[27]

St. Louis and Milwaukee

In 1897, St. Louis and Milwaukee tried out various plans for reorganizing the school boards in those cities. Civic, professional, and business leaders in St. Louis persuaded the Missouri legislature to authorize a new charter which would substitute "at-large" for "ward" election of board members and would reduce the board size from twenty-one to twelve. The 1897 charter also transferred the function of nominating professional staff to the superintendent, who also assumed responsibility for curriculum, supervision, textbook selection, the suspension of teachers, and the selection of instructional clerks. The board was empowered to add other executives to the four who already reported directly to the board (the superintendent of instruction, the commissioner of school buildings, the secretary-treasurer, and the auditor) so the board decided to hire an attorney and a commissioner of supplies, which brought the total of top administrative division heads to six.[28]

The Milwaukee board grew in size to forty-two. A "widespread and growing feeling of discontent" emerged over what amounted to selection of each school board member by the alderman of that ward and with the way the board ignored the superintendent's recommendations for the selection of teachers and texts.[29] Although supporters of radical reorganization wanted to bypass wards entirely, since some wards had no men "fit to serve as school officers," the best they could obtain was a plan to reduce the board size by half, direct the mayor to appoint a fourman commission with no more than two from any one party, and authorize these four "citizens of suitable character and education" to appoint the board of school directors.

St. Louis officials later revealed that their ideas for the 1897 reorganization were borrowed from a draft of a New York City school reform bill of 1892, one that was not passed by the New York State legislature that year.[30] Nevertheless, St. Louis chose not to depart from the twelve-man board elected at large. Milwaukee, on the other hand, had tried to find a way to keep selection of board members out of the hands of aldermen or political parties, but it did not anticipate some of the consequences that might accrue to its innovation. The four-man commission immediately became "bi-partisan" and thus very sensitive to the question of the political affiliations of board appointees, a question which the critics of the new commission felt was irrelevant to education.[31]

Baltimore

Baltimore postponed adoption of an 1880 citizens commission report on the reorganization of the school board in that city. Like Milwaukee, the city council had been appointing the board of school commissioners prior to the new City Charter of 1898. Each councilman nominated a school commissioner from his own ward, which was "equivalent to an election by virtue of so-called 'senatorial courtesy'." [32] Twelve years later a team of investigators of Baltimore's schools, assembled by the U.S. Bureau of Education, recorded that they had been told how "the school commissionership was very frequently used as a stepping stone to the council," in effect as a low rung on the ladder of political mobility. The 1898 charter placed the appointment responsibility in the hands of the mayor, who was to appoint nine instead of twenty-two commissioners, although the city council was to consent to the appointments. On the advise of several university presidents the new board selected Denver Superintendent James Van Sickle to improve the schools of Baltimore, which Joseph Mayer Rice had found to "compare unfavorably even with those of New York." [33]

San Francisco

Like Buffalo, San Francisco elected its superintendent of schools and its board of school directors. San Francisco superintendent John Swett, in his 1892 annual report, complained about the method of selecting teachers in San Francisco. He judged the system to be "the worst in the world," based largely on patronage, and "worse each year" since 1875, although the board ceased in 1872 to be selected by wards.[34] The advocates of charter revision failed in major attempts in 1883, 1887, and 1895 to get an unpaid board of five members appointed by the mayor, but in

1898 they agreed to a compromise plan which established an appointive, bi-partisan board of school directors who would be paid for full-time direction of the schools in addition to the full-time salaried elective superintendent. Nicholas Murray Butler at once predicted the inevitability of conflict between a board of education and a superintendent of schools responsible only to the electorate, both working full-time on the management of the San Francisco schools. Conflict did, in fact, arise, but Ellwood P. Cubberley in 1901 reported that in the first two years the board successfully modernized the curriculum, economized on operating expenditures, and was cooperating with the new state normal school in San Francisco.[35] Despite the apparent incongruity of multiple yet autonomous governmental structures for the schools, this arrangement persisted in San Francisco for twenty-five years.

REORGANIZATION IN THE OTHER CITIES

Conditions in six other cities were similar to those which had precipitated organized protests elsewhere and the reorganization of the six board structures described. The writings of Joseph Mayer Rice in 1892 and 1893 informed individual citizens and groups in Chicago, Boston, and Philadelphia of the shortcomings of their city schools. For different reasons in each city, reorganization did not take place during the 1890's. Proposals for reorganization in these cities met with more opposition than support until the early 1900's. Some changes in board structure were attempted but, in retrospect, these can be categorized as either internal, temporary, or inconsequential.

Los Angeles, Detroit, Pittsburgh, and Houston

Los Angeles adopted election by wards in 1889 and was still small enough to avoid criticism of that method. Detroit in 1889 made the decision to revert to the ward method of election after dissatisfaction with the behavior of members selected in at-large elections. Pittsburgh citizens, perhaps preoccupied with industrialization and labor strife (at a high point in 1892 during the Homestead strike), neither surveyed nor reorganized the schools of their city until well into the next century. Meanwhile, Houston, until 1900, was a city with less than 50,000 inhabitants.

Chicago

In Chicago the functioning of the board of education had been cursorily reviewed in 1893, but the law was revised so slightly that reform mayor Carter Harrison in 1897 called for a study of the legal basis for the management of Chicago schools. After one year of work, a commission headed by William Rainey Harper of the University of Chicago identified "grave defects in the present plan of administration," criticized the board's reliance on committees and the low status of the superintendent of schools, and urged a reduction in size of the school board to eleven members.[36]

The report provoked considerable opposition from teachers, who objected to transferring so much of the board's power to the superintendent. Margaret Haley, aggressive leader of the new Chicago Teachers Federation, opposed the Harper report and advocated giving each school faculty the right to select courses and materials. The teachers killed the Harper proposal in the Illinois legislature, where they had recently won several pension and salary battles.[37]

Boston

The Boston school committee remained an elective board of twenty-four members throughout the 1890's despite testimony before a legislative committee by Harvard President Charles William Eliot to the effect that a smaller board would be less political and more effective. One source of delay in reorganization was the success of Republican women who for school elections built an effective voting machine capable of mustering 10,000 lady voters, motivated in large part by fear of Catholic domination of the public schools. These women were reluctant to see altered a political solution which they had made to work. To some extent this feeling postponed reorganization, since the feminine vote in the 1890's made it more difficult for members they thought irresponsible to stay in control.[38] In 1895, A. Lawrence Lowell of Harvard ran for and won a seat on the board and persuaded the school committee to strengthen the authority of the superintendent and supervisors in the nomination of teachers. Lowell fought along with other members for the abolition of both the standing committees for administration and of the sub-committees, which made decisions about personnel in schools in each district. Actually his success and style pleased the leaders of neither political party and Lowell was defeated in 1898. The power of the various board committees was quickly restored and the sub-committees were revived.

A Public School Association was formed in 1898 as a successor to the Protestant and Feminist Independent Women Voters. P.S.A. candidates between 1899 and 1901 won enough seats to control Boston's school board for a brief time.[39] During the 1890's the major reorganization of the school administration had been made from within, which was a somewhat unique achievement. But the reformers, even with the strong turnout of women voters eager to use their limited suffrage for some noble cause, were unable to stay in power and retain the changes.

Philadelphia and Detroit

The judges of Philadelphia had since 1867 chosen the members of the board of controllers, but the central school district was divided into many smaller sections each with its own twelve-man elective board. These local boards kept the power to appoint teachers and janitors in the schools of their section. At the turn of the century an observer noted that this division of authority had led to contention and dissatisfaction, but that efforts made at two sessions of the legislature to change the Philadelphia system were unsuccessful, although the central board had grown to thirty-eight members by 1897 with just as many sectional or ward boards.[40]

Detroit citizens, with the support of the Detroit *Free Press,* were successful in 1881 in getting a smaller board of twelve citizens elected at large. This change was repealed in 1889 after Republicans and other citizens in the outlying wards found that a tight bloc of inner-city Democrats had captured the board and allegedly accepted bribes from the ubiquitous textbook agents. Only the notion of a smaller board was retained in 1889; one board member rather than two would be selected from each ward. However, the city was sufficiently concerned with the unbusinesslike methods of the board in the 1880's that legislation was enacted in 1893 which curtailed the financial powers of the board of education. Thereafter, no money could be expended without the approval of the board of estimates, the body which

would specifically determine the amount of money expended for
building and maintenance purposes.[41] The city controller and
city treasurer were to disburse the funds of the board of education, and the Mayor was also given a veto power over expenditures. Detroit contributes one of the clearest examples of a structure stripped of certain functions after a perceived failure to
discharge the functions assigned to it by the state.

THE CENTRALIZING OF CITY SCHOOL BOARDS

The origins of city school boards have been traced to committees appointed by the New England town meeting and to the
administrative supervision of schools by boards of selectmen, aldermen, or city council sub-committees. As cities became formally
incorporated in the years between the presidencies of Thomas
Jefferson and Andrew Jackson, the values of decentralized local
government and participation by the common man were exemplified in the establishment of small school districts within the
city, each with visiting committees or boards of school inspectors.
The local school districts most often were coterminous with the
minicipal wards.

During the second half of the nineteenth century, the cities
grew very rapidly and those boards which gave representation to
one or more representatives from each ward swelled to unman-
ageable proportions. The city school district or department was
only one of several major structures captured by new elites as the
ward bosses and city political machine leaders filled the numerous seats on boards. Ward board trustees or ward-elected central
board members yielded to the demands of aldermen, councilmen,
or ward leaders that they nominate to teaching or administrative
positions those people who were related to, friendly with, or properly grateful to the political organization, irrespective of a candidate's qualifications to teach. Textbook salesmen found certain
members of the school boards vulnerable to bribery and took advantage of the situation. School boards had no franchises to
grant, but the opportunity for graft appeared when school construction or repairs were administered by sub-committees which
made decisions on projects and contracts.

The increase in the number of schools in a city, and the
growth of the curriculum to include more specialized subjects,

began to require closer coordination and supervision than the
part-time lay school board could afford to give. By 1860, all of
the city boards except Philadelphia and the yet-to-be organized
Houston schools had selected superintendents of schools. Although two of the cities continued to select a superintendent by
popular election, eleven others by 1900 chose a superintendent of
schools by direct board appointments.

By 1900 the initially limited advisory powers of some superintendents had been broadened to include the functions of nominating teachers and principals and recommending textbooks, although not all city boards were willing to relinquish or share
these functions by that time.[42] Many of the cities added business
agents or directors, assistant superintendents, and other supervisory personnel to relieve central or district boards of some of the
chores of visiting each school, a responsibility which lay citizens
had been performing in some New England towns and cities for
at least two centuries.

The superintendent reported directly to the board in most
instances but was one of several executives in charge of major divisions or functions, usually that of instruction as contrasted with
business or school construction or supplies or auditing. Cleveland's use of an elective and higher-paid director to fill the central leadership role was a drastic and unique reform,
comprehensible only in terms of the experimentation of the
1890's.[43] If adopted elsewhere it may have meant the removal of
school boards from school administrative decision-making.

The second major trend discernible in the latter half of the
century and most sharply in the 1890's was the reorganization of
the procedures for selecting board members. This was more than
a matter of reducing the size of the board. That goal was cou-
pled with the vigorous drive to eliminate ward leader domination of the process of appointing both board members and,
through him, the teachers in the district schools. Five of the cities abandoned the selection of central board members by ward
representation. Six of the boards had been reduced during the
1890's. Only Chicago's board of education continued to increase
in size.[44]

Many of the city schools formerly were administered at a district or ward level where teachers were hired and supervised by
laymen, while high schools and special schools serving the total

school system were governed by the central board. Sub-committees of the large central boards were assigned administrative functions over high schools, kindergarten programs, floating schools, special schools for the deaf and dumb, city-wide schools for racial minorities, and over school construction and finance.

Advocates of city school system reorganization, such as Butler in New York or Lowell in Boston, struck out at what they saw as the major obstacles to "good government" of the schools —the hiring of inadequately trained teachers at the ward or district levels and the use of sub-committees for city-wide school administration. The central boards were too large to screen and select teachers, discuss problems, and make decisions. Until the size of the board was reduced to manageable proportions, sub-committees had to continue to perform the major functions.

The articulate school reformers of the 1890's were obviously groping for a way to strengthen the overall coordination of the schools, which meant considerable centralization of authority. The boroughs surrounding Manhattan had been gradually preparing for school consolidation over several decades. The 1897 confederation of the borough school boards was a major step toward the more complete city merger that would come later, although separate borough school superintendents remained powerful for a few more years. San Francisco and Cleveland each sought a strong school executive, yet provided close supervision of that administrator by the four full-time directors in San Francisco and by the seven-man council in Cleveland's "Federal Plan." Buffalo added five examiners to see that the elective superintendent would screen more carefully the teacher candidates. St. Louis, in reducing the number of board members, simultaneously added two more executives to help the board manage the business of the schools.

The reorganizations of big-city school organizations in each city were very different. As remedies, some collapsed later because they were no one's ideal but rather a compromise of the moment fraught with logical or administrative inconsistencies. A city school specialist in the office of the U.S. Commissioner of Education in 1900 wrote that the last four years "have been preeminently a period of change and experiment. The variations from what was then the normal type have been so radical, so numerous, and of such importance that it would be difficult now to say just what the normal type is." [45] He pointed out how sharply the Milwaukee plan differed from the old mode of electing school trustees at district meetings. Now, he explained, "The people elect the Mayor, the Mayor appoints the commission, the commission appoints the board, the board selects a superintendent, the superintendent, in practice, selects the principals." City schools were becoming centralized but the process of recruitment, both of board members and of staff, was also becoming more complex.

ANALYSIS: POLITICAL CHANGE
OF THE CITY SCHOOLS

The manner in which board member selection procedures were revised during the periods prior to and during the 1890's warrants some explanation and interpretation. The struggle to improve the schools required first the articulation of complaints or demands by at least some citizens and their leaders. Especially during the 1890's this function seemed to require the formation of civic club committees on education and the creation of public education associations, especially in those East Coast cities which eventually agreed to exchange ideas at annual meetings. These new groups were assisted by clergymen, college presidents, and the press in sorting out and ordering the demands and preparing legislation or charter revisions to effect the structural changes advocated.

During the brief but intensive period from 1896 to 1898, the proponents of reorganization had a most dazzling array of talent on which to draw. Urban school reformers worked closely with professional educators who contributed their time, ideas, and prestige to the movement: Goodnow at Columbia, Charles William Eliot of Harvard, and Professor of Government A. Lawrence Lowell, later to be Eliot's successor as President of Harvard. While Lowell served on the Boston board, Johns Hopkins President Daniel Coit Gilman was appointed to the Baltimore board, although neither served more than a few years nor were able to effect permanent changes.[46] William Rainey Harper, the President of the University of Chicago, led the 1898 Chicago investigation. Most of these men, though proud and able administrators, were unable to change the schools of their cities either as board members or outside investigators; their frustration and the success of Butler of Columbia in political reform demonstrated that structural reorganization required a more extensive mobilization of popular and legislative support.

Few periods in American education have seen such intense interest in city school administration by so many eminent leaders of higher education—Butler of Columbia, Draper of Illinois, Gilman of Hopkins, Eliot and Lowell of Harvard, Harper of Chicago. These men traversed the boundary which subsequently separated the state and city systems of public education from the great public and private universities in order to try to help the city school improve the performance of their intended functions.[47] It was not so much their failure as it was their interest and support which helped to rally the reformers and broaden the base from which interests could be expressed and aggregated. Butler himself helped recruit and organize the prominent upper-class ladies of Manhattan whose leaders were instrumental in changing the New York City Board.

The tactics and alliances that the New York reformers found it necessary to adopt show that the educated elites had in effect lost control of the New York City School Board and needed as a tactical matter to include in their platform the new curriculum and services which the followers of Jacob Riis demanded. Therefore, Butler, Goodnow, and the various municipal reform groups had to form a temporary coalition if either group of advocates were to influence the city schools. The Boston reformers, meanwhile, had thought they could, through revising the rules of the organization, make changes in the functioning of the school committee, but they were unable to make the changes permanent. The board member selection procedure was such that any group opposed to reorganization could gain a majority periodically and easily reverse the board's rules and regulations.

Eventually, rather than continue to try to reorganize the boards from within, leaders in several of the cities proposed to state legislatures new rules for school board recruitment. The Cleveland, Milwaukee, and San Francisco "experiments" were the more drastic of the innovations, although Cubberley pointed out that in San Francisco and elsewhere full-time paid boards had been used to supervise police and fire protection functions. Meanwhile, Cleveland's "Federal Plan" was, in fact, a counterpart of a similar plan simultaneously adopted by the municipal government of that city in order to strengthen the role of the mayor, one of the prime objectives of municipal reformers of that era. The less drastic revisions made by St. Louis and Baltimore simply streamlined the boards and tried to remove the *de facto* recruitment and selection of board members from the hands of ward political leaders.

At the same time that the board selection procedures were changed, the teacher selection function was altered so that the superintendent and his assistants (for Buffalo the lay board of examiners, and for San Francisco the teachers and principals elected as full-time directors) could advise the central board on the selection of teachers. Rice's suggestions about restructuring the arrangements by which new board members were selected as a step toward improving educational services were in at least seven instances heeded: in Cleveland, Milwaukee, San Francisco, New York City, St. Louis, Baltimore, and Buffalo.

A little is known about the way in which the legislatures aggregated the demands and responded to the requests for revised statutes and new charters. There is evidence to suspect that teachers and principals, at least in New York, were mobilized by ward politicians to testify or sign petitions aginst the reorganization proposals and that state legislators were often as corruptible as city council members in cities they were to reform.[48] For this reason, some of the city school board reorganizations were either deferred, as they were in Pennsylvania or Massachusetts, or watered-down from the viewpoint of the reformers, as in Wisconsin.

THE IMPACT OF IMMIGRATION

Almond's research on political cultures has illuminated the close connection between the more general political socialization of the members of a political system and the process of political change. Some analysis may be attempted of what may have happened to the level of political socialization in America between the 1840's, when ward boards were popular and apparently effective, and the 1890's, when the ward boards and district committees had become prime targets of reform.

Alexis de Tocqueville, critical of the culture and of schooling which had as yet produced no great poets, historians, or jurists in America, nevertheless was impressed with the level of instruction about the "political world" of the 1830's. He found the American "familiar with the mechanism of the laws . . . (which he learns) by participating in the act of legislation; and he takes a lesson in the forms of government from governing." [49] He labeled the emphasis in the schools and in the social order on preparation for public life as a great contrast to the ends and approach of European education.

Between 1840 and 1890, millions of Europeans migrated to America. When Lord Bryce asked Seth Low, the former Mayor of Brooklyn, to write a chapter on American cities, Low began immediately with the explanation that America was now governed "from the top down" by "governing classes" in the manner to which the immigrants had been accustomed. The newcomers, he complained, lacked experience with self-government, "nor do they always share the ideas which have expressed themselves in the Constitution of the United States." [50] Especially since "this foreign element settles largely in the cities of the country" (he estimated that 80 percent of New York's population was either foreign-born or the children of foreign-born parents), "the problem of learning and applying the art of government is handed over to a population that begins in point of experience very low down." He then pointed out that the problem of instructing "large and rapidly-growing bodies of people in the art of self-government" is compounded by the fact that they are not homogeneous and therefore must simultaneously be assimilated into American modes of living in a community. This sentiment was widely shared by other upper-class reformers who did not want the newcomers to run their own schools.

Henry Emerson, the elected superintendent of Buffalo schools, in 1894 complained that his position had become more precarious because of "the increasing proportion of people who are unacquainted with our institutions and traditions and have no feeling of attachment to them." He said that from 1880 to 1890, when "thousands of foreigners" came into Buffalo, the relatively simple system of governing the schools "grew vicious" and the new charter was sought as a remedy. He felt that an administrator, even an elected superintendent, was safe only "as long as there is an aroused public interest," and he concluded that no machinery of government "can be devised which will run itself." [51]

Emerson in effect made two points. The first was that an insufficiently socialized populace can, by its lack of familiarity with the institutions of school and government, impair the functioning of a superintendent or allow the selection of a less qualified educational leader. He clearly wanted to be protected from the new masses rather than become their educational spokesman. The second was that the selection procedure itself was no guarantee of continued satisfaction since any system of governance is dependent on the attitudes of the enfranchised masses. Neither he nor the other spokesmen for the old elites would admit that the less literate newcomers ought to have more of a voice in the selection of staff or even of the school programs offered.

The advocacy of reorganization can be viewed as a reaction to the diversion of school resources by the new urban politicians to their organizations and supporters. This diversion of resources from the political sub-system of the schools was due in part to a greater emphasis on awarding "jobs" than on providing educational services. The ward leaders wanted to expand the range of services and emoluments which the ward organization could provide to the past and potential supporters of their organization. Many of the new voters did not seem to object to the way this structure, the ward organization, gradually assumed the functions assigned to the boards and committees. The diversion of resources, of course, may also be traced to loss of support of the legitimate structure from business elites who profited from other liaisons with the ward and city machine leaders, as Steffens explained to the nation in such luminous detail.[52]

As the city school governmental machinery fell into the hands of the newcomers, the old political leadership had to recast the board structure in such a way as to regain control. Except in the case of Cleveland, the conspicuous leaders were not businessmen or neighborhood leaders, but were drawn from the ranks of the writers and social critics, the college professors and presidents, and the Protestant women and clergy. Neither political party can be identified with this reorganization movement; in fact, the desire for non-partisan school politics was what the reformers in part meant when they articulated the desire to lift the schools above or out of politics.

The process of reorganization was not finished in 1899. Even the cities which had modified the structure once or twice could not be sure that subsequent reorganizations might not be necessary. Ellwood P. Cubberley asked in 1901 that the San Francisco innovation, "be regarded as simply a stage in the evolution of the city's educational system." He labeled it "a start," warned other cities not to copy the plan, and urged the study of the problem by the public-spirited members of several San Francisco clubs.[53]

The parallel development, that of handing over functions of teacher recruitment and school system management to a chief school administrator, was also in an early stage. Centralization of professional power in the superintendency was fought by at least two sets of teachers—the unionized Chicago teachers who wanted decisions made at the school level, and those teachers elsewhere who owed allegiance to the ward leaders and boards who appointed them. Other laymen searched for ways to build barriers to keep personnel matters out of partisan politics. They fought to establish boards of examiners, directors, bi-partisan commissions, and the appointment of independent executives potentially accountable for the flow of funds. The stage was not yet set for a strong superintendency, but power was wrenched away from wards and local districts toward city-wide agents. Thus it was that urban school reformers in the 1890's set into motion mechanisms that tried to remove educational decisions from wards and districts and shift them to a central agency or agents.

NOTES

1. *The New York Times* (January 7, 1895), referred to in Sol Cohen, *Progressives and Urban School Reform* (New York: Teachers College of Columbia University, 1964), p. 34.

2. See reference in A. M. Schlesinger, *The Rise of the City, 1878–1898* (New York: Macmillan, 1933), to the books by Ward McAllister, 1890, and Jacob Riis, 1890.

3. Schlesinger, *op. cit.,* pp. 64–68.

4. *Ibid.,* pp. 87–109. However, the cities were also expanding the range and improving the quality of municipal services in the 1880's and 1890's, especially by the improved lighting and asphalt paving of streets and the building of bridges and trolley lines.

5. *Ibid.,* p. 112.

6. Ernest S. Griffith, *The Modern Development of City Government* (London: Oxford University Press, 1927), p. 141.

7. *Ibid.,* pp. 16–25.

8. *Ibid.,* p. 27.

9. Lincoln Steffens, *The Autobiography of Lincoln Steffens* (New York: Harcourt Brace Jovanovich, 1931), p. 422.

10. Schlesinger, *op. cit.*, p. 191.

11. James Bryce, *The American Commonwealth* (New York: Macmillan, 1895), p. 643.

12. *Ibid.*, pp. 644–645.

13. *Ibid.*, p. 646.

14. Andrew S. Draper, "Education Organization and Administration," in Nicholas Murray Butler (ed.), *Education in the United States,* Monograph no. 1 (Albany: J. B. Lyon, 1900), p. 13.

15. Steffens, *op. cit.*, p. 451.

16. Dr. Joseph Mayer Rice, *The Public School System of the United States* (New York: The Century Co., 1893), p. 76. See also Lawrence Cremin, *The Transformation of the School* (New York: Knopf, 1962), pp. 3–8 on Rice.

17. Schlesinger, *op. cit.*, p. 160.

18. *Ibid.*, pp. 168–171.

19. Cohen, *op. cit.*, p. 8.

20. *Ibid.*, p. 34.

21. Mrs. William E. D. Scott, "The Aims and Work of the Conference of Public Education Association," *The Annals,* vol. XXV, no. 2 (March 1905), pp. 169–172.

22. Henry P. Emerson, "Improvement of City School Systems," *Journal of Proceedings and Addresses, 1894* (St. Paul: National Education Association, 1895), p. 125.

23. The N.E.A. group was actually a sub-committee of the Committee of Fifteen and was chaired by Andrew Sloan Draper, former Superintendent of Schools in Cleveland, President of the University of Illinois, and later the first Commissioner of Education for New York State. The report of the committee indicated the concern of the profession itself for a reorganization of city school board structures. The force of Draper's personality and the fact that he had been both the President of the N.E.A. Department of Superintendence and the first Cleveland superintendent appointed under the plan helped to gain the N.E.A. endorsement of the reorganization scheme. (N.E.A., *Journal of Proceedings and Addresses, 1894, op. cit.,* pp. 305 ff.).

24. Raymond Callahan documents how William Bruce vigorously attacked the Draper Report in his American School Board Journal. Bruce dubbed Draper's proposals as "Educational Tyranny" and "The Czar Movement." He then organized a National Association of School Boards. Callahan in Frank W. Lutz and Joseph Azzarelli (eds.), *The Struggle for Power in Education* (New York: Center for Applied Research in Education, 1966), pp. 19–30.

25. Cohen, *op. cit.*, pp. 35–38. Cohen's study on the Public Education

Association cites both Butler and Jacob Riis as acknowledging the critical role of this organization in the passage of legislation establishing a new school board for New York City.

26. *Ibid.*, p. 40. It would be misleading to conclude that all respectable citizens were against the ward trustee system. Not even the reformers agreed on the desirability of abolishing ward boards; some of the politically "progressive" reformers voiced a strong preference for retaining any structure that maximized popular participation.

27. *Ibid.*, p. 44.

28. James Desmond Logsdon, *The Development of Public School Administration in St. Louis, Missouri*, Ph.D. dissertation (Chicago: The University of Chicago Press, 1965), pp. 49–50.

29. Duane Mowry, "The Milwaukee School System," *Educational Review*, vol. XX, no. 2 (September 1900), p. 141.

30. Although Draper's committee had convinced the N.E.A., most cities saw dangers in the one-man-rule of a single director, so Milwaukee "experimented" with four. Nicholar Murray Butler later noted in the *Educational Review* that New York had subsequently developed a better scheme than the one borrowed by St. Louis.

31. Mowry, *op. cit.*, pp. 143–146.

32. Report of the Commission to Study the System of Education in the Public Schools of Baltimore, no. 4 (Washington, D.C.: U.S. Bureau of Education, 1911), pp. 29–30.

33. Rice, *op. cit.*, p. 55.

34. *Annual Report of the Superintendent of Common Schools of the City and County of San Francisco, 1892* (San Francisco: The Board of Education, 1892).

35. Ellwood P. Cubberley, "The School Situation in San Francisco," *Educational Review*, vol. XXI, no. 4 (April 1901), pp. 364–381.

36. *Report of the Educational Commission of the City of Chicago*, Introductory Statement and "Article 1" Chicago: The Riverside Press, 1899).

37. *Chicago Teachers and School Board Journal*, vol. I (March, April, October 1899), especially pp. 211–213, 377.

38. S. A. Wetmore, "The Boston School Administration," *Educational Review* (September 1897), pp. 105–106.

39. George A. O. Ernst, "The Movement for School Reform in Boston," *Educational Review*, vol. XXVIII, no. 5 (December 1905), pp. 433–444.

40. Truman DeWeese, "Better City School Administration," *Educational Review*, vol. XX, no. 1 (September 1900), pp. 60–71.

41. Arthur B. Moehlman, *Public Education in Detroit*, (Illinois: Public School Publishing, 1925), p. 141.

42. The device of a board of examiners, either lay or professional,

came from recognition of the undesirability of allowing the board, superintendent, or school trustees to have the sole authority to screen and rate the candidates without objective rules and some formal evaluation of the candidates.

43. In effect, the Cleveland "director" was both business manager and general superintendent, who then selected a reputable educator as superintendent of instruction. It must be remembered that the major criticism of the plan, identified at that time by superintendents in other cities as well as by school board defenders, was the fact that it gave so much power to one man.

44. The 1897 New York City board rose again in size when the boroughs were consolidated, but the new total of 45 was less than the total of the separate boards; i.e., New York 21 and Brooklyn 45, etc.

45. *Report of the Commissioner, The U.S. Bureau of Education* (Washington, D.C.: U.S. Bureau of Education, 1900), p. 1492.

46. Editorial note by N. M. Butler in the *Educational Review,* vol. XIII, (February 1897), p. 207. There was little if any sentiment for reorganization on the part of teachers in the public schools, due in part to the modest growth of teacher organizations prior to 1914. Margaret Haley, after her establishment of a teachers union in Chicago, began to involve teachers in social reform, but in many cities teachers were loyal to the existing arrangements through which they had obtained their teaching positions. Superintendents Swett in California, Draper in Cleveland, and Maxwell in Brooklyn and later in New York City, were among the few articulate advocates of reform actually working in city school systems in the late-nineteenth century.

47. Previously, Eliot and Butler had taken the lead in the redefinition of the secondary school curriculum (The Committee of Ten, 1894) and well into the twentieth century the interest of these two college presidents in educational organization persisted. In recent years, James B. Conant has been one of the few university presidents who has continued to study and write on public school or urban educational problems.

48. Lincoln Steffens, *The Struggle for Self Government* (New York: McClure, Phillips, 1906), pp. 40–78, and Bryce, *op. cit.,* p. 646.

49. Alexis de Tocqueville, *Democracy in America,* vol. I., The Henry Reeve text, Phillips Bradley (ed.), (New York: Vintage Books, 1945), p. 330.

50. In Bryce, *op. cit.,* Chapter LII.

51. Emerson, *op. cit.,* pp. 123–126.

52. Lincoln Steffens, *The Shame of the Cities* (New York: McClure, Phillips, 1904).

53. Cubberley, *op. cit.,* p. 381.

* * * * * *V* * * * * *

THE ERA OF EFFICIENCY, 1900–1920

INTRODUCTION

AT THE TURN OF THE CENTURY the "Great Cities" superintendency was considered equal with or coordinate with other administrative positions established by the board, except in Cleveland where it was subordinate to another executive.

Simultaneously, the schools began to take interest in the new methods of teaching and testing proposed by psychologists and philosophers. The Gary, Indiana, schools in 1907 hired a student of John Dewey, William Wirt, whose Gary plan or "platoon school" attracted wide notice and was tried elsewhere during the second decade of the century. One student of the schools in this period traced the popularization of measurement and organizational innovation to the national enthusiasm over "scientific management," an approach to "efficiency" and economy devised by Frederick W. Taylor.[1]

Beginning in 1910, the possibility of applying the tenets of "scientific management" were explored by a relatively new group —school of education deans and professors of school administration—whose influence began to be felt through the school surveys and speeches they made and the textbooks they authored. But did this "cult of efficiency" influence plans to reorganize city boards of education? The city school boards in Chicago, New York, Buffalo, and Detroit were reorganized in 1916 and 1917. These four reorganizations lend themselves to analysis of the question whether these changes grew out of previous drives for reorganization or as an outcome of the later effort to increase the efficiency of the city school system.

THE STRUCTURES AND FUNCTIONS
OF CITY SCHOOL BOARDS IN 1900

At the turn of the century, the members of six of the city boards under study were appointed by other governmental officials and, in six other cities, the board members were chosen at popular election. (See Table 8.) The Pittsburgh central board members were chosen by the members of subdistrict boards. Buffalo had no school board at that time.

The size of the boards ranged from four members in San Francisco to forty-six members in New York, although the membership of the thirty-nine Pittsburgh sub-district boards (each of six members) totaled two hundred thirty-four, and that of the forty-two Philadelphia ward boards (each with twelve members) totaled five hundred and four. Six city school boards still had more than twenty members, two had between ten and twenty members, and five had less than ten.

Each of the six appointive boards was unique in one way or another. The New York appointments made by the mayor were parceled out to each borough. Both Chicago and San Francisco mayors appointed city school boards without geographical restrictions, but in San Francisco the appointees filled salaried full-time positions. The city council had to approve the appointments made by the mayor of Baltimore, but in Milwaukee the mayor's control was indirect, since he appointed a bi-partisan commission which then appointed the board members. In Philadelphia, board member selection by the judges of two courts was still another unique pattern.

Four of the elective boards were chosen at large and two by wards, as of 1900. The thirty-nine district boards of Pittsburgh were elective, and from their membership were drawn the members of the central board. The Buffalo city council, an appointed five-man board of examiners, and the elected superintendent of schools performed for Buffalo the functions ordinarily assigned to a board of education.

Which mode of selection of board members was accompanied by the right to approve the total amount of money to be raised for the city schools? All of the six appointive boards submitted the annual school budget requests to a city council or

City	Method of Board Member Selection	Size	Approval of Total Amount To Be Raised for Education*	Approval of Funds for School Construction	Selection of Superintendent	Nomination of Teachers**
New York	A. Mayor, by Boroughs	46	Board of Estimate and Apportionment	School Board	Board	Borough Superintendent
Chicago	A. By Mayor	21	City Council	Committee of the School Board	Board	Superintendent
Philadelphia	A. By Judges, Wards	42	City Council	Committee of the Local Board	Board	Local Boards
Baltimore	A. By Mayor	9	City Council	School Board	Board	Superintendent
Milwaukee	A. By Commission, Wards	21	Common Council	Board, City Council, Board of Public Works	Board	Board Committee
San Francisco	A. By Mayor, full-time	4	Board of Supervisors	Board of Public Works	Popular Election	Board Members
St. Louis	E. At large	12	Board—State Millage Limit	Committee on School Building	Board	Superintendent

City		Size of Board				
Boston	E. At large	24	Board—State Levy Limit	School Committee	Board	Superintendent
Cleveland	E. At large	7	City Tax Commission	Elected School Director	School Director	Superintendent
Houston	E. At large	7	City Council	Committee on Buildings	Board	Board
Detroit	E. By Wards	17	City Council	Committee on Real Estate	Board	Superintendent
Los Angeles	E. By Wards	9	City Council	Committee on Buildings	Board	Board
Pittsburgh	A. Sub-district boards, one man each	39	Sub-district and District Board of Education	Sub-district Boards	Board	Sub-district Boards
Buffalo	No Board, by City Council	—	Superintendent of Education	City Council	Popular Election	Superintendent

Each column, except for "Size of Board," is a function. In each row the structure or role-performing function has been entered.

* Budget approval for operating expenses.

** Invariably the board appoints, and an examining board or personnel officer screens, the candidates. Hence, the power to initiate or recommend names of teachers has been chosen.

CODE: A. = Appointive; E. = Elective

Source: Chronologies of big-cities school systems and Frank Rollins, *School Administration in Municipal Government*, Ph.D. dissertation: Columbia University, New York, 1902.

other elective board, which then determined the total amount to be raised for the schools. Of the elective boards, four submitted the budget requests to a city council or commission and two others had some autonomy, but within a levy limit established by the state. Both the Pittsburgh sub-district and district boards could levy taxes, the former for the local district (elementary schools), the latter for high schools and other purposes. The Buffalo superintendent, directly accountable to the electorate, could determine the total budget for the Buffalo schools.

Decision-making about school construction was a function of school boards or their sub-committees for four of the appointive boards and four of the elective boards. For two of the appointive boards, a city public works department handled school construction; for Cleveland, the elective school director made decisions about school construction.

Eleven of the superintendents were appointed by the board, one chosen by the school director, and two elected by the populace. In 1900, three of the six superintendents serving appointive boards and two serving elective boards had the authority to nominate candidates for teaching positions. The alternative pattern was nomination by board members. The superintendent in Buffalo nominated the teachers but in Pittsburgh the sub-district boards chose the teachers for the schools in each district.

The differences in the functions assigned to the different structures seemed almost random; two of the elective boards had construction performed by the city government rather than under the jurisdiction of the school board. The elective Cleveland school director and the Buffalo superintendent had more functions assigned to them than other superintendents, but the elective San Francisco superintendent had the least number of functions assigned to him.

THE SCHOOL BOARD
REORGANIZATIONS, 1901–1911

During the latter half of the 1890's Nicholas Murray Butler threw himself into the leadership of the "school war" in New York City, in which passage of the Compromise Bill of 1896, which reorganized the board, the school board appointments of Mayor Strong, and the hiring of Brooklyn's William Maxwell as superintendent were viewed as victories. Starting in 1897, Butler extended the boundaries of the battlefield to include other cities where reorganizations were imminent. In that year he published Boykin's summary of school board structures in the larger cities, noted with approval the appointment of Gilman from Johns Hopkins University to the Baltimore board, and published an article by a former Boston school committee member on how the school textbook publishers tried to bribe a city board of education. Butler watched very closely the San Francisco innovation of a full-time paid board and repeatedly voiced his own criticism and skepticism of that arrangement. However, Butler allowed Ellwood Cubberley space in the *Educational Review* to evaluate objectively the genuine accomplishments of the board after almost two years of trial.[2]

Butler himself was an unrestrained critic of city school board organizations. Through the medium of his journal, the *Educational Review,* Butler continued to discuss the New York City board, its crises and decisions, for the next ten years. But during this period he also printed articles on the new St. Louis charter and the five years of accomplishment which followed the 1897 charter revision in that city. He published several articles on Boston and several on Philadelphia, each of the articles sharply critical of existing structures. Noting the refusal of the Boston school committee in 1900 to accept one of Superintendent Scaver's teacher nominations, Butler quoted a Boston newspaper on the possibility of political intrigue and in a footnote cried out, "the sooner the reformers lay an ax to the roots of the Boston School Committee, the better." [3]

Although Butler forged no formal organization of school reformers, his communications with other prominent and activist educators and his encouragement of young educators like Cubberley and Strayer contributed to the overall success of the school reorganization in various cities. Joseph Mayer Rice may have been the first to point out the need for structural reorganization in the larger cities, but Nicholas Murray Butler maintained the running commentary and forum which helped other educators to evaluate the various proposals advanced for the reorganization of the city school boards. The murmuring of discontent with existing structures became clarions when articulated in his magazine. The *Educational Review* served as the communications link between aroused laymen in each city and educators concerned about the zeal with which reformers attacked the school boards. Butler's interpretation of the movement helped to knit a coalition of lay critics, academics, and schoolmen behind the tenets of school board centralization.

THE APPOINTIVE BOARDS

New York

The consolidation of boroughs had saddled the New York schools with a complex council of delegates from borough school boards, to whom the central superintendent legally was little more than an advisor. Superintendent Maxwell was quite open in his denunciation of borough autonomy and criticized the separate deficiencies in each borough. Although Maxwell personally advocated a twenty-one man board, the charter revision of 1902, approved by Mayor Seth Low and the state legislature, provided for an executive committee of fifteen which would handle most of the administrative work for the larger board. The same charter provided for the establishment of forty-six local boards, but with much less power than the former trustees could wield. Two new professional boards were created, a board of examiners, and a board of superintendents which Maxwell would chair and on which the borough superintendents would rank as associates under Maxwell.[4]

Houston

Although the city of Houston had not yet reached the 75,000 population mark, an innovation in that city's government in 1905 resulted in an eighteen-year hiatus in the use of elections to select school board members. The success of nearby Galveston with a new commission plan of government prompted Houston to abolish all elective positions and the mayor was given the authority to appoint the school board. Four years later the superintendent reported that "the schools of Houston can secure all the money necessary." The once debt-ridden city began to pay its bills on time so that bids on school contracts were much more competitive, and a "high type of business man" was appointed to the board.[5] Another Houston commentator intimated that without twelve aldermen, each representing a ward, "politics is obliterated from the public schools." He declared that now, "the teachers are selected for their fitness. No commissioner can even suggest the name of a teacher to the board." [6]

Milwaukee

Milwaukee leaders were not satisfied with the unintended effects of selection of board members by a politically conscious bipartisan board which combed each ward to select a board member. Rejecting a proposal for direct appointment of a smaller board by the mayor, the Wisconsin legislature passed a law in 1905 providing for the selection of a twelve-member board by the circuit judges of the city of Milwaukee. However, the Supreme Court of Wisconsin declared that act unconstitutional, so in 1907 another law was passed which specified an elective board of fifteen members elected at large for six-year overlapping terms, an arrangement which has persisted since that year. The statement of the Supreme Court did not rule out the possibility of separating the city schools from city government, and so the new law established the Milwaukee schools as a separate and quasi-municipal corporation distinct from city government. [7]

Philadelphia

Meanwhile, Philadelphia, whose appointment of board members by the judiciary had been imitated by Milwaukee, was itself contemplating board reorganization. Three school directors, members of the sectional boards, were convicted of "conspiracy, bribery and extortion for taking money from teaching applicants." [8] Clinton Woodruff, the prominent Philadelphian whose success in aiding educational reform in other cities preceded his success locally, complained that sectional board members were nominated at party primaries controlled by the bosses and the posts were treated as the "first steps in political preferment." He further revealed, in Butler's review, that in 1902 the "Republican City Committee sent every male teacher a letter requesting a voluntary contribution with a two percent assessment" of salary marked in blue pencil on each notice. Woodruff expressed a fervent hope for the eventual abolition of "the present board system." A reform act was passed in 1905 which cut the Philadelphia board in half, to twenty-one, with members to be appointed at large rather than by sections. The sectional boards were stripped of all powers except the right to hire janitors and to inspect schools. Although the central board gained the power to select teachers, the allocation of funds to the school was transferred to the city council.

Pittsburgh

The patronage problem in the Pittsburgh schools was becoming intolerable, but reform was deferred there longer than in any of the other cities. A survey of the city conducted by the Russell Sage Foundation in 1905 denounced the Pittsburgh schools as antiquated and corrupt. Despite the militance of the Voters League, the *Pittsburgh Post-Gazette* years later reviewed the extent of the misdeeds:

Many school boards were a public scandal in themselves—made up of saloon keepers, proprietors of gambling houses and "joints" city employees, common loafers, and contractors who openly accepted contracts for school buildings in direct violation of the law. . . . Janitors were political powers in the wards and sometimes were even responsible for placing principals in their jobs. . . . There was solid public opinion behind the new school code when it was brought before the Legislature in 1911.[9]

The Pennsylvania legislature in 1911 reduced both the Pittsburgh and Philadelphia boards to fifteen members each. The Pittsburgh sectional boards and Philadelphia ward boards became boards of school visitors, still elected on a ward basis but with power only to select janitors, visit schools, and make reports on conditions. The state also gave both city schools the control of funds, the power to tax within specific limits, and the authority to borrow for construction. Pittsburgh citizens were very much pleased with the new procedure and defended it vigorously six years later when the legislature was considering some changes suggested by Philadelphians. Pittsburgh and Philadelphia had been among the last of the large cities with appointive boards to undergo extensive surgery and restructuring, including stripping powers from ward boards, but this delay in reform was characteristic of both cities in other municipal matters as well.[10]

THE ELECTIVE BOARDS

Boston and Los Angeles reorganized once again in the early 1900's, and Cleveland abandoned certain features of its "Federal Plan" after a twelve-year trial.

Los Angeles

Los Angeles, although less than half the size of the smallest of the midwestern cities in this study, became disillusioned with the politics of ward selection and in 1903 the city school board was reduced from nine to seven, each member to be elected at large.[11] However, each political party nominated candidates, and in 1905 the fear of a "spoils system" brought forth the adoption of a non-partisan election, with no party affiliation to be used at all.

Boston

Financier James Jackson Storrow, a former school committee member, decided Boston needed a new school organization and in 1905 drafted a petition to the legislature which 100 citizens signed. The document was a classic piece of school reform propaganda in that letters were collected from mayors and superintendents in other cities, and statistics on the reduction of the size of school boards made by other cities were cited. On the basis of a survey made by Professor Paul Hanus of the Harvard Graduate School of Education, Storrow proposed the appointment of a three- to seven-man board by the mayor. The signers of his petition, an accompanying pamphlet points out, "are resident of all sections of the city, are both Republican and Democratic, are Catholics, Protestants and Hebrews, and represent nearly every race among the population." [12] Two former mayors of Boston joined Storrow in testimony before the state legislature.[13] The broad, cosmopolitan base of the reform and the alleged "sympathy of many parents and teachers" was enough to secure a reduction in size of the school board from twenty-four to five. But the members were to be elected at large as before, since women in Boston otherwise would lose one of their few rights to vote for public office.

Moreover, both Los Angeles and Boston in 1905 took steps to increase the power of the superintendent, especially in authorizing him to nominate teachers and recommend the textbooks to be selected. Both cities selected as new superintendents men who knew the city and were sympathetic with the aims of the reforms, yet, at the time of their selection, were not associated with the city schools.

Cleveland

The Cleveland plan had worked until 1900 when the director lost an election and the superintendent felt compelled to submit his resignation because the major issue had been the dismissal of two students from the normal school in Cleveland. The Cleveland school director also admitted in his annual reports that he perceived that instruction was the main task of the schools, hoping that he "may be pardoned for holding and expressing views" on the educational program. When the school code was revised in 1905, the Cleveland school council remained an elective board of seven, (two by districts, five at large), but the post of school director, no longer elective, was made optional, and the function of appointing a superintendent was transferred to the council. However, the director continued in Cleveland, as an executive of the board, to report directly to the board, and to manage an "executive department—at least until 1918—at which time he became the head of the "business department." [14]

THE SUPERINTENDENCY AFTER 1900

Frank J. Goodnow, writing on municipal government in 1908, noted that school boards tended "to differentiate between physical (business) and educational administration, placing a superintendent of schools or similar officer over the professional expert force." [15] The differentiation of the two roles had been strongly advocated and endorsed by Andrew Sloan Draper and other leading educators at the turn of the century. [16]

William E. Chancellor, lecturer at Johns Hopkins and the University of Chicago, also superintendent of the Washington, D.C. schools and one of the first textbook writers on city school administration, wrote in 1908 that:

. . . it is usually best to create a small elective board of education with large general powers that it should be required to exert through three coordinate officers—a superintendent, an architect, and a business manager—with the assistance of two other officers, an attorney and a secretary. [17]

This organizational arrangement of three executives, each of them equally responsible and reporting directly to the board, was what Chancellor preferred. This organization was not necessarily what existed in all cities of 100,000 or more population, the group for which Chancellor was advocating this organization. However, Rollins, in one of the early dissertations on school administration, found that the superintendent was the administrative head of the school system "on its purely educational side" in most of the 110 large cities he studied.[18]

Other authorities had begun to advance the proposition that the superintendent of schools should be the major coordinator of all administration for the schools. John T. Prince wrote in 1916 that:

Besides the superintendent of schools there should be employed by the board several executive officials, whose duties so far as they bear directly upon the work of the schools should be under the direction of the superintendent. These officials are a business manager, a physical director, one or more attendance officers, and one or more medical inspectors.[19]

In the early 1920's, when Ellwood P. Cubberley revised his major text on public school administration, he not only advocated making the superintendent chief executive officer of the board, with supervisory responsibility over all departments, but he drew elaborate organization charts of both the proper and incorrect forms of city school organization for a large-city school system. He was adamant about the necessity of making all appointments, including those of janitors (of whom he makes special reference), only on the initiative of the superintendent of schools.[20]

During the early years of the century, several of the city school boards delegated additional functions to their superintendents, as Cubberley urged. Gilland's study established the fact that as the board size diminished and board committees were reduced in number or abolished, the superintendent of schools was named chief executive officer of the board and was assigned the function of nominating for appointment at least the teachers if not the custodians.

Superintendents and urban school reformers placed a priority on seizing control of the teacher selection process. Cleveland, Baltimore, and Detroit delegated the power of nominating teachers to the superintendent during the 1890's. New Yorkers altered the teacher recruitment procedure so that by 1898 a board of examiners rather than the district trustees screened the teacher candidates and the superintendent chaired the board of examiners (from 1898 to 1920). The Boston superintendent of schools was given the authority to recommend candidates to the board in 1898, but lost it back to a board sub-committee in 1899. Later, as part of the major reorganization of the Boston school committee in 1906, the superintendent acquired authority over all appointments and promotions. Prior to 1904 the Milwaukee board included the superintendent as a member of a selection committee, but when the board was reduced to twelve members in 1904 the superintendent became the sole appointing authority. The Chicago and Detroit superintendents were not given full responsibility for the teacher nomination function until the boards in those cities were reduced in size and the functions reassigned in 1917.[21]

The superintendents in several of the cities, therefore, acquired one or more important functions at the time of the reorganizations in the 1890's and early 1900's. Although some textbook writers still approved of a dual executive or multiple administrative control of the staff, later texts stressed the desirability of unitary control and the ascendancy of the superintendency to chief executive status. The acquisition of greater authority by superintendents tended to accompany the reduction in size of the city school boards. The transfer of functions was often associated with the general reorganization of the boards and was usually contemporaneous with the abandonment of a board sub-committee on teacher appointments or the curtailment of the teacher selection powers of ward boards or district trustees. The superintendent of schools moved from an advisory and supervisory role to one which enabled him to control the quality of teachers selected, sometimes with the help of boards of examiners who helped to establish rating lists of eligible candidates.

One consequence of school board reorganization, then, was the strengthening of the chief professional executive. It need not have turned out this way. School board members could have assumed the personnel and central management functions themselves if they worked full time, as San Francisco members did. Or, as the Chicago teachers desired, a school board might have given the faculty of each school substantial say in developing curricula and the hiring of colleagues, such as colleges enjoy. Instead, big-city education went the way of the railroad or other heavy industry. The board members would work on broad policy matters and leave the details of management and staffing to a highly paid officer called a superintendent. Implicit in this decision was a distrust of the ability of teachers to take part in many professional decisions. These ingredients—a smaller board, a stronger executive, decreased lay participation but also minimal teacher participation—were essentially elitist, conservative, and a reaction against the immigrant ethnic groups and their interest in getting control of the schools to maximize the economic mobility of their people.

Much has been made of the slogan "efficiency" to explain what took place during this period of reorganization. The term was useful as a way to justify the new modes of governance and administration, but what is now called the efficiency movement came toward the end rather than the start of the developments already described.

THE MOVE TO MAKE EDUCATION "EFFICIENT"

Between the years 1895 and 1910 Frederick W. Taylor developed an approach to industrial management based on the detailed analysis of factors affecting productivity. The "Taylor System," which gained acceptance under the rubric of "scientific management," was developed first on engineering and manufacturing processes and relied heavily on studies of more efficient methods of work.[22]

Taylor also advocated the standardization of tasks, bonus and incentive plans for workers, the employment of "Functional foremen" who would teach workers more efficient methods, and the creation of planning departments to develop the scientific rules for performing each job. The most widely cited application of this theory was the work of Taylor in quadrupling the daily output of pig-iron handlers at the Bethlehem Steel plant in Pennsylvania.

The Taylor System received heavy publicity in the fall of 1910 when lawyer Louis Brandeis introduced the testimony of efficiency experts during a hearing of the Interstate Commerce Commission on a freight rate case. The testimony was spectacular, and although the commission decided the case against the railroads on other grounds, the term "scientific management" was brought before the public eye by this case. During 1911 at least 200 articles on scientific management appeared in both the specialized and popular journals.[23]

Callahan documents the great and immediate interest in "scientific management" shown by leaders in American education at that time—Cubberley of Stanford, George Strayer of Teachers College, Columbia, Edward C. Elliot of Wisconsin, Paul Hanus of Harvard, Franklin Bobbitt of the University of Chicago, and Leonard Ayres of the Russell Sage Foundation. These men, most of them universtiy deans or professors of school administration, applied the ideas almost at once to their work in investigations or surveys of school systems which sought to be evaluated after 1910. The same men collaborated with some of the alert city assistant superintendents of schools who had also grasped the possibilities of scientific management applied to the schools—Stuart Courtis in Cleveland and both Frank Ballou and Frank Thompson in Boston.[24]

Criticism of the public schools was then intense across the country, a fact which Callahan connects to the rapid acceptance of scientific management and the norm of "efficiency" by educators. The World Book Company sponsored the publication of several surveys of city schools and related books under the heading "The School Efficiency Series," edited by Paul Hanus. The N.E.A. meetings in 1912 and 1913, especially the sessions on the problems facing superintendents, were very much concerned with the application of scientific methods and engineering efficiency to education. Major reports on several of the big-city school systems stressed the need for increased efficiency in both the instructional and business activities of the schools and urged the acceptance by city educators of the tools of science then available—tests, growth charts, child accounting, and record-keeping tables.[25]

What did the term "efficiency" mean to laymen and educators at that time? Although used by those who wanted to cut school costs, it was generally thought of as a concept in engineering.

"It is distinctly the business of the engineer to lessen waste —wastes of material, wastes of friction, wastes of design, wastes of effort, wastes due to crude organization and administration—in a word, wastes due to inefficiency. The field is the largest and richest to which any worker has ever turned." [26]

The efficiency movement, as suggested by the second sentence quoted, became a kind of social gospel or missionary movement as engineers sought to find new applications of the concept and methods of study. "Scientific management" began as a very specialized field of study of industrial operations, exemplified by analyses of machine shop management and time-and-motion studies made with stop watch in hand. The emphasis on streamlining mass-production techniques is generally credited to Taylor, but the fact that his work gained attention so rapidly was in part because schoolmen and others were searching for ways to reduce the number of failures and prove that they too could spend money wisely.

THE RAPID ACCEPTANCE
OF THE "EFFICIENCY" IDEAL

It is Callahan's thesis that the acceptance of the Taylor approach to educational administration made the superintendent a business manager, forced "mass production" techniques on the schools, and ultimately generated dozens of articles and doctoral studies on trivial topics. Callahan calls the indiscriminate acceptance of business values and pseudo-scientific efficiency by school administrators and their professors an "American Tragedy." [27]

The principles of scientific management, however, were quite readily adopted, not only because superintendents were vulnerable to criticism from the business-minded public, but also because educators aspired to establish education as a respectable applied science. Some used "efficiency" as a shibboleth to achieve this end. The long-term residue of the "era of efficiency" for the city schools was neither the platoon school à la William Wirt or the "service station" concept of William McAndrew, but the increased attention to evaluating education and to collecting data on achievement, promotions, and "retardation" and teacher performance.

Granted that the zeal of some leading educators in pursuing the possibilities of "educational cost-accounting" was excessive and to some extent debilitating to the embryonic profession of school administration, the efficiency movement, nevertheless, must also be analyzed as one outgrowth of the Progressive movement which started prior to Taylorism. And the quest for efficiency can be linked to several salutary developments which persisted thereafter.

Some of the men and the developments which were part of the earlier movement to establish a science of education were:

1. G. Stanley Hall, William James, Francis Parker, John Dewey, and other psychologists and philosophers, who provided the beginnings of a scientific base for the criticism of traditional curriculm and school organization.[28]
2. Lewis Terman (trained by Hall) and Edward Thorndike, who were active in developing and popularizing the measurement of educational aptitude and achievement.[29]
3. The development prior to 1911 of specific instruments to test achievement in arithmetic, reading, and other basic skills.[30]

During the period 1910 to 1920 the following developments occurred in the city schools. The "efficiency" drive accelerated and legitimatized these developments:

1. The school survey movement was launched, and both the U.S. Bureau of Education as well as the universities provided teams of observers and evaluators who grappled with new problems of collecting data for evidence and establishing yardsticks where heretofore neither were available.[31]
2. The self-survey or self-evaluation function began to be assumed by city school districts, beginning in 1911 with the first establishment of bureaus of educational research whose immediate focus was on problems of pupil programs and placement within schools.
3. To accomplish the purposes of evaluation in both the external and self-surveys, the tests and measurement movement was accelerated and, through child study and the emphasis on science, educational research and experimentation began to become acceptable vehicles for revising curricula.

Thus, in education, the "scientific management" movement took its own course and was related to the growth of psychology as a science as much as to the causes of industrial efficiency. Some of the by-products of the "efficiency movement" were lasting, some were ephemeral. Many of the projects were ill-conceived or the tools primitive by latter-day standards, but some of the new functions such as record-keeping or educational measurement meant that data became available on which to base rational decisions or to explain the needs or accomplishments of the school to the citizenry. School boards or superintendents in cities before 1910 or 1911 gathered very little statistical information to assess the accomplishments or needs of the schools, although sporadic studies had been conducted to determine what schools were doing or not doing well. The schools were accused of being wasteful or extravagent; both boards and schoolmen lacked the data by which the charges could be verified or disproven.

Actually, many precedents for school surveys and the measurement of school achievement existed, and the marvel is that it took an efficiency movement to persuade city school boards to adopt approaches to evaluation that had been advocated in the time of Horace Mann.[32]

The municipal reform movement already had been imbued with a desire to implant efficiency in all phases of public services, of which only one phase was education. One of the men most zealous in pursuing efficiency (and a thorn in the side of New York schoolmen) was William H. Allen. Allen, in his 1907 book on efficiency, advocated the use of measures which would assess a child's physical welfare, a child's progress in school, curriculum changes, teacher accomplishments, school equipment, costs, and the work of school trustees. On the latter he raised the provocative question:

Would your community have better schools if instead of 15 or 20 or 46 trustees who volunteer such time as they can conveniently spare from their own affairs, there was one board of 3 or 5 commissioners, at least one of whom being paid to give his entire time and held strictly responsible for efficiency in the use of that time for studying school administration? [33]

Allen's many remedies for the ills of city schools included studies of the efficiency of compulsory education (the extent to which all children were in fact being sent to school), studies of the use of time in education, better reporting and ranking of student achievement, greater emphasis on child study, and conducting statistical studies on most of these topics or problems. It is

dangerously easy to read into the statements of an irascible gadfly
of the schools the accepted tenets of one-half century later. At the
very least, however, it must be acknowledged that these questions
were raised prior to 1910 and that the need for data, for studies,
and instrumentation to obtain data had been proclaimed in advance of the acceptance of "Taylorism." The fact that educators
felt under pressure to base management decisions on more acceptable and verifiable types of evidence helps to account for the
astonishing rapidity of the acceptance of "scientific management"
bureaus of educational efficiency and the enthusiasm for testing
and school surveys.

Although Taylor's ideas on efficiency had in 1911 only
begun to attract support, the size of most city boards had already
been reduced by that year, New York and Chicago being the
major exceptions. Moreover, Cleveland, Buffalo, Houston, and
San Francisco had each experimented with variations of the commission plan, the "expert director" notion, or the "paid board
member" idea elaborated by Allen. Also of interest is the fact
that these cities had rejected, or would soon reject, the use of
full-time businessmen in these capacities and would turn instead
to full-time educational directors assisted by boards of supervisors, superintendents, and professional examiners. Furthermore,
school boards were considering placing educators over the business manager rather than vice versa.

In summary, then, the efficiency movement in education can
be viewed as a movement related to that of applying science to
many dimensions of education other than efficient business management narrowly defined. Efficiency in the classroom was not
tied to economy motives alone but also to the desire or need to
know more about the effectiveness of the program. During and
after the movement toward scientific management, there was also
an increased use of data-gathering devices, tests, and surveys,
some of which became institutionalized in city school bureaus
specializing in data collection on children and school programs.
Boston, for example, started a department of Educational Investigation and Measurement to assess school performance. Other
cities created the same type of bureau ostensibly to provide the
kind of information which could improve performance.

Samuel Haber has pointed out that the message of Taylor
and others impressed social reformers far more than it did many

businessmen.[34] Progressive reformers already were interested in increased social efficiency as a goal; thus, they were quite eager to adopt scientific or scientific-sounding approaches. This offers an important alternative to the "business values" assumption from which Callahan started his inquiry.

Finally, the movement to make governments more efficient had already begun even before Frederick Taylor's ideas became popular. If "scientific management" became a vehicle for the internal improvement (or distortion) of school administration, it certainly did not inspire the external or governmental reorganization which, chronologically, preceded the movement.[35] Whether "efficiency" was a concept linked to subsequent reorganization of city boards is another question which will be analyzed.

THE LARGEST CITIES
REDUCE SCHOOL BOARD SIZE AGAIN

Most of the elective city boards had been reduced in size during the late 1890's and the early years of the twentieth century. Not until 1917 did the Chicago and New York school boards become similarly smaller, despite the availability of clear recommendations to do so, such as those of the Harper commission in the 1890's. Buffalo, the same year, changed to an appointive superintendent at the close of the career of long-time superintendent Henry Emerson. Detroit, maverick among the elective boards, turned away from ward representation for the second and last time in 1916, when its citizens voted to accept a state law allowing the board to cut its size by more than one-half.

Detroit had not rushed to take advantage of the legislative enactment of 1913, which permitted it to reduce the board to seven members, elected at large if the voters so desired. The existing board majority opposed the change and moved to block or delay any change by proposing a plebiscite. Finally, with the full support of the press, the amendment to elect seven members at large passed in 1916 by a vote of 61,806 to 11,342.[36] The new board greatly increased the authority of the superintendent of schools, who was named chief executive officer, and transferred to educators the function of selecting texts, appointing teachers and principals, and developing courses of study. Committees of the ward-elected board had previously performed those functions.

Chicago business and civic leaders in the early 1900's formed a smaller board of nine members and a strong superintendent. The highly organized teachers, along with several vigorous labor unions, fought the business-oriented board on many fronts. Jane Addams later explained their differences in ideological terms: "The whole situation between the superintendent supported by a majority of the Board and the Teachers' Federation had become an epitome of the struggle between efficiency and democracy." [37]

Organized labor in 1905 helped elect judge Edward Dunne as mayor. Mayor Dunne appointed pro-labor board members who selected Ella Flagg Young to the superintendency. The board and new superintendent authorized teacher councils at each school to participate in educational decisions. The teachers' triumph was actually short-lived. The newspapers actively opposed the new teacher-organized labor alliance. Dunne's successor, Mayor Busse, removed all of the Dunne appointees, an act later declared illegal but one which was a step toward restoring a business-oriented board of education.

Teachers, reformers, and businessmen later found common cause in opposing the actions of "Big Bill" Thompson, first elected mayor in 1915. William Hale Thompson, rogue and demagogue, saw the Chacago schools as a source of spoils and felt educators ought to follow his lead in denouncing British tyranny over Ireland, an issue that won Thompson the loyalty of several hundred thousand Irish–American voters.

Teachers needed allies, first in a fight for organizational survival, but also for tenure rights. Jacob Loeb, a board member, in 1916 pushed through a new school regulation forbidding teachers to join a union or to hire non-teachers as officials of a teacher organization. The teachers obtained a court injunction against this rule but the board in June of 1916 refused to reappoint sixty-eight teachers and principals. When these educators, many of them union members, lost their appeal to the courts on that issue, they shifted their expression of concern to the legislature.[38] The Chicago Federation of Labor logically considered both the rule and the firings as an attack on its status, too, and threw its full support to the teachers.[39] The Women's City Club, a militant "watchdog" group, joined in the struggle for teacher tenure and supported, along with many other civic groups, the passage of the Otis Law, which in 1919 reorganized the Chicago board. One bill, which had received extensive support in 1917, called for a board of seven members, elected at large, who would be paid $1,500 a year.[40]

The Otis Law, somewhat less drastic than the 1917 bill, reduced the board size to eleven but retained the method of appointment by the mayor with the consent of the common council. Although the superintendency was strengthened by the specification of a four-year term and acquisition of the power to recommend textbooks, appointments, and promotions of employees and other duties, the law also added two other coordinate executives—a business manager and an attorney.

Despite the new law, the reorganized board experienced great difficulties just in establishing itself. Mayor Thompson kept the Chicago schools in constant turmoil for the next two years, during which time both the old twenty-one-man school board and several sets of eleven-man boards fought in the courts, with each other and sometimes with Thompson. When the old board appointed Charles E. Chadsey of Detroit as superintendent in 1919, that board having been declared the legal board for Chicago schools by order of the state supreme court, Mayor Thompson made Chadsey's removal an election issue. Within months, Chadsey was locked out of his office by Chicago police and, although his right was to the superintendency was upheld in the appellate court, he resigned the position in protest over the interference by city hall. One outcome of this incredible affair was the conviction of several board members and the board attorney for conspiracy, after which they were fined and served short jail sentences.[41]

These same board members returned to serve on the board, however, and the next four years in Chicago were rife with scandal over the conduct of school business. The Municipal Voters League and other civic groups demanded a series of investigations which culminated in 1922 in several grand jury inquiries and more than forty indictments of Chicago school board members and their associates. Ample evidence was amassed to prove that the school system had been systematically plundered by the Thompson appointees. Chicago voters in 1923 rejected the incumbent mayor and elected William Dever, a reform mayor. Dever's new board appointees decided to hire William McAndrew, an efficiency-oriented New York City associate superintendent, to lead the Chicago schools.[42]

REORGANIZATION IN NEW YORK

The New York City board after 1898, with forty-six members, remained the largest of the big-city school boards. It remained large in part because the appointments of several mayors pleased the urban pressure groups who were temporarily satisfied with the flow of services and the adoption of new programs. But when John P. Mitchel was elected mayor in 1913, he placed high priority on new programs and on a school reorganization plan already agreed upon by the Seth Low-Butler-P.E.A.-City Club coalition of "urban progressives." Mitchel endorsed a campaign for restructuring the board, a campaign formally launched in early 1914 at a P.E.A. sponsored meeting where Charles William Eliot and Frederick C. Howe urged a smaller board as one prerequisite for "Efficiency in Public School Administration," the theme of the meeting.[43]

During 1915 and 1916, bills to reduce the board to seven members failed of passage despite endorsement by the Citizens Union, *The New Republic, The New York Times,* the P.E.A., Abraham Flexner, and other notables. An act was passed in 1917 which enabled Mitchel to appoint an entirely new board of five men and two women, who took office January 1, 1918.[44]

The reduction of board size at this time, Lowi concludes, pushed the board into the vortex of politics, since the various boroughs and religious groups, from that time on, struggled to gain representation on the smaller board in order to articulate and defend their interests.[45] Lowi also found that the number of members listed in the New York City Social Register dropped from approximately one-third to none within a few years after the 1917 change.

Soon thereafter, Mitchel lost in his own campaign for re-election as mayor, partly because of popular objections to the Gary Plan (for a more efficient school on a platoon basis), which he had helped to introduce in New York, but which many New Yorkers thought had been forced down their throats. Mayor John F. Hylan governed New Yorkers through World War I and into the 1920's. Hylan, a Tammany Democrat, made a campaign promise, "a seat for every child," which he fulfilled, apparently without scandal or charges of misappropriation.[46]

THE BUFFALO REORGANIZATION

The Buffalo schools in 1917 underwent the most radical reorganization in the educational history of that city, following a highly critical report on the organization of and conditions in the Buffalo schools by the New York State Department of Education. The report, requested by the Buffalo superintendent and submitted by the state's survey team in 1915, excoriated the school system organization as "ineffective and inefficient" and recommended that the common council no longer manage the schools. The major recommendation was the "absolute divorcement of all school affairs from the municipal and political affairs of the city." [47]

Buffalo was in the process of changing to a commission form of city government and in 1916 a board of education was established, the five members to be appointed by the mayor and confirmed by the council. A council member was to serve as commissioner to supervise and appoint all new offices and employees of the public school system. The board of education was also to be placed under the control of the council, the body which also selected the superintendent of education.

The following year, 1917, a state law empowered the Buffalo board of education to select a superintendent of schools and Ernest Hartwell became the first appointed superintendent in Buffalo since 1853. Still, the common council retained fiscal control. Despite later survey reports recommending increased fiscal autonomy for the Buffalo board of education, the municipal authorities continued to retain close control over the education budget in Buffalo. The mode of selecting board members has not changed (although the number of members was later increased to seven).

EFFICIENCY AND SCHOOL BOARD
REORGANIZATION

Only in New York State did the "efficiency" motif surround the drive to reduce the size of the boards, in Buffalo and, especially, in New York City. There the speeches of Eliot, and especially of Frederick Howe, identified reorganization of the New York City board with the possibility of applying standards of efficiency to the schools. However, the application of that doctrine in New York City was much more clearly associated in the public mind with the activities of the mayor and board in introducing the Gary platoon school plan than it was with reducing the size of the board.

The changes in the Chicago board were connected both to the row over teacher membership in labor unions and in part to the pursuit of educational efficiency through new vocational programs which the teacher unions opposed. Another test of the impact of the efficiency doctrine on the change would arise from the identification of the source of the ideas incorporated in the Otis Law of 1917. The bulk of the changes can be traced to the recommendations of William Rainey Harper and the late-nineteenth century commission which Harper chaired.

The Chicago board hired William McAndrew, one of the apostles of the efficiency camp, as superintendent. McAndrew's regime, until it was interrupted by Thompson's accusation of pro-British, un-American behavior, was characterized by vigorous attempts to apply the canons of business efficiency to the school setting.[48] However, after McAndrew's departure, the efficiency movement in Chicago lost most of its momentum.

The Detroit board modifications in 1916 represent a continuation of (or delayed reaction to) the earlier efforts in the 1880's to remove the schools from ward politics. The schools in Detroit were steeped in political conflict during the terms of several superintendents, especially of Wales C. Martindale and Charles E. Chadsey. The acceptance of the 1913 law providing for at-large elections represented, for Detroit, the final effort to shake the incubus of ward politics.

In the main, the movement to apply the tenets of engineering efficiency to education was accomplished through internal reorganizations: the establishment of research bureaus, the application of cost accounting principles to attendance and promotion data, and the surge of interest in educational testing and measurement. Although it was difficult for the two movements—for school board reorganization and for increased efficiency of school operations—to remain separated, these facts must be pointed out:

1. Between 1911 (year of Pennsylvania reorganizations and the first year of general enthusiasm over "efficiency") and 1923, only four of the fourteen cities reorganized the school boards.
2. All four cities in question reorganized in a short span of two years, between 1916 and 1917, although the campaigns had been underway at various degrees of intensity for from two to twenty years.
3. Only in New York State (Buffalo and New York City) was the slogan of ideal "efficiency" specifically attached to proposals for restructuring the mechanisms for controlling city schools.

Several of the reorganizations can be linked with the efficiency movement, but it is equally possible to view the changes as deferrals of previously identified needs for structural modifications. Buffalo Superintendent Emerson and New York's Maxwell had each expressed their preferences for reorganizations more than fifteen years earlier.

UNSUCCESSFUL CAMPAIGNS
FOR REORGANIZATION

Before leaving the 1900 to 1920 period, it is worth mentioning that Philadelphia in 1917 mobilized a campaign to establish an elective board of five members. Bruce M. Watson, a former superintendent, had been brought to Philadelphia as director of the new Public Education Association, and under his leadership that group fought for four years to secure the passage of legislation to gain a smaller, elective board. The 1919 bill was defeated by a very narrow margin but moved the school board to agree to another of Watson's proposals, that a survey be made of Philadelphia schools. The outcome of the survey was a heightened awareness on the part of the judges of the need for selecting as board members citizens who would worry about the quality of the schools as well as the costs. The Philadelphia board was also persuaded by the survey to "bring in an outside man as superintendent and the character of the schools began to change at once." [49]

The Chicago city school investigators later interviewed Watson and learned from him that Pittsburgh citizens had been instrumental in defeating the proposal for an elective board for

Philadelphia. Apparently Pittsburgh, from 1911 to 1917, was just as satisfied with the appointments made by the judges as the citizens in Philadelphia were dissatisfied. The Pittsburgh board president is said to have observed that all the decent citizens of Philadelphia seemed to be in favor of the change to an elective board while all the decent citizens of Pittsburgh opposed such a change. Henry and Kerwin see in this comment evidence for the proposition that the method of selection neither determines the quality of board member selection nor insures "the kind of administration that good citizens want." [50]

This episode would indicate that certain "state effects" of legislation concerning city school board organization in states where there are two or more very large cities cannot be ignored. The passage of the 1911 Pennsylvania law, directing that both Philadelphia and Pittsburgh boards consist of fifteen members selected by the judges of the Common Court, reflected the impact of one city's school board selection structure on another within the same state. However, when the city which had used selection by judges for the longer period of time wished to reorganize the procedure, the citizens of the second city blocked the conversion. The legislature, in listening to conflicting testimony, was unable to weigh the demands of Philadelphia citizens as more legitimate than the glowing reports of satisfied Pittsburgh citizens. The Philadelphia court judges, instead, were pushed to consider more carefully their function of selecting board members. For the time being, the improvements that Philadelphia sought were established through increased attention to the selection function rather than a change in the methods by which board members or superintendents were chosen.

After 1920, the number and kinds of school board reorganizations diminished. Controversy over the relationship of city schools to city government, and of school superintendents to school boards, continued, and several of the larger cities continued to search for a system which would insulate the schools from what was felt to be the sordid side-effects of city politics.

ANALYSIS OF THE REORGANIZATIONS

The thirteen "Great Cities" which had boards of education in 1900 can be categorized as either elective or appointive, with

Pittsburgh's board members appointed by the elected members of sub-district boards. Five of the boards had more than twenty members; eight others had less than twenty members, of which five boards had less than ten. The total amount of money to be raised for education was approved by city councils or other boards in ten instances, in three cases by the school boards, and in one case by an elective superintendent. Ten of the cities at this time used the school board or committee of the school board to approve school construction, three used a city agency, and one used the elective school director to make these decisions. Teacher nominations were made by superintendents in eight instances and by boards or board committees in six.

During the period from 1901 to 1920, ten of the city school boards were reorganized, six before the end of 1911. Some of the school governance experiments of the 1890's, such as the Cleveland "Federal Plan" or Milwaukee's bi-partisan nominating commission, were ended during this period. Several board selection innovations were inaugurated, such as Houston's commission plan of government, which required a shift from elective to appointive members, or Milwaukee's short-lived plan to use judges to appoint the board members, a plan that was ruled out by the courts. Eight of the boards were reduced in size, Philadelphia twice, so that in 1920 even the three largest boards had a maximum of fifteen members. Selection on a ward basis was abandoned by five more cities and in New York City the powers of local school trustees were diminished.

Usually the authority of the superintendent of schools was increased when the number of school board members and of sub-committees was reduced. Another change in the superintendency was the shift in the appointment authority for that office from the director to the school board in Cleveland and from election to appointment in Buffalo. A trend toward granting the superintendent of schools the authority to nominate teachers usually accompanied the reorganization of the boards. School administrators and textbook authors began to advocate the designation of the superintendent of schools as chief executive officer.[51]

The strengthening of the superintendency was advocated by many of the same people who wanted a smaller more centralized school board. Essentially an elite board would itself select a manager to see that its policies were carried out. Gone was any faith in the capacity of local citizens in each ward or school neighborhood to manage their own school. The reformers believed less in the people and more in the possibility of philosopher-kings. In fact, they strongly believed that schools run by the people would not serve the purposes of an orderly, industrialized society as viewed from the vantage point of company executives and college presidents. Their view of an efficient society could not accommodate the ideal of widespread citizen participation in all major school decisions. Nor would they trust the teachers to do any more than obey the orders sent down by a chief executive.

Citizens whose boards were reorganized early in the century argued for the change on the basis of taking the schools out of, or placing them above, ward or partisan politics and of ending corruption or favoritism. A later movement to adopt more efficient methods of administration had some effects in New York State in the campaign to reorganize the city boards of Buffalo and New York City. But in Detroit and Chicago older proposals and blueprints for change were used. If the efficiency movement had any lasting impact on city school boards, this impact can be identified through the creation of new bureaus of research, the adoption of formal testing programs, and the increased use of records.

Urban school reformers viewed the major school board reorganizations as the triumph of reason over "politics." What did that really mean? The changes in fact took power away from the neighborhood or ward level, from the newer European immigrant groups—at least for a time. Ward leaders had begun to recognize that jobs as custodians and teachers provided economic security and even social mobility to their people. The triumph of the working class was never so clear as when custodians actually had a hand in naming principals, as reported in Pittsburgh. The transfer of powers to smaller city school boards and especially of employee screening functions (except for janitors) to a superintendent or examining board created new barriers to employment opportunities. Occasionally a mayor such as Thompson of Chicago would join the new masses in obstructing such changes. This forced the businessman–university–journalist coalition to insist next on taking the schools out of municipal politics—out of ward politics first. Then the problem was defined as reducing the power of a mayor to appoint his henchmen or otherwise intervene in the operation of city schools.

By 1917, the pace of reorganization seemed to slow down, since most of the boards were reorganized away from the ward basis, and some of them buffered from the mayor by reliance on the judiciary to name members. Philadelphia was stymied by citizens of Pittsburgh in its attempt to change to a smaller elective board.

The next chapter will examine the structures and functions of big-city boards in 1920, the several reorganizations which came in the early 1920's, and the continued move within administrative circles to increase the status and upgrade the profession of the superintendency. Several criticisms of city school boards and the brief campaign to abolish school boards also will be examined. The major new device adopted between 1945 and 1965 was that of a nominating commission or selection board to help the mayor make appointments to the city school board.

NOTES

1. Raymond Callahan, *Education and the Cult of Efficiency* (Chicago: The University of Chicago Press, 1962). The acceptance of "scientific management" and acquiescence by school administrators to demands for more efficient schools constitute the motif or theme of Callahan's book.

2. Various issues of the *Educational Review*, 1897 to 1904, especially vols. XIII to XXVIII.

3. Editorial comment by Butler in the *Educational Review*, vol. XX, no. 1 (September 1900), p. 107.

4. Samuel P. Abelow, *Dr. William H. Maxwell* (Brooklyn: Scheba Publishing Co., 1934).

5. P. W. Horn, "City Schools Under the Commission Form of Government," *Educational Review*, vol. XXXVIII, no. 3 (November 1911), p. 905.

6. Jerome H. Farbar, "Results of Commission Government in Houston, Texas," *The Annals*, vol. XXXVII (1909), p. 365.

7. Superintendent of Schools, Milwaukee, Wisconsin, *Our Roots Grow Deep*, The Eighty-Fourth Annual Report of the Milwaukee Public Schools (Milwaukee: Board of Education, June 1943), pp. 78–79.

8. Clinton Rogers Woodruff, "A Corrupt School System," *Educational Review*, vol. XXVI, no 5 (December 1903), pp. 433–439. See also the slashing attack on the "low class amateur service" rendered by the reorganized 21-man board in an article by Scott Nearing, "The Working of a Large Board of Education," *Educational Review*, vol. XXXVIII (June 1900), pp. 43–45.

9. June 20, 1933.

10. Harold U. Faulkner, *The Quest for Social Justice, 1898–1914* (New York: Macmillan, 1933). The sectional or sub-district boards lost the other powers in 1931.

11. J. M. Guinn, *History of California: Los Angeles and Environs,* vol. I (Los Angeles: Historic Record Co., 1907), p. 332.

12. *Shall the Boston School Committee Be Reorganized?* (A petition, with arguments and information on city school boards elsewhere). Boston (February–March), 1905.

13. Henry Greenleaf Pearson, *Son of New England: James Jackson Storrow* (Boston: Thomas Todd, 1932), p. 50.

14. Harry N. Irwin, "Dual Administrative Control in City School Systems—A Case Study of Its Origin and Development," *The Elementary School Journal,* vol. XXIII (April and May 1923), pp. 573–585 and 664–675.

15. *City Government in the United States* (New York: The Century Co., 1908).

16. Andrew S. Draper, "Education Organization and Administration," in Nicholas Murray Butler (ed.), *Education in the United States,* Monograph No. 1 (Albany: J. B. Lyon, 1900), pp. 14–15.

17. *Our Schools: Their Administration and Supervision* (Boston: D. C. Health, 1904), p. 49.

18. Frank Rollins, "School Administration in Municipal Government," Ph. D. dissertation (New York: Columbia University, 1902), p. 58.

19. *School Administration* (Syracuse, New York: C. W. Bardeen, 1906), p. 35.

20. *Public School Administration* (Cambridge, Massachusetts: The Riverside Press, 1929), Chapter XVI. The "incorrect" charts showed several executives reporting directly to the board.

21. Thomas McDowell Gilland, *The Origin and Development of the Power and Duties of the City School Superintendent* (Chicago: The University of Chicago Press, 1935), pp. 163–169.

22. Callahan, *op. cit.,* p. 29.

23. *Ibid.,* pp. 19–21.

24. These were among the men who worked with Paul Hanus as advisors to the "School Efficiency Series," World Book Company, 1912.

25. The major surveys of Baltimore in 1911 and New York City in 1912 were immediately connected in time and in ideology. The survey of Cleveland in 1915 was by far the most comprehensive. The 1916 survey of St. Louis was an exception since, as Callahan recognized (*ibid.,* p. 117), it was directed by Charles Judd of the University of Chicago who emphasized educational goals above scientific management.

26. Harrington Emerson, *Efficiency as a Basis for Operation and Wages* (New York: The Engineering Magazine, 1911), p. 17.

27. Callahan, *op. cit.*, p. 240 ff., especially Chapter X, "An American Tragedy in Education."

28. Lawrence Cremin, *The Transformation of the School* (New York: Knopf, 1962), pp. 100–101, 115–126.

29. *Ibid.*, pp. 110–115, 130–135, and 104 (on Terman).

30. *Ibid.*, p. 186. The acceptance of testing was probably accelerated in 1911 by the efficiency movement, but the tests and instruments for measuring intelligence and achievement in the 3 R's had already been refined to the point at which they could be used.

31. Hollis L. Caswell, *City School Surveys: An Interpretation and Appraisal*, Ph.D. dissertation (New York: Teachers College, Columbia University, 1929). Caswell placed the start of twentieth-century surveys as 1910 (The Boise, Idaho survey), with an increase in the number of surveys each year until 1918 and a second surge upward in the 1920's.

32. Otis W. Caldwell and Stuart A. Courtis, *Then and Now in Education* (New York: World Book Co., 1925). This book recalls the precedent for achievement testing in the Boston "survey" of pupil progress in 1845, during Mann's debates with the Boston masters over the quality of education in Boston schools.

33. William H. Allen, *Efficient Democracy* (New York: Dodd, Mead, 1907), pp. 122–123.

34. Samuel Haber, *Efficiency and Uplift: Scientific Management in the Progressive Era, 1880–1920* (Chicago: The University of Chicago Press, 1964).

35. It could be argued in Parsonian terms that the reorganization of school boards was a change at the "institutional" level whereas the ideas of Taylor were applied to the "managerial" level where the work of the teachers was supervised and evaluated. However, men at both levels felt pressure to obtain more objective "data" to guide decisions. Cf. W. S. Deffenbaugh, *Significant Movements in City School Systems*, U.S. Department of the Interior, Bureau of Education, Bulletin no. 8 (Washington, D.C.: Government Printing Office, 1923).

36. Arthur B. Moehlman, *Public Education in Detroit* (Illinois: Public School Publishing, 1925), pp. 190–191. The fight for a reducing the size and functioning of the board was actually long and bitter. The board was usually divided on that issue and on other issues and the superintendent was a controversial innovator, himself an election issue in 1909 and 1911. Under the ward-elected board it was frequently charged that janitors and engineers were political appointees. This, too, was changed in 1917 (pp. 174 and 190–191).

37. Jane Addams, *Twenty Years at Hull House* (New York: New American Library, 1961), p. 234.

38. George Counts, *School and Society in Chicago* (New York: Harcourt Brace Jovanovich, 1938), pp. 53–56.

39. *Ibid.*, p. 192.

40. *Ibid.*, p. 221.

41. *Ibid.*, pp. 251–258.

42. *Ibid.*, pp. 259–264.

43. Sol Cohen, *Progressives and Urban School Reform* (New York: Teachers College of Columbia University, 1964), p. 94.

44. *Ibid.*, pp. 93–95.

45. Thedore J. Lowi, *At the Pleasure of the Mayor* (New York: The Free Press of Glencoe, 1964), pp. 31–32. Nationality groups began to complain about their lack of representation on the smaller board.

46. Cohen, *op. cit.*, pp. 98–112.

47. Thomas E. Finegan, Elementary Education, II, Report for the School Year ending July 31, 1916. The Thirteenth Annual Report of the State Department of Education (Albany: The University of the State of New York, 1917), pp. 38–47.

48. Callahan, *op. cit.*, pp. 226, 236–237.

49. Nelson B. Henry and Jerome C. Kerwin, *Schools and City Government* (Chicago: The University of Chicago Press, 1938), p. 27.

50. *Ibid.*, p. 28.

51. Not all the cities under study moved in this direction. Not only did Cleveland and St. Louis retain the dual or multiple executives, each reporting directly to the board, but some other cities (e.g., Boston in 1906) *added* executives for business functions at the time of reorganization.

THE QUEST FOR STABILITY
1920–1944

INTRODUCTION

DURING THE TWENTIES AND THIRTIES the profession of
school superintendent became more highly organized and a
greater amount of communication flowed among superintendents.
While the expertise of the superintendent attracted more attention, the city school boards themselves drew criticism from
George Counts, who found them "unrepresentative," and from
Charles Judd, who thought boards ought to be abolished rather
than continue to obstruct the professionals. However, the actual
changes in city school board organization between 1924 and
1944 were negligible.

The year 1924 marked the end of a long series of immigrant
waves and a tapering of the growth trajectory of the older cities
(see Table 9). City schools managed to assimilate and socialize
the ethnic groups already present in large numbers; city school
boards changed their form very little after immigration slowed to
a trickle. The debate about how best to select school boards continued, but the upper-class elites and the considerably strengthened top professionals did not want to change the selection system. What kinds of arguments were advanced by social critics
during the 1920's and 1930's? Under what conditions were
changes reluctantly agreed to by the successors to those who had
reduced the sizes of the several boards? But before turning to
these questions it makes sense to review the school board arrangements in each of the cities as of 1920 with special reference
to the power of mayors to appoint board members and make
other key decisions.

Table 9 BIG-CITY POPULATION, 1870–1930

	1870	1880	1890	1900	1910	1920	1930
Los Angeles	5,728	11,183	50,395	104,266	319,198	*576,673*	1,238,048
San Francisco	149,473	233,959	298,959	342,782	416,912	*416,912*	*634,394*
Chicago	298,977	*503,185*	1,009,850	1,698,575	2,185,283	2,701,705	3,376,438
Baltimore	267,354	332,313	434,439	*508,957*	558,485	733,826	804,874
Boston	250,526	362,839	448,477	*560,892*	670,585	748,060	781,188
Detroit	79,577	116,340	205,876	290,277	465,766	993,678	1,568,662
St. Louis	310,864	350,518	451,770	*575,238*	687,029	772,897	821,960
New York	1,478,103	1,911,698	2,507,414	3,437,202	4,766,883	5,620,048	6,930,446
Cleveland	92,829	160,146	261,353	384,111	*560,663*	796,841	900,429
Pittsburgh	86,076	235,071	343,904	462,801	*533,905*	588,343	669,817
Philadelphia	674,022	847,170	1,046,964	1,293,697	1,549,008	1,823,779	1,950,961
Houston	9,382	16,513	27,557	44,633	78,800	138,276	292,352
Buffalo	117,741	155,134	255,664	352,387	423,715	506,775	573,076
Milwaukee	71,440	115,587	204,468	285,315	373,857	457,147	578,249

The first tabulation of more than 500,000 is italicized.
Source: Statistical Abstracts, U.S. Census.

THE STRUCTURE AND FUNCTIONS
OF CITY SCHOOL BOARDS IN 1920

By 1920 all fourteen cities had school boards. Buffalo had chosen in 1914 to follow the board-superintendent pattern used by other cities in New York State and elsewhere. Members of eight boards were appointed by other governmental officials (themselves elective officers) and six boards were elective, in each case chosen at large. The ward unit of representation was no longer employed for either appointive or elective board members (see Table 10).

The size of the "Great City" school boards in 1920 ranged from four to fifteen members. Three boards had fifteen members and the most popular size (for five boards) was seven members. Three boards had less than seven members and the size of three others fell between eight and fourteen.

The mayor alone was responsible for naming board members in four cities; the mayor's choices were confirmed by the city council in two cities. In both Philadelphia and Pittsburgh the judges of the Court of Common Pleas named the school board members. The San Francisco school board members remained full-time salaried officers of the city and county.

Five of the eight appointive boards in 1920 submitted the annual school budgets to a city council or board of estimates, as did three of the six elective boards. Three boards in each category made budget decisions within millage limits established by the state.

No longer did any city department of public works perform the school construction function. The city councils or other city boards handled school construction for five of the appointive boards; the other three appointive boards could approve school construction but usually only within indebtedness limits imposed by the state.

Five of the six elective boards were similarly empowered to construct schools, but only within state limits or with voter approval of a bond issue. The Boston school committee could request school construction but the mayor's schoolhouse commission constructed the buildings.

All of the superintendents, with the exception of the elective

Table 10 THE STRUCTURE AND SELECTED FUNCTIONS OF BIG-CITY SCHOOL BOARDS, 1920

City	Method of Board Member Selection	Size	Approval of Total Amount To Be Raised for Education	Approval of Funds for School Construction	Selection of Superintendent	Nomination of Teachers
New York	Appointed by Mayor	7	Board of Estimate and Apportionment	Board of Estimate and Apportionment	Board	Board of Supervisors
Chicago	Appointed by Mayor	11	Board—State levy limit	Board with concurrence of City Council	Board	Superintendent
Philadelphia	Appointed by Judges	15	Board—State Millage limit	Board—Bonding limit	Board	Superintendent
Baltimore	Appointed by Mayor with Council	9	Board of Estimates	Mayor and Council	Board	Superintendent
Buffalo	Appointed by Mayor with Council	5	City Council	City Council	Board	Superintendent
Houston	Appointed by Mayor	7	Mayor and Council	City Commission	Board	Superintendent
Pittsburgh	Appointed by Judges	15	Board—State Millage limit	Board—Bonding limit	Board	Superintendent

San Francisco	Appointed by Mayor	4	County Board of Supervisors	Board—Popular vote on bonds	Elective	Superintendent and Board from Civil Service list
St. Louis	Elected at large	12	Board—State Millage limit	Board—Popular vote on bonds	Board	Superintendent
Boston	Elected at large	5	Board—State levy limit (Mayor)	School House Commission	Board	Superintendent
Cleveland	Elected at large	7	City Tax Commission	Board, popular vote on bonds	Board	Superintendent
Detroit	Elected at large	7	City Council and Board of Estimates	Board	Board	Superintendent
Los Angeles	Elected at large	7	County Superintendents and Board of Supervisors	Board—Popular vote on bonds	Board	Superintendent and Committee
Milwaukee	Elected at large	15	Board—State Millage limit	Board	Board	Superintendent

Source: W. S. Deffenbaugh, *Current Practices in City School Administration,* Bureau of Education, Department of Interior, Bulletin 1917, No. 8, Tables 1, 3, 4; and G. C. Morehart, *The Legal Status of City School Boards:* New York Teachers College, Columbia University, 1927), data through 1923, p. 11. State statutes were consulted by the author to verify 1920 status.

(See Table 8 for an explanation of the format used in this table.)

superintendent of schools in San Francisco, were appointed by
the city boards of education. The superintendents all participated in the nomination of teachers, either with sole power or
with the assistance of a board of superintendents, as in New
York. Only in Los Angeles did the superintendent subject his
nominees to a preliminary review by a committee of the board.

The major changes between 1900 and 1920 occurred in the
realm of reductions in the size of the board membership, increased autonomy for some elective and appointive boards over
budgets and construction, and the substantial gain in the superintendent's power to nominate teachers. Eight boards were
greatly reduced in size, and Buffalo added a board of education.
The Cleveland school director, no longer elective, became the
"business manager" and the board appointed a superintendent.

The appointive and elective boards both gained some independence from city control of expenditures, but the elective
board gained more autonomy over school construction. Nine superintendents won increased control over teacher nominations, a
function no longer assigned to or shared with school board committees except in Los Angeles.

What did this mean, besides the upgrading of the big-city
school superintendency? This meant that the school reformers
had succeeded in removing the power to hire teachers and spend
money from those who lived and led people in the city wards.
Samuel P. Hays, historian of municipal reform, concludes that
the reform movement was largely "an attempt by upper class advanced professional, and large business groups to take formal political power from the previously dominant lower and middle
class elements so that they might advance their own conceptions
of desirable public policy." [1] The dominant groups did not want
immigrant groups running their own schools. They felt that the
schools should make the newer Americans accept the canons of
those who had already prospered. Stated most bluntly, the reformers looked down on workingmen and saloon keepers as
urban school decision-makers.

Hays quotes a Pittsburgh 1911 Voters League reform pamphlet to document this disdain for immigrants, or at least for
their occupations:

Employment as ordinary laborers and in the lowest class of mill work
would naturally lead to the conclusion that such men did not have suf-

ficient education or business training to act as school directors. . . .
Objection might also be made to small shopkeepers, clerks, workmen
at many trades, who by lack of educational advantages and business
training, could not, no matter how honest, be expected to administer
properly the affairs of an educational system, requiring special knowledge, and where millions are spent each year.[2]

Using Pittsburgh as an example, he documents the effects of
the shift from ward election to selection by the judges of the
Court of Common Pleas in 1911. He discovered:

Of the fifteen members of the Pittsburgh Board of Education appointed in 1911, and the nine members of the new city council, some
were small businessmen or white collar workers . . . the Board of Education included ten businessmen with city-wide interests, one doctor associated with the upper class, and three women previously active in
upper class public welfare.[3]

The fifteenth member was an official of the Iron, Steel and Tin
Workers Union. Hays suggests that many of the Populist innovations, such as the referendum and recall, were used artfully to
disguise the essentially elitist or oligarchical nature of the
change.

Boston is another case in point. Storrow's biographer tells
why the turn of the century school committee provoked reform
sentiment.

. . . many members of the Committee were concerned chiefly in representing the local constituency which had elected them, in getting jobs
for teachers and janitors in the schools of their districts, and in obtaining whatever else was desirable and profitable for Charlestown, South
Boston, or Dorchester, as the case might be. Since the "Master" of each
school was beholden to the district committee for his appointment, it
was with its members that he was wont to consult, rather than with the
superintendent.[4]

Starting in 1906 and lasting into the 1920's, a majority coalition
of Yankee businessmen and Irish-Catholic professionals controlled the Boston school committee. They firmly enforced what
they felt was an impartial examination system for staff appointments, but most of all worried about the proper way to "Americanize" the newcomers and teach them respect for hard work,
trade, and industry, establishing many new programs and several
new high schools for just those purposes.

The weak forty-six-man advisory board for New York City
was changed in 1917 to a seven-man board with five men retired

from "business and professional commitments" and two women "who had already devoted a lifetime to civic work." [5] Gone was much of the ethnic and religious representation, and some borough leaders complained about that very noisily. But the era of growing working-class representation was over. The new business and professional leaders were frightened and appalled at the use of schools to enhance the social and economic advancement of adults; they prevailed on the state legislature, even then more rural than urban, to make a moral decision for the sake of the children and good government.

The Hays critique of the disparity between Progressive-era rhetoric and real intentions was anticipated by a few social and education critics such as George Counts. Transferral of power to a smaller centralized board deprived the working classes of a chance to express their educational preferences as directly as they had formerly. College graduates would be much more likely to serve on boards than vocational school graduates. The newcomers must then climb the same educational ladders as those before them climbed in order to succeed. The mid-1920's marked the end of an era of school governance designed to keep the schools relatively close to parents and immediate neighborhoods.

THE REORGANIZATIONS OF THE 1920'S

During the 1920's, the boards of San Francisco and Houston were changed at the request of citizens in both cities who voted to reorganize the two city school systems. These were the only boards of education reorganized during the 1920's despite the dissatisfaction of some civic groups with the behavior of the mayors toward the school boards in New York and Chicago.

San Francisco

The ideas for both the San Francisco and Houston changes first came to the attention of citizens well before 1920. The San Francisco Chamber of Commerce in December 1914 contacted the United States Commissioner of Education concerning the possibility of a survey of the San Francisco schools by the Bureau of Education. During 1915 the San Francisco Board of Education agreed to cooperate with the study, but a Chamber of Commerce committee had to raise $8,500 by private subscription to defray the expenses of the survey. The survey was conducted under the leadership of Philander P. Claxton, the U.S. Commissioner of Education, whose report to the San Francisco Board was released in 1917.[6]

The report was replete with statistical reports and graphs in the tradition of the "efficiency-oriented" surveys conducted by university professors over the previous six or seven years. The investigators dealt harshly with the organization and administration of the schools, suggesting that many of the evils "cannot be eradicated . . . until the dual organization and control has been abolished by amendment to the State constitution and the city charter." [7]

The report labeled the relationship of the elective superintendent to the full-time salaried board as "unique," "unnatural," and "unwise." [8] A plan whereby the board would approve its own budget, construct school buildings, and appoint the school superintendent was recommended so that the people of the city could hold one board responsible "for efficiency" in the conduct or management of their school affairs.[9] The report includes an extended quote from a survey of Denver schools by Franklin Bobbitt, one of the foremost advocates of scientific management among educators, whose ideas on the "principles of administration to govern corporations" compare a manufacturing corporation with a "School Corporation Employing 1,500 People." [10]

The Claxton report was noncommittal about which it preferred of three alternative methods of selecting nine board members from the city at large, either by popular election or appointment by the mayor with confirmation by the board of supervisors, or appointment by the judges of the superior court.[11] The superintendent of schools, the report recommended, should no longer be a member of the board of education but would head a board of examiners to certify the qualifications of teacher candidates.

The elective superintendent, Alfred Roncovieri, defended the schools and the way they had been organized.[12]

The report was controversial and Proposition 37, a proposal to make the superintendent the single executive responsible to an appointive lay board, passed by a narrow margin in 1920. A seven-man board appointed by the mayor took office in 1921. The mayor's school board appointments henceforth were also submitted to the electorate for a vote of confirmation or rejection. Joseph Marr Gwinn, previously the New Orleans superintendent of schools, took office in 1923, the first appointed superintendent for San Francisco schools since 1856 and the first "outsider." [13]

Houston

The proposal to modify the Houston school organization and its relationship to the city can be traced to the superintendent's complaints about the problems of depending on the city of Houston for annual appropriations, approval of all expenditures, and the control of school sites and buildings. Even with a dynamic mayor who had pledged to build schools to relieve overcrowding, the school officials felt it necessary to obtain fiscal independence for the schools. P. W. Horn, the superintendent of schools, was instrumental in building the case for school district independence, and beginning in 1914 complained of the difficulties encountered in working with the city. Ill-feeling between the schools and the city arose, and Horn resigned in 1921. R. V. Cousins, a former state superintendent of schools in Texas, agreed to accept a three-year term in Houston. An election was held and the voters indicated their interest in obtaining an independent school district for Houston and a delegation was sent for that purpose to Austin. On March 20, 1923, the Houston Independent School District was formed by the passage of Senate Bill 402.[14]

This act provided for an appointive board unless the citizens would vote immediately on an elected board, which they did. Since 1923, the Houston school board has remained a seven-man elective board, although the length of term has varied (two years originally, six years after 1941, and since 1951, four years).

The new district was made independent with a tax rate limited by a state legislative maximum and a popular vote required whenever any group desired to increase the local rate. Both a superintendent and business manager were appointed as coordinate executives of the board. The dual control system was abolished in 1954, but the very powerful incumbent in that role, H. L. Mills, remained in office until 1958, actually not retiring until 1959.[15]

San Francisco is a clear case of a businessman's campaign to make the schools more businesslike. Educators support and even

document the case for a single, strong appointed school executive
on the corporate model. Houston came close to accepting the appointed board concept as well, but citizens were unwilling to lose
the right to vote for a school board. In both cases school superintendents actively involved themselves in the study and debate
over changes in structure. This signals the rise of the superintendent to the role of an expert, not only on teacher selection (if not
on janitors) but on matters of school governance.

THE AFTERMATH OF REORGANIZATIONS

Chicago and New York City

Civic group leaders in Chicago and New York expressed
their displeasure with the mayors in these cities, for it became evident that the reduction in size and related reorganizations had
not achieved the purpose of taking the schools out of politics.
The Chicago battle, largely in the courts and lasting through the
rest of Mayor Thompson's first administration (ending in 1923),
has already been described, a battle wherein a superintendent
was prevented from taking office, board members were jailed for
conspiracy, and a series of grand juries were convened to sift the
extensive evidence on "gross irregularities and extravagances." [16]
Despite the four-year interlude of reform, "Big Bill" Thompson
was returned to office in 1927 and promptly filled board vacancies with agents who would fulfill his campaign promise to oust
Superintendent McAndrew. In 1927 the board suspended McAndrew for "insubordination." After five months of harrassment
and being confronted by an array of witnesses who accused the
superintendent of unpatriotic and even treasonable activity,
McAndrew resigned in protest.[17]

Meanwhile, a Tammany mayor, John F. Hylan, took office
in New York City and was successful in influencing several school
appointments, including the termination of William Ettinger's
service as superintendent in 1924. As soon as Hylan was elected,
the Public Educational Association began to draft legislation
aimed at making the schools fiscally independent and curtailing
the mayor's appointment power. One measure, suggested in the
Meyer-Ullman Bill in 1922, would have placed the power to appoint board members in an "educational commission" consisting
of the mayor and those members of the New York State Board of

Regents who lived in New York City. The bill received little support even in the city itself and the bill died in committee. Throughout the 1920's, even when "Jimmie" Walker succeeded Hylan as mayor, the P.E.A. and several groups interested in "merit" (the several City Clubs and the Civil Service Reform League) were unable to secure passage of legislation making the superintendent a stronger executive and basing all school appointments on merit alone.[18]

The earlier reorganizations in Chicago and New York had neither guaranteed the well-being of the schools nor the appointment of selfless public servants to the city boards of education. The one variable which it seemed at that time defied reorganization was the mayor's office, the incumbent of which could appoint whatever manner of man he saw fit to a school board.

Boston and Buffalo

During 1929, scandal broke out in Boston where it had been established that the chairman of the school house commissioners had been counsel for the contractors who built some of the schools. When the roofs of several new buildings leaked and the beams were discovered not to have been installed, the commission was replaced by an unpaid board of commissioners of school buildings who were authorized to hire an expert superintendent of school construction to spend money authorized for land and buildings, school alterations, and repairs. The new commissioners were to be appointed as follows: one by the mayor of Boston, one by the Boston school committee, and the third member by the first two members (or failing agreement, by the governor of the Commonwealth of Massachusetts). This change ostensibly extended to the school committee equal say in school construction without entrusting that body with the power to spend money on school buildings. A survey of the schools in 1930 by the Boston Finance Commission recommended enlarging the Boston school committee to nine members and urged the abolition of the separate school buildings department. No action was taken on either proposal.[19]

The Buffalo schools were surveyed in 1930 by the Buffalo Municipal Research Bureau which arranged for the U.S. Office of Education to evaluate the "educational service" of the schools while the local bureau pursued possible economies. Both the U.S.

Office consultants and the bureau staff considered the question of school board size and organization. The federal surveyors would not make an outright recommendation but reported friction between the board and council each year over the budget and observed that the general practice around the country was to elect the boards of education. It urged an increase in membership to seven and suggested that if the board were to be made elective, the board of education might be made fiscally independent.[20] The Research Bureau in the second part of the report considered the materials summarized by the U.S. Office consultants and strongly urged consideration of a fiscally independent elective board, seven members to be selected at large, with fewer meetings, a new research department, and more delegation of details to the superintendent of schools. The only action taken was an increase in board membership to seven.

The late 1920's and early thirties were not years in which to launch reform. The groundwork for the San Francisco and Houston reorganizations had been laid in the 1914 to 1920 period. The last total reorganization of any city school board for some decades took place in 1923.[21]

CITY SCHOOL BOARDS IN THE THIRTIES: UNREPRESENTATIVE AND OBSTRUCTIVE?

During the 1920's school superintendents had strengthened their professional organization in several ways. The Department of Superintendence of the N.E.A. was reorganized under a constitution of its own during the summer of 1921 and a full-time executive secretary was hired. The leaders decided to publish a yearbook on some broad topic of interest to superintendents; the first yearbook, in 1923, was entitled *The Status of the Superintendent.*[22] The department grew from 2,470 members in 1925 to 4,013 by 1931, the year when a second yearbook on the superintendency was issued. *Educational Leadership: Process and Possibilities* summarized several ten-year trends in the development of the superintendency. For example, by 1931 the percentage of superintendents who had earned their master's degree moved from 32 to 57 percent of all superintendents and to 65 percent of the superintendents in sixty-three cities of more than 100,000 population.[23] The superintendents exchanged via the yearbooks a wealth of information about their experience, income, travel opportunities, and perceptions of impediments to professional leadership.

The professional viewpoint on the role and functions of the superintendent of schools in the large cities was in the process of changing. Cubberley, in the 1929 revision of his text, *Public School Administration,* described the trend by which the superintendent of schools in smaller cities had become the chief executive officer of the school system, while larger cities had appointed several executives, one for business, one for educational services, and sometimes one for buildings.[24] Cubberley repeated his earlier verdict in favor of unitary rather than divided or multiple control (and criticized plans advanced by business managers to secure rank equal with that of the superintendent).[25] Fred Engelhardt, then teaching at Minnesota, agreed with Cubberley except on the position of the school board treasurer, the only office other than the superintendent for which Engelhardt advocated direct responsibility to the board, if the city or county treasurer had not assumed this responsibility.[26] Otherwise, all business functions, he thought, should be placed under the general direction of the superintendent of schools.[27]

Meanwhile, the school board as an institution in society had come under attack from several quarters. The first serious charge levied against boards was that school board members over-represented the privileged classes of society. This criticism had been voiced as early as 1917 by Scott Nearing, a University of Pennsylvania professor. Nearing based his conclusion on data collected on 967 school board members in 104 cities with populations of more than 40,000.[28]

George Struble, in 1922, made a similar study of 959 school board members and found that more than 350 were bankers, merchants, and business executives and only 54 were from the laboring classes.[29] Two authorities on school administration, Cubberley and Chancellor, had been advising in their textbooks that businessmen and professional men made the best school board members because of their experience in managing large enterprises or practices.[30]

The severest critic of boards and board membership in the 1920's was George Counts, who surveyed 1,654 school boards of all types—rural, city, state, and college—and protested that members were drawn from the conservative elements of the population such as businessmen, farm owners, and professionals. The laboring classes contributed less than 10 percent of the board members although their numbers (in cities) amounted to 60 percent of the population.[31] Counts could not prove that businessmen would tend to favor the status quo and resist social innovation in curricula or school organization, but the questions he raised suggested that businessmen might be reactionary on most, if not all, social issues.

A second line of criticism also originated with Counts, whose study of the Chicago school system revealed the failure of the board of education to protect teachers from the demands of political leaders or to protect the superintendent of schools from unwarranted attacks and possible removal on bogus charges.[32] Counts felt that the Chicago board was not only unrepresentative of the populace but had been unable to insulate the school from corrupt and vicious influences.

Counts did not believe that education should or could be separated from politics, but only from selfish or dishonest "forces." He felt that politics was an integral vehicle for improving the social order, that politics provided "the channels through which the living energies of society may flow into new forms and patterns."[33] The great problem was to find a way "to devise some means of making the school responsive to the more fundamental social realities and of enabling it at the same time to maintain an even keel amid the clash and roar of the contending elements."[34] Counts offered two solutions: first, a board of education more broadly representative of different economic strata, sexes, and religious and social classes; and second, improved training and strengthening of professional educators, especially preparing them to resist pressures and to involve all members of the staff in policy-making.

THE JUDD CAMPAIGN
TO ABOLISH SCHOOL BOARDS

Counts returned to Teachers College, Columbia University, after his year in Chicago as a visiting professor. The next articulate critic of city boards became Charles H. Judd, Director of the Department of Education at the University of Chicago. Judd, in several articles calling for a campaign to abolish school boards, carried the criticism of boards and the emphasis on expertise to some logical, if radical, conclusions.

The setting was the early 1930's and school boards had been under pressure, along with other units of local government, to curtail expenditures and reduce the tax levy until the nation worked its way out of the depression. Judd was first quoted in favor of "compact government" and the abolition of city boards of education in *How Cities Can Cut Costs,* a publication prepared and distributed by the city managers association. He accepted another invitation to write in the November 1933 issue of *Public Management* a guest editorial entitled "Abolish the School Boards." Separate boards of education, he charged, were "obstructionist," in many cases "the tools of political bosses," and for the most part "conspicuous failures." He complained that "in periods such as the present, when the taxpayers are restless under the burden of public expenditures, it is comparatively easy to induce communities to favor drastic retrenchments in school support on the grounds that those in charge of instruction are not performing effectively the services which the public has a right to expect." [35] Judd then suggested that "a movement to abolish school boards is in order and should be supported by all who believe in the simplification of government and in reliance on experts."

Another important figure at the University of Chicago in 1933 who was increasingly interested in public education in the 1930's was Charles E. Merriam, Professor of Political Science, ex-alderman, and former candidate for mayor of Chicago. Merriam wrote and edited a series of books on citizenship education beginning in 1929 and also served on the executive committee of the American Historical Association Commission on the Social Studies. This monumental five-year investigation of the place of social sciences in the school curriculum dealt broadly with the work of the school and the future of the educational profession in society. Merriam prepared one volume of his own on civic education for the commission and also helped direct the overall work, which involved close contact with George Counts, director of research for the commission. [36]

While that study was under way, Merriam and his associates in political science were working on the problems of reorganizing government on a regional or metropolitan basis.[37] Merriam's many interests were inseparable and in his book, *Civic Education in the United States,* he discussed trends in government, two of which were the reorganization of political units on a metropolitan basis and the "professionalization of administrative service." The latter development he heralded as a "new era in political competence," one in which public administration by men of high professional standards had begun to emerge.[38]

Judd shared the Merriam vision of a government improved by geographical and functional reorganization and by the employment of highly trained experts to administer these governments. Together, Judd and Merriam, in 1933, decided that a study of the coordination of schools and city governments should be co-sponsored by the two departments of which they were chairmen. This study culminated in a 1938 book reporting many instances of cooperation, coordination, or overlapping jurisdiction between the city schools and municipal governments in cities about 50,000 in population.[39]

Judd's proposal to abolish school boards, however, drew fire immediately. W. A. Bailey, editor of the Kansas City *Kansan* and a former high school principal, debated with Judd in print the question, "should the school board be abolished?" in the January 1934 issue of *Public Management.* Bailey said he agreed with Judd's criticisms but thought Judd had been overly influenced by the situation in Chicago and a few other large cities. If boards were abolished, Bailey predicted, there would be a rise of great new political machines consisting of all city employees, teachers included, and he advocated instead the hiring of an outstanding businessman as school business manager (as Kansas City had done) and the election of "higher type" board members (probably no more than six, he suggested, and elected at large). Judd responded that "virtuous reformers" were almost as bad as "corruptionists" and said the schools needed experts, not meddlers, to run the school system. Echoing Merriam, Judd foresaw an "era of good mayors; better still, experts in charge of all municipal functions." [40]

Shortly thereafter, the "abolition" proposal became a major controversy in the journals of professional educators. Judd published an article in the *Elementary School Journal* and another in *The Nation's Schools,* both along the same line as his comments in *Public Management*. He predicted that all public services would soon be professionalized, that "the ordinary mayor is a relic of an earlier age" and "boards of education are survivals, inherited from an age when professionalization of schools was far less advanced than at present." He incorporated into his statement the criticism of Counts that "board members came from the conservative levels of society," and he called for a vigorous campaign to abolish all boards of education.[41]

Theodore Reller, who had just published his dissertation on the superintendency, had seen the several statements written by Judd for the city managers. Reller, in the February 1934 issue of the *American School Board Journal*, called Judd's criticisms severe and exaggerated and expressed the opinion that the city superintendent "would once more become a politician" if placed under municipal jurisdiction. Reller reiterated the traditional argument that education is too "important" to be a municipal function.[42]

Other articles appeared in May and April in reply to Judd and in defense of the school board. Fred Engelhardt termed Judd's indictment "unfair" and "prejudiced" and claimed that the particular problems of the 1930–1934 era proved further why boards of education were required.[43] Another article acknowledged some failure on the part of board members, but felt that the abolition of boards was not the answer. Keyworth said that the functions of a board needed, instead, to be clarified and that boards ought to protect and promote the public schools and pass judgment on the quality of services rendered by educators.[44]

THE IMPACT OF CRITICISM
ON THE CITY SCHOOL BOARDS

Judd's campaign was never mounted on any significant scale and the controversy within the profession expired by late 1934. Jesse Newlon was another spokesman for public education who found some fault with the proposal, yet felt it could not be dismissed lightly since many students of government advised the consolidation of all public services. Newlon's report on educational administration reviewed the criticisms of Counts and of Judd, stated that schools were seriously affected by the chaotic "crazy-quilt of government" in metropolitan centers, and noted that Merriam had suggested a "new city-state" to recognize the existence of metropolitan regions.[45]

Newlon, however, advanced his own ideas on how a board of education might be selected in the interim years while acceptable proposals for the consolidation and centralization of government were prepared. He proposed a lay board on which "all the important groups and interest in the community are in some manner directly represented." Warning that such a board should not be too large, he further proposed that "the board might be nominated by a council created for that purpose, in which important groups and the public as a whole would be represented."[46]

More than thirty-five years have passed since Judd, Merriam, and Newlon made their predictions and voiced their suggestions about the way in which municipal, metropolitan, and school governments might be merged or reorganized. Leaders in several cities, including Cleveland and St. Louis, have tried to develop viable proposals for metropolitan governments, but only in a few southern counties (around Miami and Nashville) have these proposals been adopted. The city manager profession has been strengthened and extended to many small and medium-sized cities, but very few of the larger cities have adopted the manager plan and still fewer have retained it.[47]

Since the time of Judd's proposal for a campaign to abolish school boards more than 100,000 boards have disappeared, but because of the consolidation of smaller districts into larger units rather than any widespread agreement that the boards were "conspicuous failures," "survivals," or "obstructive." Newlon's proposal for a nominating council was adopted by Chicago in 1946. It was also adopted by New York through legislation passed in 1961, and by Philadelphia in 1965. Until the "community control" movement, the nominating council was viewed as a plausible solution to the problem of recruiting to boards men and women who would both represent the community and protect the professional staff.[48]

Counts and his predecessors had protested that boards were not representative; Judd complained that boards interfered with expertise and assisted rather than buffered the political boss. Counts' solution was to make the board more broadly representative; Judd's solution was to make the superintendent directly responsible to state or city officials and to abolish the board. Both complaints suggest the presence of disruptive influences entering the political sub-system of the school through the recruitment structure. Newlon suggested that a new structure be invented to complement the existing school board recruitment mechanism. Judd called for the abolition of the whole board, the further strengthening of the superintendency, and a division of functions between the superintendent and the rest of the city government.

Neither proposal was acted on during the 1930's nor during the early years of World War II. However, the fact that criticism was so vehement and further structural reorganization was advocated indicates that Counts and Judd thought:

1. A number of school board reorganizations, especially in Chicago, did not fulfill the hopes of their earlier proponents.
2. The superintendency, although vulnerable to outright attacks and other pressures, was gaining in strength and presumably might survive without a board of education.
3. Further experimentation with recruitment structures would be required, leading eventually to the rearrangement of all governments in metropolitan areas.

Since Judd, few analysts of the government of education have advocated the curtailment of board power or abolition of boards themselves. The notable exception is Myron Lieberman who has urged that boards staffed by professional practitioners in education make rules regarding licensing, preparation for professional education careers, and performance standards similar to the self-policing mechanisms of the legal and medical professions.[49] After 1924 and until the end of World War II, the major cities of the Northeast and Midwest began to stabilize. The flow of immigrants from Europe slowed; the migration of Appalachian whites, southern blacks, and Puerto Ricans accelerated during and after World War II. Many of the new residents of Houston and Los Angeles were already American or Americanized and, except for many Indians, Mexican-Americans, and blacks, were ready to move into single-family homes and the middle class. Neither the prosperity of the 1920's nor the poverty of the 1930's kindled the fires of reform, nor did Counts find a following sufficient to push for a redistribution of seats on boards of education.

The intellectual commentators offered suggestions that led in contradictory directions: Nearing, Struble, and Counts worried about the breadth of social-class representation on the board; Judd would have abolished the board entirely. They agreed only on the need to strengthen and professionalize further educational leadership.

Actually, the upper class and upper-middle class, who had won the earlier battles, found neither proposal at all acceptable. Power had been pulled away from the saloon keepers and ward bosses who presumably spoke for the working class. And having insulated city schools from ward politics, it hardly seemed wise to turn them over to mayors who would treat education as just one more department like sanitation or welfare.

Some of the impetus for reform diminished as the more affluent sought new houses in the rapidly growing suburbs. Between 1920 and 1930, Robert C. Wood noted:

The suburban population grew at the rate of almost 40 percent around the seventeen largest cities, while the rate of growth in the central cities steadily declined. Four cities with over 100,000 residents actually lost population, while the suburbs burst at the seams. Los Angeles provided the extreme example, when suburban Beverly Hills registered a gain of 2486 percent, but Shaker Heights near Cleveland increased 1600 percent, Grosse Point Park outside Detroit 725 percent, and everywhere gains of 200 to 300 percent were common.[50]

Wood quotes Frederick Lewis Allen on the advantages of suburban living:

The children would have the benefit of light and air and play space and their parents the benefit of constant battles over the policies of the local school boards.[51]

Urban school reform in some cities may never have recovered from the exodus of the new professionals, businessmen, and academics. The phenomenon later called "white flight" slowed down in the depression years but continued with the help of federal housing and highway subsidies after World War II. The alternative to acceptable urban schools for millions of white families was escape to suburbia.

To those who remained behind, the chief concern over centralized boards in several large cities was the role of the mayor. If ward politicians could now control only the appointment of janitors, then the mayor, through his selection of board members, could influence the more significant choices of superintendents, and through him the principals, teachers, textbooks, and equipment. Only Newlon offered an approach to curtailing the power of the mayor. And in three of the largest cities, New York City, Chicago, and Philadelphia, this became the new crusade—to curb the power of the mayor in school board appointments.

NOTES

1. "The Politics of Reform in Municipal Government in the Progressive Era," *Pacific Northeast Quarterly* (October 1964), p. 162.

2. *Ibid.*, p. 163.

3. *Ibid.*, p. 65.

4. Henry Greenleaf Pearson, *Son of New England: James Jackson Storrow* (Boston: Thomas Dodd, 1932), p. 46.

5. Theodore J. Lowi, *At the Pleasure of the Mayor* (New York: The Free Press of Glencoe, 1964), pp. 30–31.

6. *The Public School System of San Francisco, California, A Report of a Survey*, The Bureau of Education, Department of Interior, Bulletin 1917, No. 46 (Washington, D.C.: Government Printing Office, 1917). The San Francisco Public Education Society had also campaigned to obtain this survey.

7. *Ibid.*, p. 76.

8. *Ibid.*, p. 77.

9. *Ibid.*, p. 86.

10. *Ibid.*, pp. 83–88.

11. *Ibid.*, pp. 119–125. The superintendent of schools of Pittsburgh, Pennsylvania, was a consultant to the survey on administration. Although he abstained from any recommendation on the board selection question, the Pittsburgh appointment scheme was included among the alternatives for San Francisco to consider.

12. Roncovieri's defense and other reactions to the Claxton report can be found in *Transactions of the Commonwealth Club of Northern California*, Vol. XII, No. 1 (San Francisco: December 1917), pp.

13. The elective superintendency remained an issue and was voted on as a referendum "proposition" in San Francisco each year from 1921 until 1930.

14. The Texas Legislature, *Senate Bill.402, An Act Creating and Incorporating the Houston Independent School District,* 1923.

15. National Commission for the Defense of Democracy through Education, *Investigation Reports Abridgements* (Washington, D.C.:

The National Education Association, 1960). Summary of the 1954 Houston, Texas, report including the events following the investigation, pp. 57–58.

16. George Counts, *School and Society in Chicago* (New York: Harcourt Brace Jovanovich, 1938), p. 260.

17. *Ibid.*, pp. 276–280.

18. Sol Cohen, *Progressives and Urban School Reform* (New York: Teachers College of Columbia University, 1964), pp. 114–116.

19. The Finance Commission of the City of Boston, *Report of an Investigation on the Methods of Administration in the Boston Schools* (Boston: The City Printing Department, June 1936), p. 5.

20. Buffalo Municipal Research Bureau, *Report of the Buffalo Survey*, Part I (Buffalo: Turner and Porter, 1931), pp. 22–25. See also Part II, pp. 182–183.

21. Total reorganization means a major alteration of board structures and functions. The reorganizations after 1923 affected the superintendency or method of board recruitment but left the basic board structure intact.

22. National Education Association (Washington, D.C.).

23. National Education Association, Department of Superintendence, *Educational Leadership: Progress and Possibilities*, Eleventh Yearbook (Washington, D.C.: National Education Association, February 1933), p. 108.

24. Ellwood P. Cubberley (Cambridge, Massachusetts: The Riverside Press), pp. 162–163.

25. *Ibid.*, p. 97.

26. *Public School Organization and Administration* (Boston: Ginn, 1931), p. 77.

27. *Ibid.*, p. 97.

28. "Who's Who on Our Boards of Education," *School & Society*, (January 20, 1917), pp. 89–90.

29. "A Study of School Board Personnel," *The American School Board Journal*, Vol. LXV (October 1922), pp. 48–49, 137–138.

30. See William E. Chancellor, *Our Schools: Their Administration and Supervision* (Boston: D. C. Heath, 1904), and Cubberley, *op. cit.*

31. Counts, *The Social Composition of Boards of Education*, Supplementary Monograph No. 33 (Chicago: The University of Chicago Press, 1927).

32. Counts, *School and Society in Chicago*, pp. 247–248.

33. *Ibid.*, pp. 353–354.

34. *Ibid.*, p. 354.

35. Cf. Clarence E. Ridley and Orin F. Nolting, *How Cities Can Cut*

Costs (Chicago: The International City Managers Association, 1933), and Charles H. Judd, "Abolish the School Boards," editorial in *Public Management,* Vol. XV, No. 11 (November 1933), p. 32.

36. The broad scope of the work of this group is summarized by the Commission on the Social Studies, American Historical Association in *Conclusions and Recommendations of the Commission* (New York: Scribners, 1934).

37. Charles E. Merriam, Spencer D. Parratt, and Albert Lepowski, *The Government of the Metropolitan Region of Chicago* (Chicago: The University of Chicago Press, 1933).

38. (New York: Scribners, 1934).

39. Nelson B. Henry and Jerome C. Kerwin, *Schools and City Government* (Chicago: The University of Chicago Press, 1938). It is impossible to prove that Merriam persuaded Judd to advocate the abolition of boards and the fusion of school and city government, for both men were strong and independent thinkers. However, the two men shared a point of view on municipal government, often met socially, and worked together on several projects with Louis Brownlow, director of the Public Administration Clearing House, and on the Hoover Commission on Social Trends. Judd was "ably seconded by Merriam" on the board abolition proposal on the New Deal, Jerome Kerwin recalls, and had no time to help mobilize support from the public administration group. Kerwin commented that both Judd and Merriam, who directed Nelson and Kerwin in the investigation of existing city school relations, were somewhat unhappy because the report was not strong enough for them and did not reveal any urgency or great desirability for the immediate consolidation of schools with city governments. *Source:* Interview, April 19, 1965, with Jerome G. Kerwin on Judd and Merriam.

40. "Should School Boards Be Abolished?" Bailey, "No." Judd, "Yes.," pp. 17–20.

41. Judd, "School Boards as an Obstruction to Good Administration," *The Nation's Schools,* Vol. XIII, No. 2 (February 1934), pp. 13–15.

42. "School Board vs. Municipal Government Control of Education," pp. 15–16.

43. "In Defense of School Boards," *The Nation's Schools,* Vol. XIII, No. 5 (May 1934), p. 21.

44. M. R. Keyworth, "Why Boards of Education Are Both Desirable and Necessary," *The American School Board Journal,* Vol. XIII, No. 4 (April 1934), pp. 21–22.

45. *Educational Administration as Social Policy. Report of the Commission on the Social Studies,* Part VIII (New York: Scribners, 1934), p. 241.

46. *Ibid.,* p. 242.

47. Wallace Sayre, "The General Manager Idea for Large Cities," in Oliver P. Williams and Charles Press (eds.), *Democracy in Urban America* (Chicago: Rand McNally, 1961). Cleveland is one city that abandoned the manager plan.

48. See Peter Binzen, "How to Pick a School Board," in *Saturday Review*, Vol. XLVIII, No. 16 (April 17, 1965), pp. 72–73.

49. Myron Lieberman, *The Future of Public Education* (Chicago: The University of Chicago Press, 1960).

50. Robert C. Wood, *Suburbia* (Boston: Houghton Mifflin, 1959), p. 60.

51. *Ibid.*, p. 57. (From Allen, *The Big Change* (New York: Bantam Books, 1952), p. 126.)

* * * * * *VII* * * * * *

CURBING THE POWER
OF THE MAYOR 1945–1961

WHO SHOULD CONTROL big-city schools—an autonomous school board or the mayor of the city, directly or indirectly? Should mayors play a crucial role in the government of large-city school systems? What has been the record? The evidence suggests that rather than run the schools mayors typically avoid school problems as long as possible. Virtually every time mayors decide to improve the schools on their own initiatives, the attempt backfires. The majority of large-city school systems still rely on elective boards long after other departments or agencies relinquished their independence of the mayor. Even when a mayor does appoint a school board, others try to limit that power by asking that he solicit names of nominees from prestigious city-wide sources such as leaders of business, trade unions, and civic and professional associations, and from college and university presidents.

Not that mayors ever have complete freedom to select whomever they please. Theodore Lowi explains "The mayor's pleasure becomes enmeshed with the demands of his constituency; as an elected and very much exposed chief executive, he lives in an environment that he disregards only at his peril. The mayor is not a mute power, but neither is he a free agent." [1] Lowi explains that "highly prized values" are at stake and that a New York City mayor must view the appointments as a way to adjust to the competing demands made around him.

Mayors have good reason to tread carefully when making educational appointments. So much can go wrong. Three case studies deserve a close examination: Chicago, New York, and Philadelphia. In each case Newlon's suggestion of a nominating panel gains acceptance, thus limiting the freedom of the mayor to initiate his own school board appointments.

THE CHICAGO BOARD OF EDUCATION
IN THE 1940's

During the 1920's and 1930's, Chicago politics were "bitter and frenzied" because of the close rivalry between two strong Republican and Democratic machines. Reform mayor Carter Harrison (1911–1915) was followed by the corrupt and clowning "Big Bill" Thompson from 1915–1923 and 1927–1931. Thompson, allied with and financed by Al Capone and Samuel Insull, not only appointed board of education members of questionable integrity, but forced out two highly professional "outsider" superintendents,[2] Charles E. Chadsey in 1919 and William McAndrew in 1927. Both men were followed in office by former assistant superintendents in Chicago whose total impact Vieg categorized as contributing to morale and maintaining basic school services intact. Vieg, in the late thirties, commented that the last insider chosen, William Johnson, "may turn out to be a genius for sponsoring right ideas in the wrong way."[3]

In 1944, however, eight organizations requested the National Education Association Defense Commission to investigate "various aspects of the administration" of Chicago schools.[4] The N.E.A. team of investigators found that the president of the board of education, appointed in 1933, had in effect assumed administrative control of Chicago schools. Each day from a suite of presidential offices he made decisions for the board and the superintendent and played a major role in making staff appointments.[5] The inquiry noted that the report of the 1939 investigation by the state's attorney of the payment of bribes to school officials and irregularities in school business management had been suppressed. Superintendent Johnson's name as author or co-author was attached to more than twenty textbooks used in Chicago schools. Johnson was accused of maintaining a spy system and of promoting his former students and close associates from an old rating list established in 1936 and 1937 in the first year of his superintendency. The N.E.A report recommended the restriction of the board president's functions to those specified in the law and the selection of a new superintendent to "re-establish" leadership and integrity and to serve as the chief executive officer of the board. The election-at-large of the Chicago board of education was proposed as a change in the Otis Law, which governed the operations of the school.[6]

Instead of accepting the N.E.A. recommendation, the mayor of Chicago named the Heald Committee to advise him on what response to make. He agreed on the wisdom of asking a commission on school board nominations to provide him with suggestions for school board candidates. Members of the commission included five university presidents or their representatives and people selected from eleven civic organizations.[7] Their function was to screen a list of candidates and present to the mayor a list of recommended nominees.

During the summer and autumn of 1946, the superintendent agreed to accept a lesser post, the board president resigned, six new board members were appointed, and the Otis Law was changed to establish the post of general superintendent of schools. At this point the board selected Herold C. Hunt for the new post on the basis of his seven years as Kansas City superintendent.[8] By December of 1948 the new superintendent established competitive examinations for teaching and administrative positions and restored the morale of Chicago school employees.

THE SUBSEQUENT PERFORMANCE
OF THE CHICAGO SCHOOL BOARD

Since the adoption of the nominating commission or "caucus," business executives of the caliber of Sargent Shriver and Fairfax Cone have served as presidents of the Chicago board of education. Many other highly educated citizen representatives have been nominated and appointed. The three Chicago superintendents of schools, Herold C. Hunt, Benjamin C. Willis, and James Redmond, each served apprenticeships in challenging city superintendencies elsewhere. Neither Hunt nor Willis were hampered by board member interference in administration or harassed by mayors.[9] Despite many other problems the Chicago schools were commended for progress in meeting the problems of staff training, and the provision of adequate physical facilities for the schools.[10] Mayor Richard Daley supported financially both school construction programs and higher teacher salaries. Several times he re-appointed board members contrary to commission recommendations, for on the whole he was pleased with Willis and defended his work against critics.

The restructuring of the nomination procedure is, of course, only one of several plausible explanations for the comparatively stable and scandal-free years since 1945. A 1947 article by Hunt develops a rationale for the attention he felt must be given to parent groups, civic associations, the press, and other media through which the public is informed about the problems of the schools and learns about the standards of education which are attainable through increased support.[11] Through vigorous participation of schoolmen in the life of the community and the use of all available media to reach a wide variety of groups, the capacity of the school system to respond to community demands can be strengthened. These changes and the efforts by Mayor Daley to hold the support of "good government" leaders [12] may account for the unwillingness of most other city political leaders since 1946 to try to change the way the school system was governed.

New York and other cities were aware of the Chicago nominating commission, but no other major city adopted a similar procedure until 1961, when the New York state legislature inscribed in the law a similar nominating procedure for New York City.

THE NEW YORK CITY BOARD OF EDUCATION

Shortly before the 1944 to 1945 investigation of the Chicago board, the N.E.A. Commission for the Defense of Democracy through Education published a report critical of the ways in which Fiorello LaGuardia, a reform or fusion mayor of New York City, had "interfered with the independence" of the board of education. Two N.E.A. affiliates, representing elementary and secondary school teachers in New York City, requested an investigation of the mayor's appointments, his dismissal of school employees, his cutting of specific items in the budget, and his attempt to consolidate the supply division of the schools with the purchase department of the city. The investigation committee accused the mayor of "undue and unauthorized influence" on the board and urged the state to enact legislation to make the city schools fiscally independent. The investigators reported that the mayor had appointed outstanding individuals to the board (although using this power "to increase his control over school affairs") [13] and recommended that the New York City board of education members continue to be appointed, especially if borough representation was to continue. The N.E.A. judged that the schools suffered far more from the mayor's use of budgetary power than from his power to appoint board members. Therefore, no change in the latter was recommended and none took place at that time.

However, during the 1950's the Public Education Association began to advocate the creation of a "citizen advisory council" which would propose to the mayor candidates for vacancies on the board of education. This proposal received some support from the mayor's committee on management survey in 1952, but for a decade it remained on the legislative shelf. The P.E.A., during the 1940's, helped pass a bill to strengthen the New York City superintendency, but it voiced criticism of the overall centralization of authority and the neglect of the local school boards. [14]

An analysis by Lowi of the appointees to the New York City board of education has shown that the membership pattern for fifty years has "followed the shifting currents of religion and nationality." In the years following the 1917 changes, most of the seats on the New York board were filled by Protestants and Catholics in equal proportions, with provision for one Jewish member. During the 1930's "the Jews were able to make a claim for a second member" and two groups growing in size, the Italians and Negroes, made their claim for representation. The sacrifice of one seat each appealed neither to the Catholics (usually Irish) nor to the white Protestants. They could accept an increase in the size of the board to nine members, passed in 1948, ostensibly to give the Bronx and Queens equal representation with Brooklyn and Manhattan but in fact to allow the mayor to appoint three persons from each of the major denominations, including one (and sometimes a second) Italian Catholic and a Protestant Negro. [15]

The increase in the size of the board in practice served no function other than to balance the religious composition of the board. Sayre and Kaufman speculated that the ethnic, racial, and religious "balance" serves to control competition and prevent conflict between the major groups. There were through the 1960's strong pressures on the mayor to replace a Protestant with a Protestant, a Jew with a Jew, etc. One observable consequence of this allotment of memberships is the pressure to extend the religious balance to the appointment of top professionals on the school staff.[16]

The informal division of seats on an appointed board along ethnic or religious lines is not acceptable to most educators or school board members elsewhere who, in journals or policy statements, express regret that such supposedly irrelevant considerations would restrict the recruitment of school board members.[17] However, the New York arrangement serves several functions, covert but not unintended. One of these functions is that of effecting a truce between the leaders of powerful religious and ethnic factions in a cosmopolitan city. Such spokesmen watch closely and jealously the pattern of appointments to other boards, to ensure that no rival group enjoys proportionately greater access to the channels of communication and structures of rule-making. Preventing conflict among the major religious groups is an important latent function, a value also shared by the mayor.[18]

A second function performed by balancing ethnic and religious groups is that of interest-articulation. The ethnic affiliations and religious and national identification of urban dwellers remains high. Many city dwellers continue to express their aspirations through the Urban League or the Knights of Columbus, while the educated white Protestant uses as a vehicle of political communication the Public Education Association, the Fifth Avenue Association, or the other civic groups. Data summarized by Robert Lane show that religious leaders can influence votes on some referenda far more than party or labor leaders can, even across class lines.[19]

NEW YORK'S SELECTION BOARD

During the summer of 1961 the New York City board of education was ousted by the order of the New York State commissioner of education, and the legislature was asked to consider, among other measures, the approval of a "selection board" to present nominations for the board of education vacancies to the mayor.

The legislative findings, presented to the Senate and Assembly of New York during the August 1961 extraordinary session, summarized conditions in the New York City schools which "have shaken public confidence" and aroused the concern of the legislature.

These conditions included:

· irregularities in the school construction program;
· serious hazards in school buildings due to inadequate maintenance and improper repairs;
· instances of corruption among employees;
· staggering administrative complexities and needless red tape.[20]

Reports of fraud, bribery, and the neglect of buildings had been circulating in the spring and summer of 1961. The teachers of Public School 119 in Harlem bought space for a newspaper advertisement protesting the "sagging walls, unsanitary toilets, and leaking roof." The *American School Board Journal* reported that the final action of Commissioner James E. Allen followed the public revelation that "a rat . . . ran across the path of Mayor Wagner while he was inspecting 'rat and roach infested' Public School 119." [21]

The new selection board was comprised of the presidents of Columbia and New York Universities, the Chancellor of the City University of New York and the presidents of eight organizations: the bar association, the central labor council, the commerce and industry association, two parent associations, the League of Women Voters, the Citizens Union, and the Citizens Budget Commission. The selection board was instructed to accept and consider the recommendations of "representative civic, educational, business, labor and professional groups active or interested in the field of education."[22] The selection board was to submit eighteen names of outstanding citizens for the mayor's first selection of nine new members and three to five names of outstanding persons for each subsequent vacancy. The selection board had to consider the candidate nominations of community, neighborhood, representative, and other interested groups.

A NOMINATING PANEL FOR PHILADELPHIA

Judges of the Court of Common Pleas continued to select the Philadelphia board of education members until 1965. Just as the judges themselves served for as long as their health permitted, so did they reappoint for six-year terms the venerable members of the Philadelphia school board.

During the 1950's, Philadelphia's Republican machine lost control of the city to a series of Democratic reform mayors, especially two patricians, Joseph Clark and Richardson Dilworth. The reform movement at first ignored the schools and concentrated on urban renewal and transportation solutions. But in the 1960's, school enrollment rose sharply, revealing the inadequacy of both the school building program and the methods of floating boards used to supervise school construction. Philadelphia schools began to attract public attention as civil rights groups documented charges of school discrimination, and teacher leaders called for union recognition to bargain for higher wages and better working conditions.

For twenty years the board allowed Add B. Anderson, the business manager, unusual control over school finance and maintenance with far-reaching consequences. According to the *Philadelphia Inquirer:*

> He was in charge of budget, supplies and janitors. But somehow Add also took charge of education. Because any principal who didn't play ball with Add found he didn't get any supplies, didn't get replacements for broken windows, didn't get any custodial service.
>
> Add just took charge of the system. Janitors got paid more than teachers. Principals took orders from janitors and not the other way around.
>
> Add was a friend to politicians. He kept the school budget and the tax rate low. And that's the way the politicians wanted it.[23]

Most of all the Philadelphia board wanted to avoid controversy. But one member, Elizabeth Greenfield, wife of a prominent Philadelphia financier, blew the whistle.[24] Between 1960 and 1963, business and professional leaders of the Greater Philadelphia Movement (GPM) studied Philadelphia's schools and decided the major obstacle was the almost moribund board. The 1962 report called for a new school board with members appointed by the mayor on the advise of a screening panel. Meanwhile, Anderson suffered a heart attack in 1961 and died within the year.

The GPM group formed an Educational Home Rule Assembly and Governor William Scranton tied several city tax measures to establishment of a Home Rule Charter Commission. Although some civil rights spokesmen urged an elective board, GPM leaders favored the Chicago solution of a nominating panel to guide the mayor. In April 1965, such a proposal was approved by a popular referendum.

The Citizen's Educational Nominating Panel included representatives of a labor union council and a chamber of commerce and industry. One member each would be named to the panel by a public school parent-teacher association, a citizens organization established to improve education, and a federation of neighborhood or community associations. Reform zeal could be expressed by spokesmen from "a non-partisan committee for improving governmental, political, social or economic conditions" and a league for improving human and intergroup relations. Finally, an institution of higher learning within the city and a community planning council could each send a spokesman. The mayor could appoint four at-large members.

The new panel urged the mayor to appoint his predecessor, Richardson Dilworth, as school board chairman. Mayor James Tate then agreed to Dilworth's condition of acceptance, that Dilworth could exert veto power over other board appointments.[25]

By September of 1965, Dilworth moved to hold hearings and establish task forces to recommend changes in curriculum, finance, administration, and community relations. Superintendent Mark Shedd was hired from Englewood, New Jersey, as one of a series of outsiders brought in to try to move the system forward. Philadelphia then approved a series of educational innovations ranging from administrative decentralization to one school organized around the cultural center of the city.

Thus did Philadelphia jettison the system whereby judges drew on the suggestions of political party leaders for names of board members. The new business manager was placed under the superintendent, C. Taylor Whittier, Shedd's immediate predecessor. The new board accepted suggestions for opening up board meetings, integrating the staff, and decentralizing decisions at the district superintendent level.

Ostensibly the power to appoint the board passed to the mayor, who then selected a former mayor as one of the board members. But Mayor Tate, according to local observers, didn't like Dilworth but "couldn't avoid him" because of the public pressure for educational reform.[26] In effect, the right to shape the composition of the board passed to the coalition of lawyers and businessmen who ran the Philadelphia reform movement in general. Upper-class and upper-middle class citizens manage to adjust to a system even if, as in the case of Philadelphia, much of the criticism comes from civil rights spokesmen and the teacher unions. It differs from the kind of Populist broad-based participation advocated by Counts; it resembles rather exactly the prescription of Newlon for a "blue chip" nominating panel.

SELECTION BOARDS ANALYZED

The provision of the New York State law for group nominations of candidates requires brief attention. The phrase "representative group" extends logically and in practice to any ethnic or national association. The emphasis is on group rather than individual nominations. This emphasis would indicate that it was understood that an individual's suggestions would earn some consideration only after being transmitted by some civic community group in which he held membership. The amended statute spelled out in some detail the procedure by which a group (or an individual through a group) could express an interest in seeing a specific candidate considered; the identification of possible candidates was not left solely to the wisdom and discretion of the selection board.

Several years later, a mayor's "Ad Hoc Commission on Educational Selection Boards" reviewed the law on board selection procedures and reported a consensus among citizen groups that the new method was "a substantial improvement" over former procedures and that New York City had a "vastly improved board of education" because of the law. Of course, groups not represented on the selection board wanted to revise the composition of that body and raised the question of whether the mayor was free to consider names from other sources as well.[27]

Among the tasks which confronted the new 1961 board was the decision whether to retain the superintendent whose conduct had been criticized by the press. The board decided to search for a new man and it hired Calvin Gross, the superintendent of schools in Pittsburgh. After two years, this "outsider" was placed on three-months leave, and later departed—a discreet form of dismissal according to New York City observers. Selected in 1963, he was the first New York City superintendent whose major previous administrative work had been in other than a New York City educational context. Only in New York City has a tradition of local recruitment of the superintendent been adhered to for two-thirds of a century.

The similarities between the Chicago, New York, and Philadelphia developments include these features:

1. In both cities educators themselves were clearly audible in the articulation of discontent with the performance of the board of education. Chicago teacher groups invited to the city the investigatory arm of the non-unionized teaching profession to investigate the distribution of promotions and appointments. The New York teachers were prominent among those who protested in that city the ineffective and dysfunctional distribution of funds intended for construction and repair; the teachers' advertisement in the paper precipitated the mayor's inspection of the school, an event which led to the selection of a new board.[28] Philadelphia teachers through union activity precipitated the recognition of a fiscal crisis which brought down the old regime, business manager and board.

2. In neither Chicago nor New York City was the school board appointment structure drastically changed. Yet in both cities a new structure was designed to refine the board member recruitment process, to fill a perceived need for a pool of civic-minded nominees for appointment to the board of education. Philadelphia, in effect, copied the same structure. The N.E.A. recommendation of an elective board was not accepted in Chicago; the actual Chicago solution, that of the advisory nominating commission, was that adopted by New York City and Philadelphia.

The mayors in all three cities with some exceptions adhered to the spirit of the revised board member selection structure, despite the fact that it narrows considerably the actual range of their power to perform the appointment function. The mayors agreed to appoint men and women of demonstrated capacity for service in public life. The increased stature of the board, and of individual members of the board, seems to be related to the restoration of staff morale and public confidence in the schools. In all three instances the new boards increased their willingness to recruit an outsider to be superintendent of schools.[29] Whether such a board can also effectively select among proposals for educational innovation, finance the schools at a higher level (or more economically), and solve the racial and teacher militancy problems now confronting the larger cities remains to be tested.

The board selection problems in other cities have prompted some interest in the adoption of the nominating committee device on the part of Buffalo and Boston. George D. Strayer in 1944 urged Boston to designate a panel composed of the presidents of Harvard, Boston College, Simmons, and Boston University; the chief justice of the State Supreme Court; and presidents of the Chamber of Commerce, Home and School Association, Boston Federation of Labor, and League of Women Voters. This panel would give the mayor twice as many names as needed and voters would confirm or reject the appointee two years after his initial appointment. However, no city followed the lead of Chicago for fourteen years, nor have groups in many other cities mustered the consensus needed in their statutes for the adoption of a similar plan.

One of the major effects of the four reorganizations between 1920 and 1961, in Houston, San Francisco, Chicago and New York, was a weakening of the mayor's power to name the members of the city board of education. Houston's mayor lost all control over the school board member selection process because of citizen dissatisfaction with school finance. The changes in three other cities followed the evaluation of the San Francisco schools and investigations of favortism in the Chicago schools and construction scandals in the New York schools. In all four cases the mayor lost control over the selection function either completely or in part, to popular election in two instances, and to nominating panels in the more recent modifications. In Philadelphia, the home rule charter provision forced the mayor to use such a panel rather than initiate his own choice.

SCHOOL BOARDS, SUPERINTENDENTS,
AND THEIR SELECTION

One of the most phenomenal developments in municipal administration has been the continued efforts to strengthen the city school superintendency in the very large cities, especially in relationship to the mayor. Not only have cities narrowed the choices of school board appointees offered a mayor, but in many instances the cities express their values by paying the school superintendent one and one-half times what they pay the mayor.[30] This does not suggest that the superintendent has more power or responsibility, just more esteem. But it also makes very clear the desire of some big-city school boards to purchase professional expertise of the highest caliber regardless of the salary ranges of other city officials.

Of course, the superintendent manages more employees than mayors in many instances and, other than welfare costs, may prepare and administer a larger budget. As has been explained, many superintendents supervised the instructional program but not business affairs until relatively recent times. The combined responsibilities make the selection of a city school superintendent a rather significant matter.

How do big-city school boards make such a decision? Does the behavior of appointive boards and elective boards differ, and, if so, why? Does it make any difference whether school boards promote a man from within the system or select him from an assignment elsewhere? When and why should a board consider an outsider as superintendent, and how regularly do boards make such a decision?

First, school boards often seek for the position of superintendent of schools men of considerable talent, training, and experience. Experience in the superintendency *per se* can be gained by serving first in the role of superintendent of schools in a small community and then by serving in progressively larger or more challenging superintendencies. This pattern of advancement resembles that of city managers and other professional administrators.[31]

Second, school boards realize that the selection of a person from outside the school system is one way to change an organization, since an outsider can bring with him new ideas and an objective view about the present organization, programs, and procedures.

The major work on the selection of school superintendents is by Richard O. Carlson who, in his monograph *Executive Succession and Organizational Change,* discusses the conditions under which what he calls "place-bound" and "career-bound" superintendents are selected and their subsequent performance in office, length of tenure, and eventual decisions by boards of education on the selection of successors.[32] Carlson uses the term "place-bound" to describe local men who prefer to remain in one school district rather than move to a superintendency in another community. Insiders "have a higher commitment" to one community, look with less favor on the prospect of moving to another superintendency, and stay in office longer than do outsiders.

Although school boards are inclined to appoint outsiders whether the schools have previously been well-administered or not, insiders are selected only when boards feel that the schools have been properly administered and no great changes seem necessary. Outsiders are given a mandate to make changes in the organization, tend to develop more new rules than insiders, often enlarge central office staff, and consider themselves "expendable" rather than committed to staying on in the district. He suggests that the outsider, in general, tends to be "creative" and innovative, while the insider adds little that is new to the role of superintendent and adapts himself to survive.[33] Carlson noted a tendency for larger school districts, far more than smaller ones, to promote an inside man to the superintendency.

There are many hypotheses which could be made concerning the succession patterns of big-city superintendents. However, several hypotheses are tested here because of their potential relevance to the "Great Cities":

1. Grusky has suggested that the size of an organization might affect the greater turnover of its administrators and the total number of successions within it over time.[34] It is quite possible that size itself may also be a variable influencing the pattern of superintendent selection. For example, the availability of more assistant and deputy su-

perintendents in a larger school system may serve to persuade the board of education that a sufficient pool of talent exists in the school district itself, obviating the need to seek elsewhere for an educational leader capable of directing the city schools. If that is so, then the larger the "great city" school system, the more likely it is that superintendents will be selected from among the present employees.

2. The way in which the board itself is selected may influence its decision to select a superintendent. Elective boards, relying as they do on the broad support of many individuals and associations, may be all the more aware of the local political role of the superintendent of schools and may therefore be inclined to select an insider in part for that reason. Also, elective board members may have received the help of teachers and other employee organizations during the election. The board members may recognize the fact that a chain of promotions (as many as ten or fifteen) would follow the promotion of an assistant superintendent. That many promotions would provide the greatest good for the greatest number of those school employees who have aspirations for positions of greater responsibility in the district (and rewarding loyalty or longevity). Therefore, the differential behavior of appointive and elective boards will be examined to determine whether appointed boards of education in the "Great Cities" are more likely to select outsiders than are elective boards.

3. Of course, other critical events in the history of cities or of the nation might affect the choice of superintendents of schools. It may be that school boards selected more outsiders during the reform era of municipal politics at the turn of the century, or that during periods of depression, war, or times of re-adjustment after war, a school board might more naturally turn to insiders rather than outsiders. If events or eras are important factors, then during periods of municipal reform or school reorganizations, school boards in the "Great Cities" will tend to select more outsiders than insiders and after periods of national crisis will select more insiders.

THE LARGEST OF THE LARGE

Table 11 separates the five largest school systems from the remaining large systems in this study. New York City, Los Angeles, Chicago, Philadelphia and Detroit are categorized as "largest" (above 150,000 students), in contrast with nine other cities that are also big but which have a smaller number of pupils. The largest, New York City, is more than ten times as large as the three smallest "Great Cities" as of 1970. The table is set up to reveal whether or not there are differences between the largest school systems and the relatively smaller ones in their pattern of selecting superintendents from within or from outside their own school system. In this table as "insider" (I) is a superintendent who has been chosen from within the same school system. An "outsider" (O) is a superintendent who was selected from outside the school system, most often from another supintendency.

In Table 11 the percentage of insiders to outsiders is remarkably similar; the largest cities hire insiders 63 percent of the time, the remaining cities, 60 percent. The largest cities go outside 37 percent of the time, the remaining big cities 40 percent of the time.

However, the temporary or "acting" superintendents can be discounted as a genuine category, for their terms rarely last more than eighteen months. On the other hand, men who were superintendents of schools in other communities but entered the city system as an assistant superintendent, can, for purposes of analysis, be treated as outsiders. Then ratios change for both sized cities. When the number of such former superintendents is moved from the insider to the outsider column, for the largest cities the ratio becomes 22:16 and for the remaining cities 32:29. Thus, there is relatively little difference between the largest cities and the others (with the exception of New York and Los Angeles) in regard to the number of superintendents they are willing to hire from outside the school system. The data suggest, however, that some large school systems on occasion bring "outsiders" into the school system at a position initially subordinate to the superintendency and then possibly promote them at a later date. They may import such outsiders either to develop some special program (e.g., vocational education), and later may discover he can fill the superintendency when a vacancy arises.

Table 11   THE SOURCES OF BIG-CITY SCHOOL
SUPERINTENDENTS, 1900–1970,
BY SIZE OF DISTRICT

Largest Cities	All Superintendents		Separating Short-term (less than 18 months) or "Acting," and Certain Insiders *			Acting or Short-term
	Insider	Outsider	I	O	O*	
New York	6	2	5	2		1
Los Angeles	7	3	7	3		
Chicago	5	5	5	4		1
Philadelphia	5	5	3	5		2
Detroit	4	2	2	2	2	
Sub-total 5 cities	27	17	22	16	2	4

Remaining Large Cities	Insider	Outsider	I	O	O*	
Baltimore	5	6	4	6		1
Boston	9	2	8	2	1	
Buffalo [1]	2	2	2	2		
Cleveland	6	4	5	3	1	
Houston [2]	2	2	1	2	0	
Milwaukee	3	4	1	3	1	2 acting
Pittsburgh	5	5	4	5	1	
San Francisco [3]	3	5	1	5	1	1 acting (1923)
St. Louis	6	1	6	1		
Sub-total 8 cities	41	29	32	29	5	4

N of 14 cities

Code: I = Insider
Code: O = Outsider

* Insiders who had at one time been superintendents elsewhere;
came to "Great City" first as assistant superintendent.

[1] Superintendents selected since 1917 when superintendency became
an appointive position.

[2] Superintendents selected since 1923 when board became an elective
body.

[3] Superintendents selected since 1923 when superintendency became
an appointive position.

Data not available on 1 superintendent in each of 2 cities: Buffalo and Cleveland.

Table 12 THE SOURCES OF BIG-CITY SCHOOL
SUPERINTENDENTS, 1900–1970, BY APPOINTIVE
AND ELECTIVE BOARDS

Appointive	*All Superintendents*		*Same Data with Two Sub-categories Removed* [1]			
	Insider	Outsider	I	O	O*	Act.
New York	6	2	5	2		
Chicago	5	5	5	4		1
Philadelphia	5	5	3	5		2
Baltimore	5	6	4	6		
Buffalo	2	2	2	2		
Pittsburgh	5	5	4	5	1	
San Francisco	3	5	2	5	1	—
Sub-totals	30	30	25	29	2	3
Percentages	50%	50%				

Elective

	Insider	Outsider	I	O	O*	Act.
Detroit	4	2	2	2	2	
Los Angeles	6	3	6	3		
Boston	9	2	8	2	1	
Cleveland	6	4	5	3	1	1
Houston	2	2	1	2		1
Milwaukee	3	4	1	3	1	2
St. Louis	6	1	6	1	—	—
Sub-totals	36	18	29	16	5	4
Percentages	66%	33%				

New Sub-totals
Appointive: O+O*=31
Elective: O+O*=21

Code: I = Insider
Code: O = Outsider
Code: O* = Insiders who were
superintendents
elsewhere at one time

[1] "Acting" and Insiders with previous superintendencies.

THE DECISIONS OF APPOINTIVE
AND ELECTIVE BOARDS

Some 114 superintendents were selected by fourteen "Great Cities" during the period from 1900 to 1970, a total of sixty by appointive boards, fifty-four by elective boards. As the data in Table 11 show, the appointive boards picked an almost equal

Table 13   THE SELECTION OF BIG-CITY SCHOOL
              SUPERINTENDENTS, INSIDERS–OUTSIDERS
              (Appointments Made in Different Time Periods)

Year	Total	Insiders	Outsiders	Majority*	Notes
1900–1904	5	2	3	O	"Reform era"
1905–1909	8	4	4	–	"Reform era"
1910–1914	11	6	5	I	"Efficiency" era
1915–1919	10	8	2	I	No more than two insiders a year were selected. World War I
1920–1924	11	6	5	I	Post-war
1925–1929	4	4	0	I	Prosperity
1930–1934	4	3	1	I	Start of depression
1935–1939	7	5	2	I	Depression
1940–1944	7	4	3	I	World War II era
1945–1949	10	6	4	I	Post-war era
1950–1954	7	3	4	O	Korean War
1955–1959	10	5	5	–	Four outsiders selected in 1958.
1960–1964	9	5	4	I	Civil Rights era
1965–1970	11	5	6	O	Vietnam War
	114	66	48		

Code:
*O =Outsider
  I =Insider
  Buffalo entries began after 1917; San Francisco after 1921; Houston after 1923.

number of insiders and outsiders, whereas the elective boards chose thirty-six insiders and eighteen outsiders. In other words, the appointive board chose approximately one outsider in every two selections, whereas the elective board chose outsiders one time in three. When those assistant superintendents who had been superintendents elsewhere are added to the "outsider" totals, and if this sub-category of insiders is entered under the outsider column for elective boards, the ratio changes from 2:1 to 3:2. The elective boards hired twice as many insiders as outsiders but promoted some insiders who had been superintendents elsewhere. The appointment of such an insider may make some innovation possible, at the same time allowing a number of other personnel inside the organization to be promoted.[35]

The major point is that elective boards seem to select insiders a greater proportion of the time than do appointive boards. The data show that both appointive and elective boards select outsiders less than 50 percent of the time.

Table 13 shows the number of superintendent appointments of insiders or outsiders according to the time period in which they were made. An attempt was made to distinguish between pre-war and post-war eras, the depression of the 1930's, and the World War II and Vietnam periods. The data arrayed in this fashion show that the number of outsiders appointed exceeded the insiders only in the first five-year period of the century, during 1950 to 1954, and 1965 to 1970, and in these periods by only a narrow margin. In all other periods the number of insiders selected as "Great-city" school superintendents equaled or exceeded the number of outsiders.

THE SELECTIONS SUMMARIZED

The following generalizations about the decisions made by school boards in the "Great Cities" from 1900 to 1970 concerning superintendent successions may be ventured on the basis of the preceding data.

1. The size of the city school system alone does not explain the preference for insiders, except for the two very largest cities, New York and Los Angeles, where the number of insiders has been twice that of outsiders in the past fifty years. Other very large boards, Chicago and Philadelphia, have hired as many outsiders as insiders while boards in somewhat smaller city school systems, Boston and St. Louis, select insiders most of the time.

2. Appointive boards, with the exception of New York City, select as superintendents outsiders approximately as often as they do insiders. Elective boards, especially those in Los Angeles, Boston, Cleveland, and St. Louis, show a marked preference for insiders, whom they select more than twice as often as outsiders. When the number of insiders who have been promoted from an assistant superintendency but who previously held a superintendency elsewhere are tabulated separately, it becomes evident that elective boards are willing to recruit occasional outsiders

to be assistant superintendents and at a later date consider them for the superintendency itself. In this way, elective boards may try to bring in fresh talent while minimizing complaints from their constituents, including other employees seeking promotion.

3. Examination of the selection patterns over time reveals that during three five-year periods the boards selected outsiders more often than insiders, but that during most time periods insiders were selected more often. Both the reform era and the post-war periods were time periods when outsiders were selected in approximately equal numbers. Insiders were selected most often between 1925 and 1939, during times of prosperity as well as economic depression. Since 1944, as many outsiders as insiders have been selected.

The most consistent difference seems to be between the selection practices of most of the appointive boards and most of the elective boards, the latter choosing insiders twice as often as outsiders. The elective boards showed some tendency for promoting to the superintendency insiders who had been superintendents elsewhere, in lieu of going outside to make the selection. Size (except for New York City school superintendency selections) does not appear to be a variable which distinguishes among the cities in this study. To test fully this conclusion would require a "case analysis" of the reasons for selecting insiders or outsiders in each city during the period studied. For example, key school board elections or financial scandals may provoke a change in superintendents, as happened before several big-city boards adopted the nominating panel concept.

THE STRUCTURES AND FUNCTIONS
OF CITY SCHOOL BOARDS IN 1961

In many ways, 1960–1961 marks the end of one era and the start of one characterized by intense debate over how city school boards must change to respond to racial, community, and teacher welfare challenges. The Stanford University research staff which collected data on city school expenditures in the early 1960's also identified the existing governmental structures. As of 1961, members of seven of the city school boards under study were appointive and members of seven boards were elective (see Table 14). The numbers of members on the various school boards ranged from five to fifteen. Only one board in 1961 had less than seven members, six boards had seven, and three boards had fifteen members.

Although Los Angeles school board members received $50 a meeting or a maximum of $500 a month ($6,000 per annum), no other city school board member received more than token compensation, if indeed any recompense besides the prerequisites of a school board job (office, telephone, secretarial services).[36]

In 1961, two of the fourteen mayors were assisted by nominating panels who screened possible candidates for board vacancies. Two mayors had to send their nominations to the council to be confirmed, one mayor submitted the names to the voters, and judges continued to select the members for Philadelphia and Pittsburgh. Members of all seven elective boards were chosen at large.

Five of the seven appointive boards submitted annual budgets to the city officials, as did the elective board in Boston if the city school budget requests exceeded an amount specified in a statute regulating the school expenditures of that city. Two of the appointive boards and six of the elective boards in 1961 spent money for city schools either within state millage limits or voter approved limits, or both. The details of the process of establishing the millage limits warrant close attention beyond the scope of this study; it is sufficient here to note that city officials more often participated directly in the budget approval process when the school board members in these cities were appointed, rather than elected. City officials rarely approved the budgets of "Great-city" schools if the board members were elected. The budgets of elective boards tend to be limited by state millage levy limits or by tax rates approved by the voters, although some appointive boards may have similar limits within which to raise money from taxation, too.

City agencies approved school construction requests for the funding of school construction for three appointive boards and shared in the decision-making with one other appointive board. Three appointive boards submitted decisions on construction (or bonding for that purpose) to the electorate as did up to six of

Table 14 THE STRUCTURE AND SELECTED FUNCTIONS OF GREAT-CITY SCHOOL BOARDS, 1961

City	Method of Board Member Selection	Size	Approval of Total Amount To Be Raised for Education	Approval of Funds for School Construction	Selection of Superintendent	Nomination of Teachers
New York	A. Mayor, from list from selection board	9	Mayor, Council and Board of Estimate	Mayor, Council, City Planning Commission, and Board of Estimates	Board	Superintendent
Chicago	A. Mayor [1]	11	Mayor and Council	Board, with consent of City Council and voters	Board	Superintendent
Philadelphia	A. Judges	15	Board—State levy limit	Board—within bonding limit	Board	Superintendent
Baltimore	A. Mayor and Council	9	Mayor, Council and Board of Estimate	Mayor, Council—Board may select sites	Board	Superintendent
Buffalo	A. Mayor and Council	7	Mayor and Council	Mayor and Council	Board	Superintendent
Pittsburgh	A. Judges	15	Board—State levy limit	Board—within bonding limit	Board	Superintendent

			County Board of Supervisors		Board	Superintendent
San Francisco	A. Mayor, voters to confirm	7	County Board of Supervisors	Board and voters	Board	Superintendent
St. Louis	E. At large	12	Board and voters	Board and voters	Board	Superintendent
Boston	E. At large	5	Board—Mayor and Council (over a limit)	Board—Mayor, Council, and Commissioners of School Buildings	Board	Superintendent
Cleveland	E. At large	7	Board—Voters can approve limit	Board	Board	Superintendent
Detroit	E. At large	7	Board—Voters can exceed limit [2]	Board and voters (state limit)	Board	Superintendent
Los Angeles	E. At large	7	Board—Voters can exceed limit [3]	Board and voters	Board	Superintendent
Milwaukee	E. At large	15	Board—State levy limit	Board	Board	Superintendent
Houston	E. At large	7	Board—Voters can exceed limit	Board	Board	Superintendent

See Table 8 concerning format.

[1] Bound by custom, not law, to choose from names suggested by a nomination commission.

[2] The budget is also submitted to the Wayne County Tax Allocation Board for approval.

[3] The county superintendent and county board of supervisors review the budget but approve all legally authorized amounts.

Source: Reports of field observers, Stanford Great Cities School Finance Project, and state statutes.

the elective boards. Boston was again an exception among the elective boards, although the school committee received in 1929 the privilege of naming one man to the school building commission, the mayor appointing a second man, and these two men then choosing a third colleague.

All the superintendents in 1961 were selected by school boards and all the teacher nominations were made by the superintendent, often with the help of boards of examiners, to the city school board.

The boards of 1961 differed from those of 1920 in several ways. First, three boards had grown slightly larger—New York's from seven to nine, Buffalo's from five to seven, San Francisco's from four to seven. More significant was the fact that four mayors in 1920 made appointments on their own initiative, but no mayor in 1961 escaped the legal or moral obligation to consult a nominations committee, a city council, or the voters before the appointments were final.

The contrast between the 1961 and 1900 city school boards is far more dramatic. Not only did the size of boards decrease and the superintendents become responsible for teacher nominations, but the elective boards, other than in Boston, gained legal autonomy from the city and became free to take to the voters or to the state legislature their requests for additional funds. Two of the appointive boards with a measure of fiscal independence in 1961, Philadelphia and Pittsburgh, lost that independence in 1963 when the state legislature gave each city council authority to approve the city school budgets for those two school systems. Most of the elective boards by 1961 were given more of an opportunity to present school construction needs to the electorate or to seek a new limit from the legislature, when necessary, than was the case in 1900.

However, it is quite clear that none of the city school boards under study now has full authority to make the final decisions about current operating budgets or capital outlay. The final authority to make these decisions is lodged in the office of the mayor, and is often shared with his city council or board of estimate, or placed with the state legislature, or with the electorate. The "fiscally independent" city school board does not make the final financial decisions any more than does the appointive dependent board, nor is there implicit in fiscal independence any assurance that more funds can be obtained from sources other than a benevolent mayor and council. The possibility, in theory, exists that for so-called "independent" boards the state legislative limits may be less flexible or responsive to changes in need. Or the necessity of persuading a large body of voters to authorize a higher tax levy may create a great burden on the time and ingenuity of city school boards, their staff, and their citizen supporters. Nevertheless, the structure which provides for an elective board seems to be associated more often than not with independence from the municipality, a development which began to appear before 1920 and which continued thereafter.

The fact that urban school departments managed to shake loose from city hall perplexes and even angers political scientists and public administration theorists. They argue strongly that:

1. the same local tax base furnishes the revenue for all municipal services, not just for education, and
2. the mayor and city council represent the citizens in making the difficult decisions as to what cuts, expansions, and "trade-offs" should be made in any given year—in widely different city departments, from sanitation to recreation, libraries to public works, education has no right to be separate while the need for other human services are pitted against the other budget priorities, and
3. education, to be most effective, should operate not independently but in close concert with city planning, parks and recreation, police and fire, public health, economic and manpower development, and anti-poverty agencies— all of which normally fall under the supervision of the mayor.

The third argument appears to gain validity as other city agencies cooperate in "multi-service center" efforts to assist families and individuals with health, welfare, legal, job counseling, and other related problems which affect the learning potential of children in schools. City school staffs in recent years have also found themselves developing very close relationships with police and drug treatment officials as violence and narcotics problems increase in and around public schools.

The first and second arguments, however, serve as deterrents to educator agreement that all local agencies should be governed by mayor and council. Supporters of the schools worry about the local tax base and possible cuts. They fondly point to state constitutions which say that city schools are really state schools and show that the state usually contributes anywhere from one-quarter to two-thirds of the annual school system operating costs. The state usually shares the costs of new school construction as well. Indeed, if control of the school shifts away from local school boards, it will probably be to state school boards as the states consider—or are forced by court rulings—to equalize taxation for the public schools.

Other arguments against giving more control to city hall were summarized by David Seeley, an attorney and educator who tried to help a reform mayor, John Lindsay, change an urban school system:

1. "The memories of the spoils system and Boss Tweed are still strong in the minds of New Yorkers. New York's Tammany has long been the textbook symbol of nepotism, bribery, and dirty politics . . . the merit system has attained a revered status—even more so in the school system where it is felt that defenseless children's lives will be violated if politicians are ever allowed to get their hands on school affairs." [37] Similar sentiments are shared by good-government groups as well as by educators in other cities.

2. Also, New York City—and several other cities—likes to think of the schools as institutions needing academic freedom and protection from "right-wing book burners who have won school board elections in some school districts across the nation." This argument suggests that not only city hall but "any kind of political interference" is the enemy.

Who do these arguments really serve and what does the separation of city schools from city government really accomplish? First, the educators themselves are served for they are insulated not only from much of the employment scandals that still plague city government but also protected, to a degree, against budget cuts generally denounced as "political." Of course the political innocence of teachers fades rapidly during and after prolonged teacher strikes when teacher leaders extract improved salary settlements from the city treasury.

The alleged purity of the schools also serves the original coalition of elites—the established business firms, the university professors, and the newspapers. The reputations of their cities and the behavior of future employees depend on well-ordered and fairly predictable schools. Only in the early 1970's have professors and journalists in substantial numbers criticized the city schools as dull, oppressive, and unproductive.[38] Until then the coalition tacitly agreed that city schools served a screening function in identifying the most able candidates for colleges and jobs and the less able for the general labor pool. (Lately, the very fact of political insulation has allowed to emerge a degree of public complacency about school graduates that even the usual supporters of the schools—employing firms and college faculties —cannot tolerate.) This leads to the current surge of school criticism and the quest for more productive approaches to childhood education generally. But all this does not suggest any willingness to turn the schools over to big-city mayors.

THE HIGH POINT OF SEPARATE
CENTRAL SCHOOL BOARDS: A SUMMARY

Mayors win very few open battles with big-city school boards. Most mayors seem to sense this and suppress the temptation to try to change the school system. As will be seen in a review of the Lindsay efforts in New York City, and as was evident in the La Guardia era, either the temptation or the apparent necessity to intervene may be quite overwhelming. But intervention may exact quite a heavy cost in each case.

Mayors such as Robert Wagner in New York, Richard Daley in Chicago, and Richardson Dilworth (in the 1950's) in Philadelphia paid little attention to schools, with few exceptions. Wagner and Daley usually agreed to try to find money for the latest teacher union contract. But they stayed out of most school issues as long as they could, despite criticism and requests to take a stand.

Other mayors, such as Chicago mayors Thompson and Kelly, by their actions provoked the response of the nominating panel concept, used in three cities in the latter 1960's (although the New York City pattern dissolved in a 1969 legislative compromise.) The nominating panel device tries to remove the school board member selection process even further from electoral politics. What it does is to try to substitute the politics of the higher social classes for the values and inclinations of immigrant or working-class citizens.

In many ways the mid 1960's represented a kind of high point in big-city school centralization of power in the hands of professional educators, buffered from city politics in many instances by a carefully chosen lay board. Appointive boards tend to search more widely and to prefer outsiders as superintendents. Their insulation from the electorate explains some of that freedom, especially given general pressure on the mayor not to interfere.

What happened in the first two-thirds of the century in many large cities was that reformers felt an obligation to de-politicize school decisions in two steps:

1. Remove personnel and instructional decisions from neighborhood or ward leaders and give them to a central board.
2. Strive to separate school governance from the mayor's influence either by retaining the elective board format or by devising ways to shape the mayors' appointments to the school board.

Many of the reforms tended to strengthen the school superintendency, at least on paper. Hunt in Chicago, Briggs in Cleveland, and Whittier in Philadelphia were among those who fought successfully to place the business functions under the superintendency.[39] This fulfilled Cubberley's dream of a strong, unified superintendency. On the other hand, this phenomenon irritated one articulate Chicago school board member to the point where he wrote a detailed account of his frustrations at dealing with so strong a superintendent.[40]

The structures, whether appointive or elective, for several decades appeared to insulate much of city school systems from the rough and tumble of urban politics. There are exceptions, notably the politics of maintenance contracts and janitorial services, which in cities such as New York and Boston occasionally generate publicity which temporarily outrages the reformer class. But the appointment of teachers and the promotion of principals with few exceptions remain apart from the oldstyle politics. So insulated from community pressures are these functions now that the newer urban minorities question whether the system can open to them employment opportunities and a chance to express preferences for school personnel. The revolt against this political insulation will be examined in the next chapter.

NOTES

1. Theodore J. Lowi, *At the Pleasure of the Mayor* (New York: The Free Press of Glencoe, 1964), p. 3.

2. The term "outsider" refers to the selection as superintendent of a man whose previous career has been in other school systems rather than "inside" the same system.

3. John A. Vieg, *The Government of Education in Metropolitan Chicago* (Chicago: The University of Chicago Press, 1939), p. 40.

4. National Commission for the Defense of Democracy Through Education, *Investigation Reports Abridgments* (Washington, D.C.: The National Education Association, 1960), pp. 7–20.

5. *Ibid.*, pp. 15–16.

6. *Ibid.*, p. 17.

7. The commission is an *ad hoc* group sanctioned only by custom, not law, and represents institutions or groups (not positions) each of which designate a representative. In the 1960's the commission consisted of 18 men and women, 6 from universities, 1 or 2 from organized labor, 1 from the American Legion, 1 each from the PTA and the Citizens School Committee and since 1963, several Negroes. The commission idea was strongly supported by the Citizens School Committee, a "save our schools" group organized in 1933 which formerly interviewed and screened candidates before the broader commission assumed this function. The mayor found it easier to accept an advisory committee than to agree to the N.E.A. proposal for elections. *Source:* Interviews of Warren Carson with Dr. Erick Oldburgh, 11-year member and chairman of the commission and Mrs. Herrick, secretary and founder of the Citizens' School Committee. Interview report dated January 24, 1965.

8. Harry B. Wilson, "Toughest School Job in the Country," *The Saturday Evening Post,* vol. CCXXIII (October 7, 1950), p. 29 ff. Hunt insisted on the merging of two executive positions, business manager and superintendent, so that the former position would be placed under a single executive reporting to the board.

9. Interview with Herold C. Hunt, March 20, 1965. Hunt and Willis had discussed and agreed on this point. Both Willis and Redmond met with considerable federal agency pressure to integrate schools and faculties. In fact, on one occasion Mayor Daley complained to President Johnson about Commissioner Keppel's threat to shut off federal funds for Chicago.

10. Robert J. Havighurst, *The Public Schools of Chicago, Survey Report* (Chicago: The Board of Education of the City of Chicago, 1964), p. 495. Only in the matter of *de facto* segregation did Willis meet with governmental opposition, and that from the United States Commissioner of Education.

11. Herold C. Hunt, "Public Relations Through Public Participation," *The School Executive*, vol. LXVI (March 1947), pp. 61–62. See also the Wilson account, *op. cit.*, which tells how Hunt continued in Chicago the communication techniques he had perfected in previous superintendencies.

12. Edward C. Banfield and James Q. Wilson, *City Politics* (Cambridge, Massachusetts: Harvard University Press and M.I.T. Press, 1963), p. 127. The mayor has long held the respect of Chicago business and other civic leaders.

13. National Commission for the Defense of Democracy through Education of the N.E.A., *Interference with the Independence of the New York City Board of Education*, A report of an investigation (Washington, D.C.: National Education Association, February 7, 1964).

14. Sol Cohen, *Progressives and Urban School Reform* (New York: Teachers College of Columbia University, 1964), p. 202.

15. Lowi, *op. cit.*, pp. 32–33.

16. Wallace S. Sayre and Herbert Kaufman, *Governing New York City* (New York: Russell Sage Foundation, 1960), p. 283.

17. "New York's New Board," *The American School Board Journal*, vol. CXLIII (December 1961), p. 40. The account reads as follows: "In making the appointments, the Mayor discarded borough lines, but perhaps unwittingly, duplicated the former custom of following occupational, racial, political and religious lines." According to Lowi or Sayre and Kaufman it is doubtful that the mayor of New York rejects or follows an appointment "custom" unwittingly. For the various religious and racial groups, the stakes are too high.

18. When New York Mayor Wagner "named a Jew to fill a 'Catholic vacancy' on the board" in May 1963, representatives from the Catholic Archdiocese, the Board of Rabbis, and the Protestant Council of the City of New York voiced their objections. Religious balance was restored eventually because of these protests. Peter Binzen, "How to Pick a School Board," *Saturday Review*, vol. XLVIII, no. 16 (April 17, 1965) p. 73.

19. Robert E. Lane, *Political Life* (Glencoe, Ill.: The Free Press, 1959) pp. 235–255. Cf. also *Beyond the Melting Pot* by Nathan Glazer and Daniel P. Moynihan (Cambridge, Massachusetts: Harvard University Press and The M.I.T. Press, 1964) for a description and analysis of the slow rate of assimilation of minorities in New York City. The phenomenon of carefully allocated representation of religious groups has been observed by Stanford School of Education

Great Cities staff members to hold for Buffalo, Baltimore, and San Francisco as well.

20. "An Act to Amend Section 2553 of the Education Law," a bill introduced to the Senate and Assembly of the State of New York, August 21, 1961.

21. "The New York Mess," editorial in *American School Board Journal*, vol. CXLIII (October 1961), p. 36.

22. Article 52, Section 2553, Education Law, McKinney's Consolidated Laws of New York, 1963 cumulative annual pocket part (Brooklyn: Edward Thompson Company, 1963).

23. Quoted in *Philadelphia* magazine (May 1969), p. 76.

24. Marilyn Gittell and T. Edward Hollander, *Six Urban School Districts* (New York: Praeger, 1968), p. 43.

25. *Ibid.*, p. 48.

26. *Philadelphia* magazine, *op. cit.*, p. 77.

27. Preliminary Report of the Mayor's Ad Hoc Commission on Educational Selection Boards," New York City (1963), (mimeographed).

28. The role of the press in both cities has also been one of pivotal importance. The "rat" incident was tailor made for the New York tabloids. In Chicago, the *Daily News* and then the *Sun* kept their readers alerted to Mayor Kelly's continued support of board president McCahey and of the controversial superintendent. See the article on "Chicago" by Warren Pierce in Robert S. Allen (ed.), *Our Fair City* (New York: Vanguard, 1947), p. 182.

29. The number of three cities, five superintendency appointments in a total of twenty years is too small to verify this capability. Moreover, the possibility that the appointive board already possesses to some extent a greater capability than the elective board will be explored in subsequent pages.

30. The superintendents of Chicago, New York City, and Baltimore in recent years have been among the highest paid public servants of all time. Usually the salary of at least one of the three has been exceeded only by the President of the United States and the Governor of New York State.

31. George K. Floro, "Continuity in City Manager Careers," *American Journal of Sociology*, vol. LXI (November 1955), pp. 245–266.

32. Richard O. Carlson, *Executive Succession and Organizational Change,* (Chicago: Midwest Administration Center, The University of Chicago, 1962).

33. *Ibid.*, pp. 69–71.

34. Oscar Grusky, "Corporate Size, Bureaucratization and Managerial Succession," *American Journal of Sociology*, vol. XXXIX (November 1961), pp. 261–269.

35. Carlson, *op. cit.*, pp. 21 and 22. Carlson feels such an insider will have less of a mandate for change.

36. The next highest maximum pay for school board members was in San Francisco, where the members receive $1,500 per year. Some board members elsewhere are the beneficiaries of gift testimonial dinners annually and can distribute patronage of a minor sort (ticket-takers, temporary guards, etc.).

37. David Seeley, "A Big City Mayor Tries His Hand at School Reform," in Frank W. Lutz (ed.), *Toward Improved Urban Education* (Worthington, Ohio: Charles A. Jones, 1970), p. 178.

38. Illustrative of the criticism are Charles Silberman's *Crisis in the Classroom* (New York: Random House, 1970) and Norton Long, "The City as Reservation," a strong indictment of city schooling in *The Public Interest*, no. 25 (Fall 1971), pp. 26–30.

39. Only St. Louis retains the divided executive, although legislation has been introduced to place business functions under the superintendent as elsewhere. Marilyn Gittell, *Participants and Participation* (New York: Praeger, 1968), p. 77.

40. Joseph Pois, *The School Board Crisis: A Chicago Case Study* (Chicago: Educational Methods, 1964). See also Robert Crain *et al.*, *The Politics of School Desegregation* (Chicago: Aldine, 1968), for documentation of civil rights leaders' disappointment with "color blind" superintendents.

RETURNING CONTROL TO THE COMMUNITY

A CENTURY OF REFORMS smashed the hold of ward leaders and tied the hands of mayors who sought to influence school politics. Until the 1960's hardly anyone complained about power ebbing away from the neighborhoods. The voices urging a stronger role for the mayor were largely those of public administration scholars who preferred a single strong executive running all city departments—either a city manager, or a strong mayor, or at any rate, a "chief administrative officer," with professional training and the power to coordinate municipal departments. Among the educators, only Judd broke ranks to agree with those who would grant the mayor greater control over city schools. Any mayor who tried to reshape the schools faced severe criticism from the National Educational Association, especially its investigatory commissions charged with defending the professional educators against "political interference."

During the 1950's and 1960's new minorities fled the farms and flocked to the industrial cities of the North, the Midwest, and the Southwest. Civil rights leaders, inspired by the Supreme Court ruling in 1954 and subsequent government support of their efforts in Little Rock, New Orleans, and elsewhere, sought to open up *de facto* segregated schools in the North. When they moved, they met with the centralized, reformed, reasonably small school boards and their very professional superintendents in these cities. The new minority leaders didn't like what they found.

City school superintendents and boards faced with desegregation proposals tended to respond in about the same pattern in each major city in this sequence:

· Rejection or refusal by the system to consider initial demands for desegregation, then
· Civil rights action—suits, demonstrations or boycotts,
· Board response—either limited agreement, rejection, or continued negotiations,
· Escalation of pressure—temporary resolution or state intervention.[1]

In very few of the larger cities could civil rights leaders and school boards implement plans to integrate completely the new minorities, black and Puerto Rican, with the existing white-pupil populations. New York City and Detroit boards responded favorably but with plans that only began to meet the objectives. Efforts to integrate the schools met with openly hostile resistance from white ethnic groups who feared the impact of the new immigrants on neighborhood customs and institutions. Parent groups arose to protest pairing, cross-busing, and attempts to redistrict elementary school districts.

Black leaders, after from five to ten years of struggle to eliminate *de facto* segregation, grew cynical in the mid 1960's about the willingness of white leaders to move decisively. Boycotts, as Crain found later, succeeded in raising the issue and forcing school board discussion but not in convincing the total community to accept as legitimate minority-group demands for quality, integrated education.

Mayors and judges, over the years, recognized the right of blacks to representation on the appointed boards. Black men in the 1960's, however, found it much more difficult to get elected to boards, unless they could build a political coalition with white liberals and the Spanish-speaking. Moreover, the first wave of board appointees were the more moderate middle-class members of minority groups, rarely the most vocal in clamoring for "integration now." In fact, their associates on the board often hoped the presence of moderate Negro members somehow could help to dampen the conflict over racial integration.

Meanwhile, even the most optimistic of integrationist leaders by the late 1960's despaired of success on any substantial scale. What gains had been won were canceled by steady increases in non-white pupil populations. A new and younger group of activists, many of them veterans of the tense confrontations in the

South (integrating lunch counters and universities or registering voters in the mid-'60's), placed little trust in the white man's willingness to correct injustices. Better to try to take over their own neighborhood institutions—the stores, the schools, the community centers. Black men had better develop their own pride, prowess, and power because the "white power structure" would not yield. Such was the rationale for a new approach.

The new approach, under various labels, was called "community control" or "decentralization" or in its most euphemistic form, "increased community involvement." Led originally by black spokesmen, the concept grew into a movement, spurred by the failure of northern city school integration measures and by the awakening of racial pride and ethnic identity among blacks.

Fundamentally, the new movement challenged the reforms of fifty years ago. The approach, if adopted, would return "power to the people," a popular if somewhat vague slogan except when defined as the power to hire and fire teachers. The new approach in effect reversed the trend to centralization, to decision-making by a small elite group, and to reliance for virtually all personnel and policy proposals on a professional school superintendent's staff.

This chapter raises several questions. Why did the centralization movement stop? What did the new terms and slogans mean operationally? What intellectual rationale lay behind the new proposals? To what extent did New York City and Detroit and other cities succeed in decentralizing their school systems? What new problems appeared, and to what extent did the new proposals resemble or differ from the ward politics of the nineteenth century? Not all the evidence is in on these questions, but policy-makers properly worry about whether a swing of the pendulum at this time means a serious loss of progress or a return to a more satisfactory equilibrium in city school governance.

THE CASE OF NEW YORK CITY I.S. 201

The most spectacular example of white resistance to racial integration was the planning of Intermediate School 201 in East Harlem, New York City. Civil rights leaders thought they had won commitment from board of education leaders to the concept of a new integrated school, even if it meant importing white students from across the Triborough Bridge. School officials made some efforts to recruit enough students but were undercut by headquarters staff. Finally, in an effort to save face, the board early in 1966 announced that the school would indeed achieve a kind of racial balance, 50 percent black and 50 percent Puerto Rican. Local leaders exploded and proposed that the community not allow the new school to open. The opening of the school was postponed several times in the period between April 1 and September 12, 1966, as a parents' council tried to gain support of Mayor Lindsay, State Commissioner James Allen, and U.S. Commissioner of Education Harold Howe, II.

Beginning in 1965, spokesmen for parents called for appointment of a black principal and for measures to increase the "accountability" of the educational system to the community.[2] By late August the parents knew that outside officials would not or could not intervene. Their demands shifted to a request for a quality segregated school run by a black principal. Since the board could not integrate the school, then it should allow the community a chance to select the staff and take part in making other school decisions. (The board had earlier promised special programs which later fell from sight.) Superintendent Donovan agreed to several of the points, including community participation in selecting a black male principal, but the board of education would not support these concessions. The school was picketed on opening day and controversy continued to rage around it. David Rogers describes how the issues attracted more attention:

> The Lindsay administration and the Ford Foundation through its new president, McGeorge Bundy, became involved in the discussions, along with board officials, the United Federation of Teachers, and parent spokesmen. Ford was interested in urban development and public education and saw the reform of New York City schools as central to that interest. And, of course, the mayor realized that the quality of the schools affected many other city problems and was a political question with which he had to deal.[3]

Rogers explained that the demands for more participation came at a time when the slogan "Black Power" was raising many fears among not only the professionals but also among white moderates and the press. White civic and parent groups expressed dismay at placing the merit system in jeopardy by relenting to the choice of a black principal.

The board countered with proposals to recognize an advisory council and to decentralize the school system to make possible greater parental involvement. At several points during the 1966–1967 school year, the board announced an intent to study decentralization. On March 30, 1967, the New York State legislature agreed to grant additional school aid to the city on the condition that the mayor would submit a plan to decentralize the school system the next year. Meanwhile, by the summer, the Ford Foundation agreed to grant financial support to planning efforts by the staffs and boards of three districts authorized by the central board to propose ways to decentralize. The three demonstration districts were:

· I.S. 201 and feeder elementary schools,
· Ocean Hill–Brownsville, a poor, predominantly black section of Brooklyn,
· Two Bridges—a multi-ethnic district in lower Manhattan.

Thus, a major struggle to define community control and decentralization had begun. It is important to try to define these concepts, both related to the struggle to return decision-making power to the people.

"COMMUNITY CONTROL"
AND "DECENTRALIZATION"

Words that have become slogans, and, to some, even epithets, tend to elude precise definition. Different people at different times used "community control" and "decentralization" to mean very different things. For example, the Harlem parents originally wanted an integrated intermediate school with a high-quality program. At first they mainly wanted the board to listen to reasons why IS 201 should not be built on a high-hazard site adjacent to a railroad. They also wanted to participate in naming the school, a courtesy ignored when the central board proceeded to name it the Arthur Schomburg School. They were promised an integrated school which would obtain university assistance to develop an innovative educational program; they got art, music,

and typing, no university, and no integration. Their request for
a black male principal was agreed to by the superintendent, then
overturned by the board. As one community ghetto leader that
Rogers interviewed explained so plaintively: "They make us into
militants and then they discredit us for being militants. We just
cannot win. That's why we want to take over the whole thing." [4]

What does the "whole thing" mean? Community control?
Boards, legislators, and professionals in many states have struggled to determine which functions might be returned to the community.

The New Urban League in Boston in 1969 defined community control of schools very broadly and yet with considerable
specificity:

> Community organizations must be set up with a cross section of
> people from the black community—parents, professionals, teachers,
> ministers and interested persons who live in the community. These or-
> ganizations must move to gain total control over the operation of the
> schools, including expenditure of monies. The money should be
> banked in a community bank with local people serving as treasurer
> and in charge of bookkeeping. The city and state should be made to
> allot money on a school-by-school basis with each community organiza-
> tion for respective schools determining how the money should be
> spent. These school–community organizations must also have control
> over principal and teacher accountability, that is, the power to hire
> and fire school officials. These school–community organizations must
> have the power to be involved in the plans for building and rehabili-
> tation of schools. Construction contracts should be given to black com-
> panies. This is community control! [5]

Advocates of community control differ over whether a central board of education would be necessary. On the one hand a
central board could help in recruiting teachers, supplying supervisors and custodians as requested, and distributing the tax funds
—collected from local, state, and federal sources. Some feel that
raising revenue would be about all that a central board would
need to do. Those who have started up their own "community
schools" feel that even the need for a local revenue agency might
be unnecessary; just give the children or their parents tax vouchers to cash in at the school of their choice.

The type of community control depends in part on the electoral machinery and in part on the size of the community unit.
Some proposals call for parent boards or parent–teacher–student

councils at the level of each school, while others call for community elections of all voters in areas which embrace twenty or more public schools. Some plans provide for recall elections, while others authorize the central board to remove members of an unsatisfactory board. Does it make a difference? Community boards under one form may worry about a single school or many; may consist entirely of parents or have a majority of members with no children in public schools; may feel that they report to their neighbors ultimately or that they work for the central board.

Some community school board districts may overlap with other political jurisdictions such as wards or legislative districts, while others may be drawn so as to minimize the potential for partisan political influence. District lines may be drawn to support school integration plans or to separate ethnic and racial groups into homogeneous districts. The only common denominator is the effort to restore to laymen in sub-sections of the city some of those powers previously given to the central school board.

The notion of "decentralization" differs both in degree and in kind. Those who seek community control label it a political concept, whereas decentralization is technically an administrative device wherein control over personnel matters remains in the hands of educators.

Decentralization proposals grow out of a willingness to reconsider the extent to which authority can only be exerted by a central body such as a city-wide board and staff. There are at least two kinds of decentralization: one very mild and indeed mainly administrative, the other somewhat more oriented to parents but still mainly advisory.

Administrative decentralization means granting certain powers to officials to exert in geographic areas smaller than the total territory governed. A central school board, for example, might designate an area or district superintendent to supervise schools with student populations of anywhere from 10,000 to 50,000 pupils.

Advisory boards or councils may exist to give the staff and central board some sense of which alternatives a community prefers, given either limited sites or limited appropriations. Such boards may be asked to conduct hearings on school budgets, school repairs, and school policies and procedures. Until about 1965, local advisory boards were thought of mainly as buffers or trouble-shooting devices.

Many cities adopted the idea of decentralization not so much to improve communication with communities but to see that policies and rules were properly enforced by other employees in the school system. Advisory boards, let alone district governing boards, prior to 1965 were scarce other than in New York City, and in that one instance virtually powerless. After 1965, the federal government asked cities to create advisory councils to plan and monitor anti-poverty programs of an educational nature.

The influx of new minorities to the cities tested the capacity of city school boards to respond to complex issues such as racial desegregation, the modification of curriculum materials for multi-racial classrooms, and the recruitment and promotion of educators from the new groups. Black groups voiced their complaints first, but by the early 1970's Puerto Ricans and Mexican–Americans articulated their demands as well. In the West, the aggrieved groups formed Third World Coalitions, Orientals included, to protest the division of the world into two warring white factions and to insist on recognition of Afro and Asian cultures.

The poverty of so many of the new city residents and the perplexity of welfare professionals over how to end poverty generated more fundamental criticisms of American society, technology, the city, and education. Welfare professionals and some social scientists proposed as one potent remedy the granting of more political power to the poor so that they too could effect a measure of control over their own destiny. This constituted the rationale for community action councils, for election of the poor to policy positions, and for action against any professionals who placed their own careers first before client concerns.

Federal policy-planners found it relatively easy to insist that parents "control" new health and educational programs such as the Headstart programs for very young children. But neither federal officials nor civil rights leaders could budge the large-city school systems for several reasons:

1. The teaching and administrative staffs had not only adjusted to the fact of centralized control but worried about

whether a decentralized or community controlled system would jeopardize their job and career possibilities,

2. Educator unions and associates during the 1960's in most of the large cities won collective bargaining and grievance arbitration rights, after considerable agitation, at the city-wide level and were not about to yield these hard-won prerogatives.

These reasons infuriated minority leaders, who judged that the "so-called professionals" were more concerned about their own welfare than that of community children. The fact that so many teachers, often poorly trained for inner-city schools, appeared to fail as teachers of minority children only escalated the level of criticism of central boards, superintendents, and the impersonal bureaucracy that sent presumably qualified teachers to ghetto classrooms.

Thus developed pressures for community control over what almost everyone had agreed were professional matters, especially over curriculum, budgets, and educational personnel. The ensuing debate forced a more dynamic definition of decentralization and its purposes. In particular, the drive for community control provoked central school boards to calculate how much of what was determined centrally could be delegated to professionals at the district level with consultation with parent advisory groups. Under pressure, central boards might even agree to share with local groups the right to pick the professional in charge of a district and maybe even the head of a school. Central boards fought, however, to retain their function as makers of overall curriculum policy, certifiers of personnel and chief budgetary and building authority. Each city had to face the division of powers question in terms of who would decide what and why.

EARLIER EFFORTS TO DECENTRALIZE
NEW YORK CITY SCHOOLS

Decentralization in the 1960's was not a totally new concept nor one unique to urban education. The Citizens' Union in New York urged as early as 1947 the grouping of community services in various districts, "For more orderly planning and decentralization of municipal services." [6] The city planning commission in 1950 proposed sixty-six districts to coordinate the planning of schools, hospitals, playgrounds, streets, and houses. Manhattan Borough President, Robert Wagner, in 1951, established twelve districts as recommended, but really only for planning. Daniel Bell concludes, "Thus, the idea of decentralization and local community organizations as the basis of new administrative and political functions was underway, slowly, haltingly, and confusedly, in the 1950's." [7]

Bell and Daniel P. Moynihan both identify, as one source of the community action and "participation" ideology, the social scientists involved in social actions and reform, especially among youth in the urban ghettos, and with a focus on the opportunities denied delinquent youth.[8] The new approach of Columbia social welfare professors Lloyd Ohlin and Richard Cloward was to combat anomie and a sense of powerlessness by providing jobs, job-training, and community organization. The Mobilization for Youth program in New York City in the early 1960's proved to be a seed bed for the later War on Poverty and its insistence on the involvement of the poor themselves in program development. This ideology of community participation never so clearly influenced a city school system as when an assistant professor of social work at Columbia, Preston Wilcox, in 1966 drafted the essential position for the frustrated parents of I.S. 201 in New York City.[9]

Even so, a persistent group of socially conscious women organized in the Women's City Clubs of New York City in 1960 advocated restoration of some powers to fifty-four district boards which, although stripped of responsibilities, lingered on as advisory boards. The 1961 city school board statute reactivated the local boards, twenty-five of them, and established selection panels to generate names for local boards (district superintendents passed the names along to the central city-wide board). Local boards could hold budget and other hearings, but otherwise controlled virtually nothing. The city-wide boards still appointed the principals and district superintendents and settled the budget. A follow-up study by the same women revealed some increase in community consultation and improved relations between the district superintendents and parent groups. But the major function served, with few exceptions, was that of a buffer between the board of education and the parents at the community level.[10]

Rogers documented an increase during the 1960's in citizen frustrations, local board member resignations, and the failure to appoint to boards spokesmen for the poor and minorities.[11] Although the number of boards was expanded to thirty-one in 1965, criticisms of poor communications and of local powerlessness continued. Thus the board of education gradually perceived the need to decentralize some decisions but continued to exploit the local boards as shock absorbers as long as possible.

HOW MUCH DECENTRALIZATION FOR NEW YORK CITY?

The I.S. 201 controversy and the state grant of additional aid to education both forced another re-examination of the New York City board of education. The legislature agreed to compute state aid on a borough basis (Manhattan property wealth inflates the city-wide average). But why not decentralize the school system into five borough school districts as a device to stimulate participation?

A borough plan was proposed by a consultant to the Temporary Commission on City Finance, political scientist Marilyn Gittell of Queens College. Her study of governance and decision-making for the commission was published by the Center for Urban Education under the title, *Participants and Participation: A Study of School Policy in New York City.* She urged a school committee and superintendent for each borough and cooperation with municipal colleges. She argued, "Such a change provides avenues of expression for local groups; and with the existence of natural interborough rivalries, it encourages competition and change." [12] A mayor would appoint a city-wide school commissioner with a small research staff, an appointed board of fourteen members (the chairman of each borough committee, chancellor of the City University, three named by the mayor, two by the city council, and three by a selection panel.) Borough boards would recruit teachers and develop programs with "varying types of experiments in community involvement."

Staten Island, as the Borough of Richmond, would gain the most autonomy from such a plan, especially given its comparatively small size. State Senator John Marchi, Chairman of the legislative committee on New York City, did not miss the implications of the proposal. But the bill authorized Mayor Lindsay to propose a plan and he in turn asked Ford Foundation President McGeorge Bundy to study the question and offer recommendations for decentralization.

The mayor's advisory panel on November 1967 proposed for New York City a community school system with from thirty to sixty community school boards governing all schools in a geographical area. Each board would assume responsibility for teacher and administrator hiring and operations and for advancing racial integration. Local parents would choose six members and the mayor, five members. The chairmen of the community school boards would suggest three names for each of five positions on a nine-man central board; the selection panel would provide names on a city-wide basis that the mayor could choose from others.[13]

Meanwhile, the United Federation of Teachers won a new two-year contract but only after a strike in which the teachers' right to deal with the "disruptive child" was a central issue. Minority groups interpreted this as an attempt to place the blame for learning problems on the child and his parents, and at several schools broke the strike.

The Bundy Plan drew criticism from many community leaders; there were those who viewed it as a threat to integration, those who worried about the excellence of city-wide high schools, those who felt extremists could capture a district of only 15,000 pupils. So the mayor exempted the senior high schools from his proposal and recommended only thirty local boards. The existing New York City board offered its own decentralization plan which permitted, but did not mandate any delegation of powers. Then the New York Board of Regents, sensing additional hostility to the role of the mayor in appointing so many members of the local and city-wide boards, presented another plan calling for fifteen rather large districts which would average about 60,000 pupils. Mayor Lindsay, whose own proposals won very little support, supported the Regents bill.

During the Spring, the Ocean Hill–Brownsville board sent termination notices to six administrators and thirteen teachers and referred them to school board headquarters at 110 Livingston Street for reassignment. This move raised a storm of protest.

Both the U.F.T. and the Council of Supervisory Associations in 1967 had questioned the appointment of demonstration school district administrators not on city lists of eligibles; now the question was defined as one of teacher and administrator transfer rights and of compulsory transfer without "due process." The unions demanded specific charges, defended the right of teachers to a hearing, and criticized Rhody McCoy, the unit administrator.

Albany in May of 1968 was the scene of impressive lobbying, especially by the U.F.T., which on May 20th sent more than 500 of its members to campaign against the Regents' bill. Union leaders pressed for a milder bill or a delay. 1968 was a presidential election year, so in late May the legislators asked the board of education to design a new plan but, acknowledging the reluctance of the existing board, authorized Mayor Lindsay to appoint four new members. After some resignations, the Wagner board became the pro-decentralization Lindsay board.

Summer of 1968 brought no resolution of the conflict between the union and Ocean Hill leaders. Michael Harrington calls the events of late 1968 "not a simple conflict of right and wrong, but an antagonism of two rights . . . effective community involvement in the educational process . . . (versus) academic freedom and due process when a professional is dismissed;" in short, "the aspect of an Antigone-like tragedy." [14]

Three times that fall the unions went out on strike, teachers and administrators and usually the custodians with them. Regents, mayor, mediators—none could bridge the gap for many weeks. Thirty-six out of the first forty-eight days of school were lost to all but a few thousand children attending the demonstration schools, which remained open.[15]

Dutifully the Lindsay board held hearings to refine a new plan, which was submitted to the Regents on January 29, 1969. The plan called for thirty community districts, each with an elected board. Safeguards for tenured employees were described in detail, and the commissioner of education was designated as "principal adjudicator of disputes," a role he had assumed by the end of the third strike in November 1969. Community boards with from eight to sixteen members would be elected by intermediate or junior high school units and from elementary schools.

Eleven high school councils of parents and community board representatives could select senior high principals and review high school budgets.[16]

The 1969 legislature reflected the Republican victory of November 1968, and state senator Marchi sponsored a bill giving very limited powers to local districts.[17] Teachers supported the Marchi bill and opposed the more liberal Regents' bill which embodied most features of the Lindsay board proposal. Antagonism between so many parties created tremendous tension and a five-week marathon of legislative negotiations for an elusive middle way. Finally, Governor Rockefeller's staff prepared a package that fully satisfied no one but provided for:

1. Thirty to thirty-three community school districts with elected boards, each to select its own community superintendents.
2. An elected central board of seven members, one from each borough and two appointed by the mayor.
3. An interim board of five, one appointed by each borough president, to serve until May 1970 (thus no mayoralty appointments for one year.
4. Appointment of a chancellor instead of a city-wide superintendent of schools.
5. Authorizations of a maintenance budget for each community board of up to $250,000 for school repair contracts.
6. Local board selection of textbooks, recommendation of school sites and budget.
7. More open hiring of teachers for schools with low reading scores.[18]

No one pretended that the final result was perfect. The U.F.T. had long fought an elected board but wanted to get rid of the existing strongly pro-decentralization Lindsay board. Marchi and the conservatives felt their interests safeguarded by the borough features. Black, Puerto Rican, and white-liberal legislators felt the number of districts was large enough even though the three demonstration boards would be sacrificed. The maintenance and repair budget would make possible a scattering of contracts to minority-group companies.

Many thought the interim board would effectively preclude

Mayor Lindsay's further involvement—he was very unpopular in many quarters of the city. He was blamed for both of the teacher strikes (1967 and 1968) as well as for tardy snow removal, an outbreak of anti-Semitism, and other ills of the city. Marchi won the Republican nomination for mayor and Lindsay's re-election in November 1969 was due not to his handling of the schools but to widespread dismay at the conservatism of the two major party nominees. In summary, the school issue and strife over the decentralization remedy almost aborted the political career of John V. Lindsay. An unusually generous three-year teacher contract negotiated in the summer may have helped re-establish his credibility as a leader who could do something for the schools without setting off a serious strike.

In the end, the community people presumably won some power over who their local board members might be and over the selection of community superintendents and, within limits, the principal. Both categories of personnel must be properly certified under the statute. The chancellor would nevertheless retain extensive powers to veto budgets, change community school district lines, and approve the overall textbook lists. A central board would hire the chancellor, could veto his decisions on courses, budgets, sites, and might serve as an appeal board. But, by and large, the chancellor could become quite powerful while the mayor receded in importance. The community regained some of the powers lost in the 1890's, including the power to shape personnel decisions.

How well did decentralization work in New York City? Opinions differed sharply. A study by the Institute for Community Studies at Queens College criticized the plan, the community school board elections, and the underrepresentation of black and Puerto Rican minorities that resulted from the low voter turnout.[19] Critics also felt that the community school boards lacked sufficient authority, including control over the senior high schools and the power to hire and fire *all* educators in the district, not just the community school district superintendent.

On the other hand, a review of the first year's operations showed that the boards were not only working on their own severe problems separately but were able to coalesce on city-wide financing issues. Furthermore, some of the boards were approving experimental programs, sponsoring in-service education pro-

grams, and effectively insisting that central office staff consult
with them on key decisions.[20]

In truth, citizen participation had increased in such a way as
to attract support from the state as well as from educators. The
Fleischman Commission (a state study of the cost, quality, and
financing of education) in 1973 recommended further strengthening of the community school boards. New York City had overcome most of the fears and concerns voiced by the coalition of established city-wide education groups and the organized school
employees. Some of the important decisions about school programs and staff leadership had been turned over to community
school boards.

The meaningfulness of this transfer of power ought not to
be exaggerated. The "communities" affected included from 20,-
000 to 35,000 school children. Several districts included three or
more racial and ethnic groups and ten or more distinct neighborhoods. Board members could hardly represent each block or village within the whole. The main outcome was the reduction of
the need for community groups to travel to 110 Livingston
Street, Brooklyn, to air any or all complaints. Instead, thirty-one
other arenas for conflict resolution shared the growing load of
dealing with community frustrations about the schools. The new
boards offered additional outlets both for testing ideas and ab-
sorbing hostility and for more immediate action by policy-makers
who if not fully responsible by statute increasingly seized the informal power to shape central school headquarters decisions.

Meanwhile, the New York State Board of Regents in late
1971 offered another alternative—the abolition of the central
board and appointment of a city education commissioner by the
mayor.[21] In place of the board the commissioner would have an
advisory council composed of community school board representatives. The immediate reaction of parents and traditional public
education groups to the proposal was adverse.

Former New York City Board Chairman Max J. Rubin was
the principal architect of the Regent's proposal. Although it
provided for reduced citizen participation at the city-wide level,
it honored and potentially strengthened the community boards
at the city level and created for education a structure parallel to
other city departments.

New York City in the 1960's and early 1970's was the laboratory for urban school reform, the hot house of experiments—of teacher militancy, community control, educational accountability —that leaders in other cities watched closely. For the successful or even popular developments spread to other cities within five years. If an idea, such as the Ocean Hill–Brownsville demonstration failed or caused excessive turmoil, other cities shied away from it. But the community school district plan appeared to work, which meant the next frontier was whether to cut the powers of, or simply abolish, the central city school board.

DECENTRALIZATION IN DETROIT

New York was not the only city to experiment with community control. Washington, D.C. was the next most popular testing ground, with major community controlled schools in the Adams–Morgan district and in Anacostia. Tensions in that city rose so high that a reluctant Congress, whose Committee on District Affairs is largely southern and conservative, authorized an elected school board in 1968. Nevertheless, the community schools and their staffs experienced great difficulty in breaking free from bureaucratic constraints and in securing and holding the necessary personnel.

Other cities tended to push ahead on the "decentralization front." Of these, the most determined was Detroit, where in March 1967 Superintendent Norman Drachler proposed a network of nine regions each staffed by a regional superintendent and two assistants.[22] Their responsibilities included staff supervision, community relations, and monitoring of maintenance and school requisitions. Budgeting and staff selection responsibilities were not included at that point although the superintendent was willing to upgrade further what had been titled field executives, each working in a region of more than 30,000 students. In 1969, they were retitled deputy superintendents.

Detroit's superintendent earlier worked as deputy superintendent for community relations and therefore placed a high priority on improved communications. He also responded to a serious high school walkout and to pressures both from the N.E.A. and A.F.T. to add staff to handle school–community conflict. Detroit in 1969 hired a black deputy superintendent for labor relations and personnel who arranged informally for community screening of eligible principals for certain districts, increasing the number of non-white principals ten-fold to fifty.

Nevertheless, the National Association for the Advancement of Colored People proposed community control as a substitute for a centralized city board. State Senator Coleman Young met with board spokesmen and union leaders to work out a moderate decentralization plan with advisory boards. Young's proposal passed the Michigan legislature in July 1969.[23]

The central board retained responsibility for general finance and construction grants, union contracts, payrolls, and school maintenance. Each regional board could hire a superintendent from a list proposed by the central board, could spend funds apportioned by the central board, and conduct pupil-testing programs. These boards could also develop and try new curricula and allocate the use of school facilities to community groups.

One reason the bill passed, in addition to the threat of complete dissolution, was legislative guarantee of teacher seniority rights, tenure, and the right of unions to bargain with the central board, along with retention of existing benefits.

Michigan at the time was also considering full state support of public education, a related issue of concern to those worried about equalizing educational opportunities between communities. The total package of union guarantees, greater community involvement, and expansion of the central board to include spokesmen for regional boards extended to the more recent minorities an opportunity to translate criticism into policy.

The 1969 plan blended the old solution of city-wide representation with regional representation, with the latter holding a majority. The size of the augmented board reversed the trend toward smaller city boards.

The *New York Times* quoted criticism by Detroit's lone Republican state representative, "It will not solve problems but create them. It will compound confusion by making multiple bureaucracy out of the one bureaucracy we have now." [24]

Actually, the greater concern was whether decentralization would increase racial isolation or could be arranged in such a fashion as to maximize integration. The board held hearings and in 1970 drew district lines which would both decentralize and integrate the Detroit schools. When the plan leaked to the press, angry white parents boycotted the schools and moved to recall the board members.

The 1970 Michigan legislature threatened to repeal the decentralization law, but instead passed a new one with eight regional school districts, each governed by a five-man elective board. The highest vote-getter in each district would become chairman as well as a member of the central school board. Eight regional chairman and five at-large members would make up the Detroit board of education.

Meanwhile, the recall campaign continued and in August 1970 the integrationist members were recalled. A school boundary commission created by the governor simultaneously laid out four white-controlled and four black-controlled regions. Then a new school board was elected, with ten white and three black members.

Superintendent Drachler resigned early in 1971 rather than continue under the new board.[25] A Detroit education editor reported a loss of black interest in decentralization and the virtual end of central board willingness to implement an integration plan.

One component of both Detroit plans was the recognition of employee rights and provision for the election of regional superintendents from an authorized list. Presumably these key features separate decentralization from the excesses of nineteenth century ward politics of the "Great Cities." Sub-committees will regain some of the authority previously forfeited, but the freedom to select teachers, principals, and superintendents will be safeguarded by the contract and by central certification of eligible superintendents. Regional school boards were granted power to hire, assign, and promote and dismiss teachers but with the right of appeal to the central board which would "overrule, modify or affirm" a regional district decision.

On the other hand, the Detroit plan in reality appeared to reduce black influence in education matters. The liberal board was replaced by a thirteen-member board that doubted not only the value of integration but some members also questioned the idea of decentralization. Much of their conservatism grew out of the earlier community blacklash against compulsory busing of whites to black schools.[26]

Thus the Detroit experience, although more daring and sweeping a plan than New York's, seemed to create as great a conflict and in the end undermined public confidence in the school system. Minorities actually found themselves with less influence. The experiment was painful for most of the participants to the extent that the new board sought mainly to reduce the liklihood of future conflict as well as to resist efforts to integrate the schools by compulsory cross-busing of students.

Elsewhere in the nation city leaders watched the New York and Detroit experiments with great interest and considerable concern about the stability of the city school systems. Parallel efforts to decentralize other school systems seem limited and bureaucratized in comparison.

DECENTRALIZATION IN OTHER MAJOR CITIES

Gittell and Hollander examined four school board decentralization arrangements other than that of New York and rated St. Louis high on certain factors, such as the power to appoint principals.[27] St. Louis district superintendents can nominate any person on an eligible list (regardless of position). Three subject area supervisors assist each district superintendent. Although one district superintendent has control over federal funds for the highly publicized Banneker Community Project, district superintendents otherwise exert little control over city school budgets.

Chicago has twenty-eight district superintendents with local advisory boards. Superintendent Benjamin Willis initially appointed the district superintendents. During 1959, some authority to adjust the curriculum and endorse budgetary requests was offered the district superintendents, but Gittell reported only minimal acceptance of the responsibility.[28] James Redmond, successor to Willis, explained "the district superintendents could not humanize their community relationships with an organizational chart that had no comprehension of their individual needs." [29]

Redmond followed recommendations of a consulting firm and appointed three area associate superintendents, each to use the district superintendents as either a community leader or specialist. He felt "multiple boards of education" not necessary but wanted "community involvement" through councils which could advise on problems within each district.

Philadelphia in 1967 had nine district superintendents but with few duties other than general surveillance and problem-solving. A survey team led Professor William Odell of Stanford recommended two more districts to make each district embrace approximately 20,000 students. Superintendent Mark Shedd in 1968–1969 increased the powers and staff of the district superintendents to whom principals subsequently would report.

In Baltimore, seven area directors supervise the elementary schools and two the secondary schools, but each under a central office superintendent. Curriculum specialists are divided into areas but maintain an office at city school headquarters.

Boston in 1966 appointed area superintendents with offices in various sections of the city but no staff other than a secretary. Principals continued to be selected from a central list of eligibles and reported to an associate superintendent either for elementary, junior high, or senior high schools. Area superintendents worked under the deputy superintendent. In 1968, two junior high schools formed an advisory council and with the help of a federal grant hired a director and other staff. The words "community control" were carefully deleted from a model cities application in 1968, but a 1969 model cities board request for recognition as a seventh district with its own superintendent never won much support, although a black area superintendent was named in 1970.

Other than New York and Detroit, the examples simply show some recognition of the ferment in each major city which requires ultimately some consideration of greater parental involvement in personnel selection, budgetary decisions, and curriculum evaluation. Most of the requests flow from the articulate black leadership with some support from white boards and occasionally from foes of school integration. Many of the new leaders come from the ranks of civil rights spokesmen, poverty council representatives, and now of model cities staff and board members.[30] They reflect the rising tide of dissatisfaction not only with the old buildings and curriculum but most of all with the remoteness of many appointive boards and the defensiveness of many elective boards.

A CRITIQUE OF CITY SCHOOL
DECENTRALIZATION PLANS

One of the greatest flaws in decentralization proposals to date is the lack of coordination or even "coterminality" of districts for interrelated social services. The isolation of bureaus draws criticism from both advocates and critics of decentralization.

For example, Paul Goodman, who urges much smaller schools, calls attention to the "new evils" so often created by decisions in the sphere of public life:

. . . housing, slum clearance, location of industries, adequate schools and teachers, transportation, clean streets, traffic control, social work, racial harmony, master planning, recreation . . . the solution of this or that isolated problem inevitably leads to disruption elsewhere. Escape thoroughfares must aggravate central traffic. Slum clearance as an isolated policy must aggravate class stratification and delinquency. New subways aggravate concentration. "Housing" makes for double-shift and overcrowded classrooms. No master plan guarantees foolishness like the Lincoln Square project. These consequent evils produce new evils among them.[31]

Daniel Bell uses the case of New York City to display the "crazy quilt" nature of community systems, "sixty-two planning districts, twenty-five community corporations, thirty-five urban renewal areas, three Model Cities projects, thirty health districts, seventy-six police precincts, thirty school districts, twenty-two urban action park forces, five neighborhood city halls, fifty-eight sanitation districts, fifteen fire department divisions, forty-two welfare centers . . . etc." [32] He argues that the attempt of each institution to define community places new conflicts on their respective agencies. He warns that in a completely open community system little or no expansion or change would be allowed by residents.

The flaw is quite serious and potentially fatal to the survival of cities. This particular problem also stems from the successful drive for total independence of schools from not only "political" but all other governmental functions. The example cited above suggests that educators may have won an impressive battle or series of battles with politicians and public administrators. But schools thereby cut themselves off from the larger wars on poverty, blight, malnutrition, ill-health, and social disorganization, problems which are at the very root of the alleged failures of urban schools. The same children, with some guarantee of family stability and personal health, presumably might learn what is taught in school. This is not to question the utility of radical reform of curriculum, for much of the curriculum could benefit from drastic revisions.[33]

This does not imply that organizations and services are coordinated when a school system is centralized. Before decentralization in New York City, the board of education was particularly isolated and resistant to inter-agency coordination. Theoretically, it might be easier to coordinate the delivery of many social services in the schools if the system were decentralized; then, outside agencies would not risk being lost in the bureaucracy of a central office. Coordination among agencies is never assured in any city without organized attempts to foster it.

Another great problem is that of defining community, an extremely difficult task in highly mobile and diversified urban settings. In setting up a new system of community boards, the 1969–1970 New York City interim board of education re-discovered the great difficulty of accomodating often contradictory criteria such as:

· Common and special educational needs of the communities
  and children involved.
· Convenient location and geographic continuity,
· Heterogeneity of pupil population, etc.[34]

Still another problem is that of racial or religious discord, especially white–black hostility and the phenomenon of anti-Semitism. The teachers union in New York City has been accused of publicizing excessively the anti-Semitic, anti-teacher sentiments by community control advocates. Yet evidence exists to show that Jewish principals were victims of anti-Semitic attacks at I.S. 201, Ocean Hill–Brownsville, and elsewhere. Black nationalism and separatism, although repudiated by most minority leaders, forced white teachers and legislators to worry about reverse racism. The anti-Semitic comments hurled at teachers were used to generate opposition to the Bundy and Lindsay plans and reinforced the teachers' intent to eliminate the Lindsay board and the three demonstration districts.[35] In fact, complaints about anti-Semitism were used to neutralize Jewish liberal support for black community controlled schools.

Some observers discount the relevance of bringing scare terms like "separatism" or "anti-Semitism" into the discussion of school decentralization. Others warn about community control that, "No more perfect script for perpetual conflict can be imagined. . . . Anyone who thinks that this majority [white-middle and lower-income] will cheerfully pay taxes so that black nationalist (with its inevitable racist overtones) can be taught in ghetto schools is being unworldly, to put it mildly." [36] Actually, the Ocean Hill–Brownsville demonstration board hired many white Jewish teachers to replace those who had walked out. Anti-Semitism is a genuine issue but opponents of decentralization thoroughly exploited the issue and in fact increased the supply of anti-Semitic propaganda just to prove a case. Supporters of decentralization feel such a specter is unlikely and point to the current problem of white racism as a greater evil, as documented in the Kerner report and elsewhere.

Other very real issues raised by analysts of the "community revolution" include:

1. The balance between selecting educators on the basis of "merit" or professional competence versus the considerations of his race or ethnicity and that of the clientele of a community (Should black children have a black, male principal?); [37]
2. The balance of parents and other community leaders (non-parents) on either a governing or advisory board (Who speaks for a community and its aspirations?);
3. The extent either of teacher participation on a board in choosing a principal or the curriculum versus the extension to teachers of local bargaining rights on matters at the school level (the school schedule, school discipline policies, materials, use of specialists and consultants, the budget, etc.).[38]

Several of the New York City and Washington, D.C. experiments emphasized the necessity of hiring a black male principal and of placing teachers and students on the community boards. In the excitement of launching a new school, serious questions about conflicts between those potentially conflicting roles may be postponed (e.g., Can one teacher serving on a school board participate in the decision to fire another? Under what conditions could a student hire a teacher or expel a fellow student?). Of course the moments of awkward conflict might be few indeed at other than the time for personnel evaluation. Adults, and professionals, need not be in perpetual conflict over providing what children need. The concept of a faculty–student–parent council or coalition may have more to recommend it despite the blurring of conventional notions about "who's in charge of whom?"

One disturbing question is whether community control will inhibit the immediate press for school integration, advocates dividing on whether it freezes the status quo or acts as an interim alternative. Integrationists worry about schemes which would perpetuate either *de facto* segregation or separatism on the part of any race. But James Farmer, former director of the Congress of Racial Equality, sees the separateness of community control not as a permanent problem but rather a period of racial pride as a prerequisite.

Thus I see decentralization and community control as really being a forerunner to integration; and, in a larger sense, a partner to integration. There really is no contradiction, no paradox in this statement. Control of the schools, an exercise in populist democracy, is essential for developing the self-image and self-respect of the black community. Only after the full flowering of the black self-image and after the elimination of cultural biases from all our institutions, can there be complete integration.[39]

On the other side, the Detroit experience shows that the two objectives may indeed conflict irreconcilably. While critics pointed out flaws, advocates, including Mayor Lindsay, spread the new gospel through such widely disseminated reports as the Kerner Report on Civil Disorders. The Kerner Commission recommendations included decentralizing the school systems of the largest cities to make education more responsive to the community and increase support for schools. Such mechanisms as parent advisory councils were recommended.[40]

The model cities program of HUD, for which 1968 was a major planning year, included a heavy commitment to model neighborhood boards. However, such boards specifically were to include city professionals and the route to federal approval must pass through the office of the mayor. Even with such safeguards, the consultation of city people had become a major tenet of federal public policy by the end of the 1960's.

PROFESSIONALS VERSUS THE PEOPLE?

Ironically, professionals spoke for several sides, for and against, in the campaign to return power to the people. Initially, the ideology and many of the concepts were defined by social scientists and either social welfare professionals or those who prepared them in professional schools.[41] Foundation officials promulgated and financed social and political experiments.[42] Universities and colleges arranged for the proposal-writing, itself a professionalized style of reform, for staffing, and for "evaluating" experiments.[43]

Other professionals, individually and collectively, either opposed or carefully reworked the concepts such as "control" or decentralization to fit the career needs of teachers and supervisors. Most dramatically, the external threat of community dismissal of faculty was sufficient by 1968 to unite two warring factions, the United Federation of Teachers and their managers in the New York City Council of Supervisory Associations. Even the teacher unions supporting community control, the Detroit and Washington, D.C. locals, quietly insisted on preserving most of the tenure and transfer rights previously negotiated with central boards.

Superintendents varied in their response from active encouragement of community control and shared school–community expenses to espousal of very modest steps toward administrative decentralization. Philadelphia and Detroit superintendents Shedd and Drachler were among those willing to transfer line authority to community-selected district superintendents while others agreed with James Redmond that there was no need for multiple boards.

The movement of the 1960's, then, did not resemble the old ward board structures in two important ways:

1. The advocates of community control or participation were so very often social welfare professionals dismayed at their own failures, or those of their colleagues, and of the "system" to adapt social services sufficient to serve the new urban minorities.[44]

2. The nature of the reform called not for substituting of citizen judgment for that of professional in such decisions as teacher recruitment or program development, but mainly for making professional educators accountable for their performance. In blunt terms, this meant professionals would be selected on the basis of their commitment to community aspirations but would be fired if they failed to

make measurable progress toward the agreed on goals. In effect this was a heightening rather than a dimunition of professionalism as a service-oriented, idealistic calling.

Of these two points, the second caused the most confusion, for not always could community spokesmen make clear in advance the conditions under which professionals might be asked to leave. This was a reason for teacher dismay at the absence, then the vagueness, of charges against teachers released from service at Ocean Hill–Brownsville in 1968. The questions of "due process" and safeguards of civil liberties educators will henceforth require relatively specific answers in the form of performance specifications. If parents can obtain greater "accountability" in the form of the right to penalize educators for failing to educate, then teachers will call for relatively objective criteria established in advance along with provision for the review of appeals of those fired for less than adequate performance.

To the most alienated and frustrated blacks, however, any objections about due process or technical complexity of evaluation smacked of racism and treachery. "Our children's minds are brain washed and white washed; in order to survive we must control the institutions which cope with the larger world," such was the rhetoric of the minority leader despairing of equity in a culture dominated by Caucasians.

THE EFFECT OF DECENTRALIZATION PLANS

What emerged in most big-city school decentralization plans, then, was a degree of transfer of authority over such decisions as curriculum, personnel, and some budgetary and business decisions to professionals on an administrative level nearer the school or neighborhood—with or without an advisory board. Community control was a concept with many meanings, varying from citizen participation in selecting a principal or district superintendent (from lists of certified professionals) to complete transfer of program development and financial decision-making to laymen.

One of the greatest problems with the community control movement was the tensions generated among those who now hold teaching and administrative positions. Educators sense that certain kinds of community control—e.g., by spokesmen for those other than public school parents—could distort the work of the schools. Parochial school parents or leaders of other social agencies could seize control of the schools in apathetic, low-voter-turnout neighborhoods. The Ocean Hill–Brownsville parents complained about the activity of a New York State legislator who saw in the schools a chance to extend his power and influence. Thus, community control may on the one hand mean increased participation and school system responsiveness. On the other hand, it can bring new kinds of coerciveness, confusion, and competition for the right to staff the schools. The movement generated new fears that the positions of educators might be seen as prizes to be distributed by local potentates rather than as professional posts allocated by cosmopolitan criteria and candidate qualifications.

The problem grows more complicated when one acknowledges the label "semi-professional" applied to teachers by Etzioni, Lortie, and other sociologists. If it is true that teaching is as much an art as a science, a matter of compassion as much as of technical competence, then objective criteria of evaluation will not suffice. What counts as much as subject-matter knowledge is an understanding of children and a rapport with the values of a minority group or community. Thus one can argue for the selection of teachers and principals not by impersonal "professional" criteria alone but by subjective criteria, too, such as whether they identify with the aspirations of a community or can empathize with its history, culture, and ideologies.

What makes this difficult is that values within an ethnic or religious group not only differ but may be at odds with larger national or societal goals—such as to pay allegiance to the U.S. government or learn to work together with all races. The state, therefore, will reserve its right to restrain any community control scheme which jeopardizes the rights of others or subverts support of major governmental policies. In the end the issue, then, is not simply professionals versus laymen, but a question of determining the extent to which ethnic or racial group values can be honored in a school system which tries to "Americanize" its young.

The other important issue is whether teaching and teachers can become more effective through additional "professionalization"—i.e., more and better training in diagnosing learning difficulties, in instructional planning and methodology; and in teacher supervision. Black communities, growing impatient with teachers who seem unable to teach their children, advocate greater use of indigenous community persons as teacher aides. Although several aide programs are called "career opportunity programs" and lead eventually to a degree and certificates, the use of aides in classrooms helps to "deprofessionalize" the school at least in the short run. Education might learn from the medical profession that the use of aides can actually abet professionalism while creating within a profession new problems of status, communication, personal development, and career mobility. One basic problem is the current under-professionalism and inadequate training of most of the teachers and supervisors in urban schools.

The pressure for more popular participation was in many ways part of a general reaction against central authority, remote boards, and out-of-date bureaucracies. Dissatisfaction was articulated by a new coalition of reform-oriented professionals, leaders of minority groups relatively new to the city, and the idealistic and critical college graduates of the "baby boom" era. The latter group questioned both the integrity and utility of virtually all social institutions; the public schools fell considerably short in their response to the openly declared "war on poverty." Thus, both the existing leadership and structures were seen as ineffective, of "failing," and in need of radical revision. The logical remedy for an over-centralized structure seemed to be a decentralized structure staffed by "new breed" professionals who would make the system work for poor people. Also, the career ladder for such professions as education must be open to the poor, but mainly so that new groups could aspire to jobs and develop careers as professionals.[45] Central boards might be stripped of powers but the profession would simply be made more open and more honest and ultimately more accountable. Professionalism would be purified but not repealed.

Would these changes suffice? Many felt city school systems could not survive without either metropolitan support or much heavier state and federal aid. Some wondered about the negative impact on integration planning; others felt integration was virtually hopeless given the mood of white parents in easy range of the ghettos. Still others felt that the public schools had outlived their usefulness and that, as the automobile replaced the horse carriage or the airplane diminished the need for passenger trains, that alternatives to the public schools must be encouraged. But these options suggest more fundamental changes in the governance and administration of urban education, and so deserve analysis in the closing chapter.

NOTES

1. Robert Crain *et al., The Politics of School Desegregation* (Chicago: Aldine, 1968), pp. 138–141.

2. Excellent accounts of the I.S. 201 struggle are found in Dorothy S. Jones, "The Issues at I.S. 201: A View From the Parents' Committee," *Integrated Education,* vol. IV, no. 5 (October–November 1966), and in Preston Wilcox, "The Controversy Over I.S. 201: One View and a Proposal," *Urban Review,* vol. IV (July 1966).

3. *110 Livingston Street: Politics and Bureaucracy in the New York City School System* (New York: Random House, 1968), p. 367.

4. *Ibid.,* p. 368.

5. Toye Brown Lewis, "Community Control of Schools Is Necessary for Survival," *Survival,* vol. 1, no. 2 (Boston: New Urban League, October 1969).

6. Daniel Bell and Virginia Held, "The Community Revolution," *The Public Interest,* no. 16 (Summer 1969), p. 148.

7. *Ibid.,* p. 149.

8. Daniel Patrick Moynihan, *Maximum Feasible Misunderstanding* (New York: The Free Press, 1969).

9. Wilcox, *op. cit.*

10. Womens' City Club of New York, *Strengthen or Abolish? A Study of Local School Boards in New York City* (New York: March 1960); and the sequel, *Performance or Promise: New York City's Local School Boards Revisited* (New York: May 1966). An exception in the late 1940's and early 1950's was the Bronx Park Community School experiment under District Superintendent Joseph Loretan, summarized in John W. Polley *et al., Community Action for Education* (New York: Bureau of Publications, Teachers College, Columbia University, 1953).

11. Rogers, *op. cit.,* pp. 370–384. See also the discussion of the frustration of one local board member in Martin Mayer, "What's Wrong with Our Big City Schools," *The Saturday Evening Post* (September 9, 1967), pp. 21–22.

12. Marilyn Gittell, *Participants and Participation* (New York: Center for Urban Education, 1967), p. 61.

13. *Reconnection for Learning: A Community School System for New York City,* Report of the Mayor's Advisory Panel on Decentralization of the New York City Schools (New York City, 1967).

14. Michael Harrington, "An Open Letter to Men of Good Will . . . " *The New York Review of Books* (January 2, 1969), p. 41.

15. For one account, see Martin Mayer, *The Teacher's Strike, New York, 1968,* New York: Harper & Row, 1969), and the documents and commentary in Marilyn Gittell and Maurice Berube (eds.), *Confrontation at Ocean Hill–Brownsville* (New York: Praeger, 1969).

16. *Plan for Development of a Community School District System for the City of New York* (Brooklyn: Board of Education, January 27, 1969).

17. The local board powers enumerated in the Marchi Bill were indeed limited. However, the language of the bill was so vague that it actually gave local boards broad powers, if they wanted to assume them.

18. The New York *Times,* May 1, 1969, vol. CXVIII, pp. 1, 39.

19. Boulton H. Demas, *The School Elections, A Critique of the 1969 New York City Schools Decentralization* (New York: Institute for Community Studies, Queens College, 1971). See also the Marilyn Gittell critique in Annette T. Rubinstein (ed.), *Schools Against Children* (New York: Monthly Review Press, 1970), pp. 262–266.

20. Joseph M. Cronin, Laurence Iannaccone, Donald M. Levine, and Peter P. Horoschak, *Organizing and Governing Public Education in New York* (Cambridge, Massachusetts: The Fleischmann Commission, 1971).

21. The New York *Times,* October 30, 1971, vol. CXXI, pp. 1, 28.

22. Marilyn Gittell and T. Edward Hollander, *Six Urban School Districts* (New York: Praeger, 1968), p. 67. In 1956, nine regional executives were appointed. In 1966, an official of the Detroit NAACP was named deputy superintendent for community relations. (p. 148).

23. The Detroit board of education was authorized to establish between 7 and 11 districts by January 30, 1970. Voters in each district would select a 9-member regional board in the 1970 general election. The 7-member at-large board would then be enlarged by 1 delegate from each regional board. Act no. 244, State of Michigan, 1969.

24. The New York *Times,* July 1969, vol. CXIX, p. 1.

25. William R. Grant, "Community Control vs. School Integration: The Case of Detroit," *The Public Interest,* no. 24 (Summer 1971), pp. 62–79.

26. *Ibid.,* p. 78.

27. Gittell and Hollander, *op. cit.,* pp. 68–69.

28. *Ibid.,* pp. 66–67.

29. On Chicago in Carroll F. Johnson and Michael D. Usdan (eds.), *Decentralization and Racial Integration* (New York: Teachers College, Columbia University, 1968), p. 167 (see also pp. 153–171).

30. Many of the community control advocates are eloquent and well informed. Many are strident, some are opportunistic, and at least a few are psychotic. See the vivid account of New York City board of education hearings by William F. Haddad in the *Manhattan Tribune* (February 18, 1969), reprinted in *The Public Interest*, no. 16 (Summer 1969), pp. 178–179.

31. Paul Goodman, *Growing Up Absurd* (New York: Random House, 1956), p. 77 (Vintage Book edition), and earlier in *Communitas*, Appendix D.

32. Bell and Held, *op. cit.*, p. 169.

33. See Goodman's other works on education for some provocative ideas and the writing of John Holt, Herbert Kohl, Terry Borton, and others who have prepared persuasive rationales for major changes in urban school curriculum and pupil motivation. See also Robert Havighurst, "Requirement for a Valid 'New Criticism,'" *Phi Delta Kappan*, vol. XL, no. 1 (September 1968), pp. 20–26, for a critique of the critics.

34. Proposed Plan for a Community School District System in New York City, Board of Education legal advertisement of a tentative districting plan (November 19, 1969).

35. Documentation can be found in Leo Blond, "Black Anti-Semitism in New York City," *Phi Delta Kappan*, vol. L., no. 3 (November 1968) pp. 176–177. And examples in 1967 are mentioned by Daniel P. Moynihan, *op. cit.*, pp. 116–117.

36. Irving Kristol and Paul Weaver, "Who Knows New York? Notes on a Mixed-up City," *The Public Interest*, no. 16 (Summer 1969), p. 54.

37. The issue goes even deeper, for what may be needed is a more precise definition of concepts like "merit" and "professional competence." Often, there is little relationship between the formal qualifications for a position and the skills and characteristics that are actually necessary to do an effective job. Perhaps "competence" as a principal in a ghetto school must be partly defined as being a man or woman who understands the needs and problems of the community.

38. This issue is argued by Arthur E. Sale, "Policy Making under Decentralization: The Role of Collective Bargaining at the Local Level," *The Urban Review*, vol. 3, no. 6 (June 1969) p. 34. Teachers would negotiate certain policies and procedures with the local board as well as with the central board, which sets salaries and general conditions of work.

39. James Farmer, "Some Views on the Relationships Between Decentralization and Racial Integration in Large City School Systems," in Johnson and Usdan (eds.), *op. cit.*, pp. 186–187.

40. *Report of the National Advisory Commission on Civil Disorders* (New York: Bantam, 1968), p. 451. In 1968 the U.S. Office of Edu-

cation invested $12 million in a "central cities task force" to allow greater citizen participation in inner-city school project development.

41. The Columbia University School of Social Work and many of its faculty were in the forefront—Richard Cloward, Francis Piven, Preston Wilcox, and several others.

42. Most visibly, the Ford Foundation supported the efforts with top leadership of the Bundy Panel and the funds for planning and development. Other city foundations—Taconic, Field, etc.—helped with studies and special projects.

43. Marilyn Gittell at the Institute for Community Studies, Queens College, was especially active. Staff members at Teacher's College, Columbia, and N.Y.U. and the Center for Urban Education were supporters. The Harvard Graduate School of Education convened a late 1967 session on "Subsystems" and otherwise tried to facilitate communications between staffs of a variety of decentralization projects.

44. Moynihan documents this phenomenon first in *The Public Interest* (Fall 1965), "The Professionalization of Reform" and later in *Maximum Feasible Misunderstanding.* Even the "citizens" groups were heavy with health, education, and welfare professionals interspersed with journalists, clergy, and some elected officials. Half of the 100 members of the Emergency Citizens Committee to Save School Decentralization and Community Control were professors or doctors on the staffs of universities, clinics, or diverse social service centers. Fifteen others represented the clergy. Advertisement "Three Strikes—and the Children Are Out," The New York *Times,* Friday, October 15, 1968, vol. CXVIII, pp. 1, 38.

45. One of the more acceptable reconciliations of the tension between professionals and the poor was that devised by Frank Riessman and associates at N.Y.U. A proposal for "new careers for the poor" and new career ladders starting as a school aide and leading ultimately to teacher status was attractive to minority groups and especially to the federal government, which tied the concept to as many federal programs as possible under the Elementary and Secondary Education Act (1965) and Education Professions Development Act (1968).

CHAPTER

* * * * * *IX* * * * *

CONTEMPORARY PROPOSALS
FOR REFORM

NOT SINCE THE DAYS of Jacob Riis and Joseph Mayer Rice did as much criticism of city school systems break into print as in the 1960's. "Our Children are Dying" and "Death at an Early Age" were two of the more pessimistic accounts of the shortcomings of urban education in New York City and Boston.[1]

But school board members themselves were speaking once again with unaccustomed candor about the frustrations inherent in the status quo, especially Joseph Pois on the Chicago board, and Martin Mayer's several articles and books based in part on his service as a district board member in New York City. Detroit Board President A.L. Zwerdling strongly advocated city and suburban school district reorganization to achieve racial integration in the Detroit metropolitan area.[2]

Critics could not agree on the remedies for the maladies of city school systems. Some wanted to try to reorganize urban education in cautious stages, some urged drastic reform immediately, and others repudiated city school systems as hopelessly intransigent and began a search for urban educational alternatives.

The reorganizers can agree to decentralize the decision-making on crucial questions but want to retain central control over finance, construction, evaluation, and staff negotiations. The central board would remain strong; schools or neighborhoods would speak through advisory groups or councils.

Reformers fell into two competing camps—those who wanted community control (essentially smaller units with considerable citizen veto power over personnel, curriculum, and contracts) and those who wanted larger units such as metropolitan school districts, especially for finance but also for planning for school integration and other purposes. The two approaches in many ways represent very different directions although some savants see possible combinations which could be compatible.

The middle road is called the Federation model or "two-tier" system of school governance, schemes which work reasonably well in Ontario and in England. Proponents of a middle way in the United States include economist Charles Benson and a group of education and political science professors at Ohio State University.[3]

Radical critics—and some reactionary voices—call for alternatives to the public schools. Conservative economist Milton Friedman urged the free market mechanism whereby parents could cash in a tuition voucher at the school of their choice. His ideas have been reworked by Theodore Sizer and others who see in the idea a chance to make schools compete for the vouchers of the poor as colleges did for war veterans in the late 1940's. Although Friedman would presumably bestow vouchers of equal worth on all, the Sizer proposal introduced a factor which enlarged the size of the tuition grant the lower the family income of the child. New-Left radicals saw the voucher plan as a chance to break the stranglehold of bureaucratic professionals. Meanwhile, separatists wanted separate schools to avoid racial integration.

This final chapter will examine the degree to which citizens in the fourteen cities seem either satisfied or outraged at existing structures. The existing evidence on the effectiveness of appointed and elective boards then warrants attention. Thus, each major proposal for reform requires analysis with concluding comments on both the likely and necessary kinds of urban school reform ahead.

LATTER-DAY ATTEMPTS TO CHANGE
CITY SCHOOL BOARDS

Racial strife, teacher miitancy, student rebellion—each brings city schools into first the newspapers, then the journals, then the books on urban education and politics. The New York City battles over education attract interest in the other great cities; such phenomena as boycotts for school integration and strikes to win teachers negotiation rights tend to appear first in Gotham and then work their way west and south.[4]

Each city since 1945 has felt some turbulence, usually over the issues of race and teacher rights. But how typical was the recent wave of school board changes in New York City? Which groups want to change the boards, and how basic are the changes sought? What changes were won at the ballot box and by what kinds of individuals? What alternatives do those who live in cities propose? First the appointive, then the elective boards will pass in review.

THE APPOINTIVE BOARDS

Baltimore

For many decades following World War I the Public School Association of Baltimore battled to prevent political opportunists from exploiting the public schools. Especially under the long-term leadership of Mrs. William Bauernschmidt, the group's executive secretary, the interest of citizens was mobilized against the unprofessional conduct or incompetence of superintendents, several of whom were forced to resign because of complaints brought to the board by this group.[5] This active "watch dog" group has been instrumental in supporting the selection of a series of competent superintendents and the maintenance of a nonpolitical aura for the Baltimore public schools.

All three major religious groups have at least one member on the nine-man Board of School Commissioners. Administrators from three higher education facilities—Johns Hopkins, University of Maryland, and Morgan State College—fill three other seats. Crain points out that the Baltimore civic and business elite provides one of their more prominent members to serve as presidents.[6]

Thus, the Baltimore board moved very swiftly in 1954 to eliminate de facto segregation. But Baltimore schools in the next twelve years grew much more rapidly than the new building program. Despite a strong bid by the Baltimore N.E.A. unit, which applied "sanctions" to dramatize the aged buildings and overcrowding, the A.F.T. won a teacher bargaining election in May 1967.

Outsiders disagree on the performance of the Baltimore

board; Crain labels the leadership as liberal as any major city school board, more so than one might expect of a border state, while Gittell reports it is considered conservative. Of course, Gittell and Hollander also report that the new mayor in 1967 expressed frustration and "a conviction that he must remain detached" while Robert Bendiner quotes Mayor D'Alessandro directly, "I believe that as Mayor it is my responsibility to provide leadership in education as well as in other essential areas." Thus, he pledged the support of city hall to improve the schools.[7]

Baltimore, by 1970, had appointed two black members to the board one of whom Crain termed "an outspoken militant on civil rights issues." As early as 1965, the board abolished local district lines, provided school buses, and actively pursued an integration policy. In 1971 Baltimore followed the lead of Oakland, California, and Washington, D.C. in appointing its first black superintendent of schools.

Other than a 1964 citizens' committee study, little community participation characterizes the Baltimore school scene; the administration is quite centralized.

In 1969–1970, the Baltimore school leaders prepared plans from ten to twelve decentralized districts but not necessarily with community control as a component. Washington, D.C., forty miles to the south, had already experimented with several types of community control while Baltimore waited to see what would happen.

Buffalo

The mayor and common council of Buffalo retained close financial control over school operating expenditures and bond issues despite complaints that began with the 1915 investigation and which were echoed in a 1951 survey, once again directed by New York State education officials. The survey report emphasized the need in Buffalo "for a revival of faith in the public schools, (and) for the active participation of all groups in improving their services."[8] The revival of public concern was deemed of such importance that it was labeled the "chief need" for Buffalo and was accorded highest priority in the list of recommendations.

As a corollary to this recommendation, the survey staff urged

the formation of a citizens' committee to serve as an advisory
committee to the mayor in recommending candidates for membership on the board of education, a committee that should be
nonpartisan in character and might include members of such
groups as industry, labor, business, parents and teachers, social
agencies and the like." [9] This proposal was clearly along the lines
of the Jesse Newlon–Chicago model. Public support was not extensive, however, and the recommendation slowly died.

Polish, Italian, and Irish voting blocs in Buffalo exert
enough influence on the mayor to guarantee two board members
each from the former and usually one each from the latter two.
During the late 1950's the growing black population, with support from labor unions, forced a 1962 expansion of the board
from five to seven members, one seat belonging to organized
labor.[10] Again, the board includes members from each of the
three major religions and one black member.

Buffalo, as a city, has declined steadily as an economic center
since the depression. Despite state aid of more than 50 percent
and a liberal superintendent of schools, many of the school
buildings are old and over-crowded. One recent mayor recruited
most board appointees from the circle of his immediate friends
and supporters.[11] Robert Bendiner elicited from a state judge
severe criticism of "the very poor method and pattern of pick-
ing people for the Board of Education. The members of the
board should be the strongest, the most notable, the most outstanding—the most feared, if you will—people in the community. . . ." [12] The judge thought that with few exceptions that
had not been the case. The black community voiced some concern about the schools and a University of Buffalo team studied
metropolitan solutions to Buffalo area problems but without
bringing about any immediate changes in governance.

Chicago

The Chicago nominating panel, already discussed at length,
has satisfied most citizens in that city and the mayor has accepted
most of its recommendations, in 1967 asking that his own candidate be added to the list.

One board member, Joseph Pois, recorded his insights on
school board decision-making after his departure from the board.
Pois voiced his strong criticism of the way in which the board is

diverted by a plethora of detail concerning the business functions of the board. He bridled at the fact that the superintendent and staff, not the board, conducted district hearings on the budget one year. Pois felt that the board was shielded from policy-making and board meeting time consumed with the discussion of often trivial matters.[13]

Any discussion of Chicago must acknowledge the persistent importance of the mayor and his political machine, which often adjusts to some of the more significant demands for progress. In the end the mayor, not the board, must agree to the financial terms negotiated with the teachers union, and the machine gets out the vote for bond issues. Much energy has gone into trying to liberalize the Democratic party in Chicago rather than to restructure the school board in recent years.[14]

One exception is an effort by the Woodlawn Organization and the University of Chicago to develop a Woodlawn Community Board for urban education projects. At the insistence of T.W.O., community members took one-third of the seats (one-third each to the University and to the Chicago public schools) and later accepted three more yielded by the University. The Chicago board of education retains a veto over W.C.B. decisions but from 1967–1970 advanced their own plan which favored limited community involvement while safeguarding teacher tenure and transfer rights.

New York City

Dissatisfaction with the nominating panel has been voiced by the leaders of religious groups in the city, as noted previously. A 1964 bill restoring to the mayor full control over appointments was passed by the legislature, over the protest of Public Education Association spokesmen, and was killed only by gubernatorial veto. Militant black groups, and some white groups concerned about the school integration proposals, objected to the monopolization of school board member nominations by the selection board and urged consideration of an elective board. Black groups have similarly complained about the Chicago panel method, even to the length of filing suit against that plan of generating nominations.[15]

Mayor Lindsay's response was the appointment of more black and Puerto Rican representatives and of white liberals

known to favor decentralization and community control. A conservative state legislature responded to teacher demands that the
Lindsay board be replaced by borough representatives and that
after 1970 the mayor appoint only two of the seven members; the
mixture of borough election and mayoral appointment was subsequently ruled unconstitutional as a violation of the "one man,
one vote" principle.

Either a five- or seven-man board will preclude the religious
balance that for New York City so long has been a *sine qua non*
of mutual trust. Granted that each borough will have one member, with a seven-man board two of the four huge boroughs will
probably have a second member. It is likely that no group will
be placated for long and that the search both for improved productivity and racial/religious equilibrium may end either in a
nine-man board, a three-man commission, or no board at all,
which latter proposal was advanced by the New York State
Board of Regents in 1971.

Actually, the borough representatives brought to New York
City schools decision-making participation virtually on a full-
time basis of a Puerto Rican, a black, and three whites—two
Jews and a Catholic. The board hired an outsider, Harvey Scrib-
ner of Vermont, as chancellor and managed the school system in
1970 and 1971 better than many critics of the "borough board"
had predicted. In fact, the day of borough elections was postponed and the appointees, by legislative vote but with general
popular approval, were given additional time to make decentralization work and find a new equilibrium for the system as a
whole.

Philadelphia

William Odell, a Stanford University professor, in 1964 led a
Philadelphia survey team into Philadelphia in response to citizen
criticism of the schools.[16] The Citizens Committee on Public Education, the Educational Home Rule Assembly of Philadelphia,
and the Greater Philadelphia Movement all voiced objections to
board selection by judges. The judges secured names of possible
candidates from a variety of sources and groups, most of them informal and private, with county political committee chairmen
endorsing various candidates. The Odell survey team observed
that the problems faced by the board were "as remediable under

the existing board selection plan as by any other that may be adopted." [17] Nevertheless, the city voters wanted a new board and adopted the nominating panel approach on May 18, 1965.

Once established, the new panel was to solicit names from organizations and individuals and then submit three names for each place. Richardson Dilworth, once appointed to the board, tried to control all other appointments but on critical issues barely held a 5–4 majority and retired from the board at the end of 1971. In 1970 and 1971, the board weathered several severe fiscal crises and then in 1972 the new mayor, the former police commissioner and a severe critic of the board, filled several vacancies with less liberal appointees.

Pittsburgh

The Civic Club of Allegheny County supported board member appointments by judges as a guarantee of board and school freedom from political considerations. Organized labor has always been strong in Pittsburgh and union leadership is usually represented on the board of education, as has been a member of each of the major religions and one or more black members.

A former superintendent, Calvin Gross, reorganized the administration in order to decentralize some administrative functions, and his successor, Sidney Marland, encouraged the formation of a Pittsburgh Council for the Public Schools to mobilize support for the city school system.

P.C.P.S. drew upon civic, business, and educational leaders who, although technically independent of the school administrations, helped to pave public opinion for financial support. After Marland stepped down, P.C.P.S. continued and in 1969 offered a plan which would make decentralization "unnecessary and irrelevant to a sound education system." [18] A select commission to study the Pittsburgh school board (chaired by Chatham College President Edward Eddy, a P.C.P.S. leader) proposed these changes:

1. A parents' council for each school,
2. District councils for sections of the city,
3. A thirteen-member board of education (six members appointed, seven members elected by districts).

Neither Pittsburgh nor the legislature moved to alter the size of the school board by the end of 1971.

San Francisco

San Francisco's mayor has long been guided by an informal custom of balancing the three religions (three Protestants, two Catholics, two Jews) and of providing representation for women, organized labor, and since 1961, a Negro on the board. The San Francisco superintendent is quoted by Binzen as supporting the religious "quota" because "it gives our people a feeling of unity," and the fact of the representation ". . . helps develop popular support for the board." [19]

Crain found that the San Francisco board on the question of racial integration was relatively impotent, partly because of the elaborate balancing of members and bi-partisan considerations (Mayor Christopher salted a Democratic board with four Republicans, one a national committeeman). Although San Francisco enjoys a cosmopolitan representation, the board at times reflects a conservative elitism in curriculum and other matters. Superintendent Spears recommended a "color blind" policy in matters of integration but the board subsequently agreed to civil rights demands. [20]

Then in 1971, a federal judge ordered San Francisco to desegregate the schools by busing approximately half of the elementary children in any given grade. The court order angered not only white voters but the substantial Chinese population (18 percent of the city) who resent any challenge to their strong community cohesiveness. A strong majority of San Francisco citizens in November 1971 voted down a major school bond issue and in favor of an elective board. Mayor Joseph Alioto, who was re-elected, voluntarily relinquished his prerogative and in fact told the voters that opting for an elective board was one way they could display unhappiness with the busing decision. [21]

Thus, as in Detroit, the mode of governance was disrupted by a strong move to racially integrate the schools. Again, the strong desire, this time of Oriental parents to maintain community identity, meant a weakening of an elite, in this case, the liberal central board. It was the first major change in San Francisco's board structure since 1921, and one of the rare instances whereby an appointive board gets changed back to elective or

vice versa. Most of all, the change was quite clearly a popular rebellion against authority and a symbolic move to restore the
schools to a majority Anglo–Oriental coalition of parents and
voters.

THE ELECTIVE BOARDS

Boston

George Strayer headed a survey investigation of the Boston
schools in 1944 and recommended at that time that certain community organizations might select nominees from whom the
mayor would make the final selection, a proposal similar to that
advocated about the same time in Chicago. The Boston Finance
Commission, after the Strayer proposal was criticized as being "a
step away from democratic government," proposed that thirteen
electors be chosen by popular vote to choose three nominees for
each vacancy, the mayor to appoint one of the three to the school
committee. The press gave favorable publicity to the proposal,
seeing in it "promise of a nonpolitical school committee" or an
end "to the use of school committee membership" as a "spring-
board to politics." The proposal failed to pass the legislature.[22]

More recently, two political scientists at the M.I.T.–Harvard
Joint Center for Urban Studies, Martin Meyerson and Edward C.
Banfield, proposed once more for Boston the Chicago–New York
nominating panel approach, with appointment of school board
members by the mayor "whose political power a board needs to
have behind it." To assure concern about keeping the schools
"close to the public," Meyerson and Banfield urged the creation
of citizens advisory committees along district lines, as has been
done in other cities.[23]

Since 1960, a group formed around Mrs. Dorothy Bisbee, a
Beacon Hill resident, and called itself the Citizens for Boston
Public Schools. The Citizens for the Boston Public Schools
screened and elected two of the five members in the 1961 and
1963 elections, but has not been able to obtain control of the
board, of whose policies the "citizens" are quite critical.

One member lost in 1965, the other in 1967, as the question
of compliance with a state racial imbalance law temporarily dominated other election issues. Mrs. Bisbee ran again in 1967 and
1969, but unsuccessfully.

The black community turned to other approaches, such as a metropolitan busing program (METCO) and enrollment in private or parochial schools. Three new community schools were established privately and the state sponsored an experimental school with urban and suburban students working together. By 1970, as many as 2,000 black students thus left the system. Federal officials negotiated a $1,500,000 grant for a central cities coalition of community council of parents and teachers at the Roxbury junior high schools and their feeder elementary schools.

During the 1969 campaign the NAACP tried to secure a court order enjoining the election on the grounds that the system did not allow minority representation on the school board, thus denying them of their rights. The request was denied, despite the dissatisfaction, and the legislature in 1970 rejected proposals for substantial community control for model city and other neighborhoods.

During 1970, two groups completed analyses of the existing school government. The mayor's Home Rule Commission recommended a two-fold change:

1. The establishment of fourteen locally elected community councils which would handle local issues affecting parks, police, schools, and other city services, and
2. Abolition of the school committee with a school commissioner selected by the mayor as a department head.

The proposals were held from the voters while Mayor Kevin White ran first for governor, unsuccessfully, and then for re-election as mayor. Meanwhile, a separate study team headed by this author suggested a nine-man school committee, three elected at large and six from separate geographical districts.[24] Although this proposal won tentative approval from the mayor and city council, the state legislature did not approve its placement on the 1971 ballot. The proposal was a popular campaign issue and advocates won several seats on both the city council and school committee.

A public opinion survey of 400 elementary school parents, however, revealed divided feelings, one quarter favoring the five-man elective board, one-quarter favoring an appointive board, one-quarter favoring a larger board with some district representatives, and the remainder undecided.[25] No clear consensus

emerged except the notion that a minority favored the status quo
and a slight majority the elective board concept.

Cleveland

During the 1930's and 1940's, prominent citizens in Cleveland were drafted to run for the school board as a result of popular indignation over the behavior of members elected in the early
and mid 1930's. The Citizens League endorsed candidates and
exerted considerable influence for several decades.[26]

The National Education Association Commission on Professional Rights and Responsibilities investigated the activities of
the Cleveland board of education, and in June 1964 it reported
that the dominant political party had endorsed candidates for
the non-partisan school board positions.[27]

Rather than counsel the citizens to reject consideration of
political party endorsements, the N.E.A. simply urged the development of "a means for securing qualified candidates for the
Board of Education who will place the welfare of the schools
above their personal and political ambitions," a somewhat vague
injunction. One concrete result of the N.E.A. recommendations
was that the Cleveland board promised the incoming superintendent, Paul Briggs of Parma, Ohio, that he would be made the
chief executive and thus end the triple-executive arrangement.

Cleveland area citizens tried to recruit a more progressive,
less partisan type of board member. Three leaders of the PACE
association, a school improvement league with some metropolitan support, ran for and won election to the board in the mid
1960's. The superintendent, Paul Briggs, actively cultivated the
assistance of business leaders and the black community, whose
support he won in part by promoting several dozen black professionals to administrative positions. Subsequently he worked
closely with the white ethnic groups as well. The concepts of
community control and decentralization attracted little support
in Cleveland, but neither did Briggs encourage any major plan
to achieve racial integration in a city which has known considerable tension between races and nationalities.

Detroit

Board elections in Detroit often draw only a few candidates.
Campaigns in the 1950's were relatively quiet, inexpensively

financed, and not associated with the city or county political activities. Although the ballot is non-partisan, the 1964 election was won by three candidates who were endorsed by the Democratic party and by the labor unions (A.F. of L. and U.A.W.). During the 1960's unions and party officials responded to the charge that the board of seven whites and one black member failed to represent a school system with a predominantly black population. Gittell and Hollander report the existence of a coalition of labor and teacher unions, Jewish community leaders, and some civil rights groups in a save-our-schools group which also endorses candidates.[28] By 1970, three black members served on the board.

The Detroit decentralization statutes discussed in the preceding chapter were very much a compromise between more militant community control proposals and the modest administrative steps already taken. The 1969 regional district plan provided for the election of from seven to eleven members, one from each region, in addition to the seven at-large members. Each region would elect its own nine-member board for four-year terms. Each board could then hire a superintendent and all other employees and then determine the budget and curriculum. The Detroit teachers acquiesced since the statute protected tenure, seniority, and transfer rights between districts, and specifically made contract negotiations a function of the central board.[29] Then in 1970 a revised statute set the number of districts at eleven. The second set of changes was very much a show of concern against racial integration and in support of using the schools to reinforce community and white ethnic identity. One school official was heard to say "the song is 'community control' and the tune is 'Dixie.'"[30]

Houston

The Houston school board elections, since at least the end of World War II, have revolved around contests between "liberals" and "conservatives," the latter group being characterized by a concern about subversive textbooks, progressive education, and school integration. The dismissal of a deputy superintendent in 1954 on the basis of alleged "Communist leanings" brought the N.E.A. "Defense Commission" into Houston.

The commission then found the teacher associations weak

and uncoordinated, the business manager more powerful than the superintendent, and the board of education meetings marked by bitter statements, charges and countercharges.[31]

Since that time the business manager has retired and his position, after a series of see-saw changes, was made subordinate to that of the superintendent (since 1959). The conservative-liberal cleavage remains, however, and integration and the acceptance of federal aid are two issues on which board members have been unable to gain a consensus.

Conservatives won a victory in persuading the legislature to change the time of school board elections to odd-numbered years, which usually reduces voter turnout and may enable older and more prosperous voters to win more elections. Again, opposition to racial integration will remain an important background issue in Houston.

Los Angeles

Vincent A. Ostrom's study of the Los Angeles board of education politics of the 1930's and 1940's concluded that non-partisan elections had not freed Los Angeles from the "usual ills of partisan politics and patronage in the school system." During the 1930's, when a shadowy group nicknamed the Four Horsemen won control of the board, nepotism and dismissals of employees became the order of the day.[32]

Ostrom reported that phantom organizations were created to back slates of candidates for each election, with politically astute campaign managers assigned to the tasks of raising money and securing a list of prominent names for letterheads and campaign posters.

More recently Ostrom concluded that a "relatively small group of economically and politically influential persons, representing a highly specialized segment of the community," have functioned in Los Angeles school elections as a political machine with great effectiveness. This group has been successfully challenged by sporadic reform groups on only three occasions in four decades.[33]

During the 1960's, a very liberal board majority worked hard to respond to the needs of minority groups. Both black and Mexican–American members won election. The Yorty–Bradley mayoralty election in 1969 created a conservative backlash on the board of education, defeating two liberal candidates. The California legislature has currently under consideration several decentralization plans which would affect Los Angeles.

Milwaukee

The Milwaukee school board elections have been subject to little criticism, for the citizens of that city appear to be reasonably satisfied with the elective process.

One observer found that "endorsement by labor seems to be of inestimable value to a candidate." [34] He was told that the names of union-endorsed candidates are printed on cards distributed by shop stewards at Milwaukee factories and that a great number of votes are decided that way. Even so, candidates campaign very actively and "no caucus or inside group is able to control the selection process."

St. Louis

During the 1940's and early 1950's, the Democratic party in St. Louis recruited candidates to run for seats on the school board of that city. Daniel L. Schlafly, elected first in 1953 as an independent candidate, formed a group called the Citizens for Action on the Public Schools (CAPS) which has endorsed candidates for the school board since the late 1950's. A grand jury in 1961 exposed a number of school board member indiscretions which enabled CAPS-endorsed candidates to gain control of the board.[35]

The CAPS group allows citizens to evaluate publicly individuals who want to run for the school board. Leaders of the P.T.A.'s, Chamber of Commerce, and League of Women Voters participate in the work of this organization. Schlafly, however, leans toward board member appointment by the mayor, with both a nominating panel beforehand and ratification by the voters afterward. He reports great difficulty in persuading qualified men and women to run because they "don't want to get involved in the campaigning." [36] He complains, "We've taken some second-rate people because of this" although his persistence has been rewarded by success at the polls. Actually, reform mayor Raymond Tucker appointed two civic-minded members in the early 1960's and several subsequent elections were uncontested, creating therefore the equivalent of an appointive board.[37]

Election campaigns in St. Louis require 6,000 voter signatures on nomination papers and approximately $30,000 to win.[38] Although Crain cites the board as very responsive to pressures for integration, Gittell labels the board as conservative fiscally and educationally with limited community participation.

Schlafly's support in part comes from Civic Progress, an elite business group. Although several black members have won election, Gittell found civil rights groups in St. Louis comparatively weak. Of course, her yardstick is New York City. Despite the success of the Schlafly board at removing the schools from partisan patronage politics, Gittell and Hollander report "some feeling, apparently justified, that the board is far too insulated from its public. . . ." with a consequent loss in support for expenditures and innovation.[39]

Again, what the St. Louis reform efforts reveal is a successful attempt by an elite coalition—businessmen, city-wide parent groups, and well-educated women—to take the schools away from party politicians. Aided by a reform mayor, the well-to-do civic leaders managed to avoid some of the rigors of electoral campaigning by appointing several of the Schlafly type elites to fill vacancies. Such a process is at least one full step away from community control but represents the St. Louis citizens' negative response to school construction scandals a decade ago.

Thus, the major cities vary widely in their degree of satisfaction with the current types of boards. Most of the cities have not adopted anything like the amount of decentralization found in New York City and Detroit, although other city boards voluntarily have allowed greater citizen participation.

The next question is whether or not it makes any difference how a big-city school board is selected.

BIG-CITY SCHOOL BOARDS: SELECTION AND PERFORMANCE

The Appointive Boards

Three of the boards adopted the nominating panel as a device to prevent the mayor from selecting his political cronies, as have some mayors in Buffalo. Meanwhile, the Baltimore mayor appears to use a variant of the panel approach in his appoint-

ments, especially in reserving seats for higher education representatives and for minority representation. But Buffalo explicitly rejected the nominating panel device, as did Boston, and
Pittsburgh continued to rely on the judges as a selection panel.
Does the selection panel make a difference? Gittell and Hollander voice skepticism: "The panel selection device in Philadelphia, New York and Chicago has made little difference in the
composition of the board as compared to other cities or as compared to memberships on earlier boards in their own cities." [40]
But the panels serve two additional functions: one, the subsequent evaluation of board member decisions, and then the asser-
tion of public confidence in the board, at least up to a point.

The installation of each school board selection panel
marked a clean break with the past and with patronage politics
in particular. In each instance the boards selected by such a
panel next sought a successful reform superintendent from outside the system. In the case of Chicago, this recruitment decision
has been made three times in a row. Of course, in the case of
New York City, the essence of the plan was jettisoned in 1969 in
the frantic search for a compromise in the traumatic struggle to
find an acceptable decentralization proposal. It is not at all clear
that the new arrangement can last in New York City, but it is
worth noting that the borough-selected members also agreed to
select a non-New Yorker as superintendent, a decision made so
rarely since 1900 yet one which suggests recognition of the need
for a new approach to city school decisions.

One fascinating characteristic of the appointive boards is the
tendency to develop "seats" for special interests, especially organized labor, the three major religions, blacks, and nearby universities. The nominating commissions often reflect these interests in
their own membership and mayors seem especially sensitive to
the need to grant various interests groups a seat on the board.
Usually, at least one woman also serves on a city school board.
This phenomenon disturbs those who feel that religion, race, and
sex are irrelevant to quality education. What difference does it
make? Lowi, who studied the ethnicity and social class of New
York City mayoralty appointees of this century, advances the idea
that appointments reflect a certain recognition of the political
importance of minority groups. Italian, Jews, Negroes, and other
minorities by their appointment received acknowledgement of

the legitimacy of their claims for political representation.[41] Their membership also made possible the diminution of distrust and resolution of conflict that characterizes the multi-racial and heavily ethnic cities e.g., conflict involving questions about the balance of personnel appointments, electives in the curriculum, the number and location of new schools, the observance of holidays, and handling of sensitive charges such as classroom bigotry in any form.[42]

Some evidence of superior performance by appointive school boards exists, but not much. Crain discovered that in eight large cities the method of selecting school board members was a major factor in distinguishing their response to school integration demands. When members of a civic elite (a loosely organized class, not necessarily a power structure) communicate their support, appointed board members tend to commit the school system to the idea of school integration.[43]

Crain also reports that the superintendents in those cities played a much less influential role than commonly assumed. But in Chicago, San Francisco, and Baltimore, the next superintendent hired in each instance held strong pro-integration views, developing further the broad commitment to integration. Superintendents hired in the 1950's were, as Crain reports, usually "color blind" and did not consider the integration of schools, especially in the North, an educational leadership function until 1964, when the Congress and some states gave a clear mandate for positive action.

Another index of appointive board performance is the finding that in large school districts, appointive boards were more successful than elective boards in passing bond issues voted on by the public.[44] But H. T. James and associates did not find appointive boards more successful than elective boards at raising revenue for school systems once various socio-economic measures such as city fiscal ability and demand for education were statistically controlled.[45]

The finding reported in a previous chapter that appointive boards since 1920 more often select outsiders than insiders as superintendents must be regarded with some caution. It is not always true that outsiders have more successfully innovated than the insiders; in fact, in several cases the outsiders failed all too visibly to satisfy the board or, more often, civil rights leaders seeking significant changes. We need to know more about the current successes of outsider-superintendents in the largest cities and the effect of their work on the school system and pupils generally.

The Elective Boards

Several large cities have been remarkably successful in making elective city school boards function in such fashion as to secure favorable reactions from observers. The St. Louis and Detroit school boards in the 1960's managed a school system relatively free from patronage politics and comparatively responsive to minority-group needs. Three other cities—Cleveland, Los Angeles, and Milwaukee—have in several instances supported leadership recruited from outside the system and made efforts to develop the minority programs requested. Only Houston and Boston have fought racial reforms, largely because of fundamental reluctance to place a high priority on school integration and related problems of black minorities.

Elective boards in recent times have hired some superintendents as distinguished as those serving appointive boards—e.g., Samuel Brownell in Detroit, a former U.S. Commissioner of Education; Richard Gousha in Milwaukee, former Delaware Commissioner of Education; and Paul Briggs in Cleveland from Parma, Ohio, and Bay City, Michigan, where his forte for building new schools drew national attention. Later Los Angeles hired a former deputy U.S. Commissioner, J. Graham Sullivan, as a top-ranking administrator. So also have St. Louis and Boston recently pioneered approaches to compensatory education and reading that other states later imitated.

On the other hand, Detroit legislators brought about a substantial change in the board member selection process largely to represent smaller districts, which certainly suggests widespread dissatisfaction with the previous arrangement. Los Angeles is under similar pressure.

The key urban school reformer in St. Louis spoke openly of his preference for an appointive board, as have Boston newspapers, radio stations, and mayors in recent years. Nevertheless, the experience of St. Louis, Cleveland, and Detroit indicates that well-organized citizens reform groups can achieve some success at the polls, especially with assistance from either the civic elite or labor union and civil rights leaders.

What happens when civic elites or other reform groups relax their efforts? Political parties very quietly step in when non-partisan groups do not actively perform a school board member recruitment function. This trend was reported in Cleveland, Detroit, and St. Louis at various points. Parties support some of the individual candidates who have won elections in Boston. Partisanship applies equally to appointive boards—to Philadelphia during the years of Add Anderson's control and to at least some of the Buffalo and San Francisco appointments. In the case of elective boards, Charles Adrian has even suggested that in some non-partisan city elections only those candidates supported by a major political party organization have much chance of being elected.[46] This situation seems to apply to several of the cities, especially between periods of reform.

Who else will step into city-wide school board election contests? Martindale discusses the extreme specialization of interest groups in large urban centers and concludes that "the selection of city officials by popular vote becomes impractical under these conditions," at least without assistance from either "political bosses or good government groups." [47]

Usually, one of those two groups steps into the vacuum in cities with elective boards. Usually a good-government group triumphs only after the disclosure of undue, even scandalous, intervention by political parties or a class of politicians termed "benefactor," one who grants benefits in the form of jobs or contracts to those more interested in patronage than quality performance. Good-government groups then recruit either the elite members of a "guardian" class, those who will fight to restore public trust in the board and insist on professional standards, or spokesmen for the "clients," men and women who speak for the parents and for programs needed by children. Good-government groups and guardians often suffer from the politically fatal handicap of dullness and thus their support ebbs away, creating a new vacuum into which the "politico" can slip.

Perhaps elective school boards more truly reflect the voting populace of their cities. But as Crain found, elective boards in working-class cities—e.g., Buffalo and Boston—may be less recep-

tive to certain changes, especially in racial matters, than even
some border-state cities—e.g., Baltimore and St. Louis—with
very active civic elites on their boards. Ironically, some of the systems with appointive boards achieve a greater religious and racial balance than systems with an elective school board.

Whether a city school board is elective or appointive may
make a difference to state officials and legislators. Detroit and
Boston lost control over certain school finance or construction
matters because of unsatisfactory management many years ago.
The states simply did not trust elective boards in those two cases
to discharge responsibilities honestly and efficiently.

This raises a more fundamental question, that of the com-
parability of city political structures. Can the city school boards
of great cities be compared? Does the form of local government
also make a difference? Chicago, with a strong political machine
and mayor, cannot allow a very strong school board, despite a
selection panel to keep watch on the mayor's appointments. Philadelphia reform politics made that city and its school board
selection in the 1960's dramatically different from the turbulent
school situation in politically fragmented New York City. And
Houston and Los Angeles are still young cities, comparatively,
with trajectories of growth yet to level or plateau as have those of
the older cities.

Banfield warns of the important structural and cultural variations which cause great differences in the role of, and constraints placed on, mayors, city councils, and, by extension of this
logic, on school boards.[48] But school boards, despite variations,
respond to the challenge of providing educational services in remarkably similar ways. Unlike city councils, city school boards
have hired superintendents. Despite state and regional variations,
city school systems all offer a basic academic program of surpris-
ing similarity. Differences in bureau titles only partially obscure
tremendous similarities in testing programs, special services, and
the internal organization of the school system.

Only New York seems to be unique, not only in size but as a
city in conflict, a port of entry for waves of immigrants "sometimes met at the waterfront by native-born New Yorkers savagely
determined to keep their own jobs." James Morris calls New
York City "This forcing house of humanity" where one finds "the
tensions of race synonymous here, or nearly so, with the tensions

of poverty and of envy." That Welsh observer likes Lord Bryce's description, "A European city, but of no particular country and never Americanized." [49]

But is New York unique, or simply larger and noisier? My visits to Buffalo and Los Angeles, my living near San Francisco and Boston, my research in Cleveland and Pittsburgh suggest that ethnic enclaves are found and fiercely defended not only in New York City but in all but the newer and most homogenized of great cities. Tensions mount when one insists on the mixing of ethnic groups until that point at which their members feel secure in achieving some new identity as Americans. So the uniqueness of a city is not in its people, but in the governmental arrangements that provide for the managing of conflict and allocating of resources sought by competing groups.

The other major question is whether any structural arrangement can guarantee that government will perform in the way intended. Lincoln Steffens pondered this problem more than sixty years ago until a "new and startling theory" occurred to him, "that the form of government did not matter; that constitutions and charters did not affect essentially the actual government." [50]

Steffens was trying to understand why cities did not stay cleaned up once reformers had abolished a branch of a bicameral city council or strengthened the role of the mayor. No system is fail-safe. T.S. Eliot expressed it elegantly when he observed that humans "try to design governments so perfect that men no longer need to be good." A structure of government simply allows conflicts to be resolved and for values to be expressed in the allocation of resources. It provides for authorizing programs, but others must assess the extent to which the programs actually achieve or fall short of perfection.

METROPOLITAN PROPOSALS FOR CHANGE

Those who despair of urban school boards managing to revitalize urban education search for other ways to govern the system. Since so many of the middle-class and better-educated citizens have left the cities for its suburbs, they say a "metropolitan system" must be devised to rescue city school systems. Peter Schrag finds the case for a metropolitan school district for Boston persuasive, as did the Boston Finance Commission, a watchdog agency which in 1966 proposed a metropolitan district to correct both racial and fiscal imbalance and to offer new educational choices to youth in all the communities.[51] Bendiner not only endorses the Metro system, with some decentralization as in Toronto, but predicts that citizens accepting the idea "will possibly have saved the city—and the suburbs and country with it." [52] He finds the concept of federation more attractive than that of the metropolitan district plan adopted in Nashville, Tennessee. Federation advantages would include proper financing, a chance for racial integration, and more protection from extreme local pressures such as those of the John Birch Society or various vigilante groups.

Others have suggested large educational parks or school complexes for some of the same purposes, especially for racial integration and choice, but the metropolitan school district or federation idea holds considerable appeal, at least to journalists who have looked at the cities closely.

Advocates of metropolitanism must confront at least two phenomena:

1. The persistent opposition of suburban and satellite city voters to merger, and
2. The emergence of equally valid conceptualizations of region and megalopolis.

On the first point, Robert C. Wood explains why Americans left the city once technology made it possible:

No longer did Americans have to tolerate the crowded neighborhoods of the city, its impersonality, anonymity, restlessness, nor endure the suspicion and misunderstanding which class conflicts provoked. No longer were they forced either to accept the corruption and arrogance of machine politicians or to join reformers to wage an uphill battle for the redemption of the city.[53]

That explains why city annexation of outlying land was so popular well into the twentieth century but petered out by 1945.

The next gambit was the "multi-purpose district" or "metropolitan county." Hundreds of studies offered variations on a theme of federation. The Toronto example, which consolidated a city with six suburban borough school districts in 1952, was exceptional in that so few other metropolitan areas followed the example. Suburban voters defeated hundreds of plans, fearing what

Wood calls "not compromise but seduction." [54] Only those solutions which did not look like super-governments seemed to pass the test: special authorities, public corporations, and special commissions or "pseudo-governments."

Wood concludes that, however unfortunate, metropolitan reorganization lacks both popular or partisan support and disturbs rather than persuades the voters. Only planners, professors, some executives, and editorial writers carry the "banner of reform." Wood predicts "that genuine metropolitan reform is not a likely prospect in our metropolitan areas for some time to come." [55]

Other social scientists who surveyed metropolitan area voters report widespread opposition to single metropolitan districts, especially on the part of suburban residents in the larger metropolitan areas such as around Buffalo, Milwaukee, and Dayton, Ohio. Zimmer and Hawley contend that despite the fact that residents acknowledge possible increases in efficiency and economy in multiple school districts, a significant majority prefers segmented local government. [56]

Zimmer and Hawley found central city residents more favorably disposed, but this phenomenon may fade as black voters elect black mayors and school board members. Enthusiasm for metropolitan government will wane if one of the consequences is a loss of minority-group jobs or participation in curriculum and personnel decisions.

The other major phenomenon is the emergence of areal conceptions of governance beyond that of the metropolitan area. The geographer Gottman coined the term "megalopolis" to describe the extended chain of communities that runs from Boston through Providence to New York, Philadelphia, Baltimore, and Washington. [57] Herman Kahn, the futurist, points out that the year 2000 will witness at least three of these elongated multimetropolities:

· Bos–Wash (Boston to Washington), or
· Port–Port (Portland to Portsmouth, Virginia)
· Chi–Pitts (Chicago to Pittsburgh)
· San–San (San Diego to San Francisco)

Since people travel up, down, and across these corridors, simple metropolitan structures will not solve the problem of combining communities with natural interests. Furthermore, the suburbs of St. Louis and Boston now include communities in two or three states. The satellite communities of Milwaukee and Chicago or Baltimore and Washington, D.C. actually overlap. Those who watch these trends advocate an even more comprehensive regional approach to the design of solutions to economic and manpower questions which vitally affect education.[58] Thus, it makes sense not to rest with metropolitan solutions (except, perhaps for immediate programs of school integration or pooling of facilities for students with unusual problems or talents). A regional, usually multi-state, approach to educational planning and financing may be worth the kind of effort formerly devoted to futile efforts at arranging metropolitan community weddings.

Then, there remain the states. States are not only imperfect vessels for reform (critics point to the inequality of educational facilities and financing currently within each state), but in many instances are either too big or too small. Had the Pilgrims and Puritans come from China and worked their way east, California now might be two or more states and all of New England one. But given existing inequities, it must be recognized that states already possess adequate legal powers to provide educational services and financing. Many of these powers, except in the state of Hawaii, have only been delegated to local communities or districts. Presumably such devices as lawsuits to protest unequal expenditures, as in Michigan, California, and elsewhere, could provoke greater gubernatorial concern over educational programs and finance. James B. Conant and former U.S. Commissioner James Allen both proposed full state financing of public education, liberating schools from the less equitable and unevenly collected local property tax.

States can serve as instruments of educational reform, as under Governor Terry Sanford in North Carolina, Edmund G. "Pat" Brown in California, and in New York State during the first terms of Nelson Rockefeller. As Theodore J. Lowi argues:

Now that cities have proven that they cannot cope with urban problems, even with Federal help, we have, in any case, no other place but the States to turn to. But relying on the State need not be thought of as an act of desperation. As already argued, the State possesses all the powers of its cities plus the advantage of containing most of the metropolitan realities that are beyond the reach of cities.[59]

Furthermore, the two major political parties agree on the need to share federal tax revenues with the fifty states, largely disagreeing on only questions of "how much" and "how soon." [60]

CHOICES FOR CHILDREN
AND THEIR PARENTS

Critics on both the left and right of the political spectrum despair of winning sufficient reform in the large-city systems, which they label hopelessly bureaucratic and rigid. The public school monopoly can be broken, they say, by a simple form of trust-busting—just by giving tuition vouchers to parents to cash in at the school of their choice. Thus schools would compete for their clientele and would either satisfy or sink financially.

Conservatives, notably Milton Friedman, urge tuition vouchers as an extension of the free market remedy to the sluggishness of quasi-socialist systems of rendering services, as in the case of state school systems.[61] Liberals view such tuition plans as guarantees of options for the poor and for victims of an oppressive white majority. For example, Theodore Sizer and Phillip Whitten advocate a "poor children's bill or rights" that would give families of low income additional amounts to make up for the education limitations of the home environments.[62]

Civil rights leaders voice some skepticism of this approach, pointing out that they have long fought "freedom of choice" plans in the South and that only racial separatists want all-black or all-white schools. It can also be charged that tuition vouchers might perpeutate the elitist academies as well as the more archaic parochial schools, both of which enjoy a considerable vogue. But the advocates see only the very optimistic side—the new schools that corporations or universities or ghetto entrepreneurs would start or the innovative learning centers that parents could reward with their vouchers. Paul Goodman and others strongly advocate a return to very small schools where children can discover their interests and work closely with the teaching staff.[63] Christopher Jencks not only acknowledges the parallel with parochial schools, but suggests that black parents at this point in time may need and want the same type of option enjoyed by Catholics in many cities for decades.[64]

The traditional charge of divisiveness may not fit the alternative schools which, under state supervision, would adhere to certain minimum standards of content and quality. Furthermore, the Greeley-Rossi study of Catholic schools found the graduates at least as well prepared for American citizenship as their public school counterparts. And either a bonus would be offered those schools with an integrated student body, or schools with a surplus of applicants would select one-half of their entrants randomly. Still, whether a U.S. plan could avoid the tension generated by alternative or competitive systems in Holland or parts of Canada remains a question.

Voucher plans may on a small scale be tested in western states, just as the Nixon family assistance plan was tried in New Jersey prior to presidential advocacy of the idea. Unquestionably, many thousands of parents would seize the opportunity. Boston parents from 1966 to 1969 created three new community schools as alternatives to the public schools which, in their opinion, would not offer the kind of quality education they sought for their children. Since money from the state even now is apportioned on a per-pupil basis, some city school systems might be stimulated to innovate and diversify further the kinds of instructional program. A successful response on the part of the existing system would, of course, keep city school systems (and boards) in business. After all, such systems would enjoy from the outset buildings, equipment, and not only the economics of scale but also a cadre of specialists in many fields with vested interests (tenure, seniority, friendship, and even past successes) in working in the big-city school systems.[65]

THE CASE AGAINST THE PROFESSIONAL

Radical critics of American social systems condemn the professionals who protect their career by serving only those who have power and resources:

- lawyers who defend the corporations and the wealthy, even as they pollute the environment;
- doctors who cater to the needs of suburbia and leave the medical problems of the ghettos unattended;
- educators who try to impose middle-class values and standards on the poor and instill feelings of guilt and insecurity in those who do not conform.

Criticism of teachers and principals can take more extreme forms, criticism of incompetence, condescension, colonialism, exploitation, and suppression, worst of all of "failure." The response of educators, as of all humans in a bureaucracy, is to respond defensively and hold on to present advantages. Anthony Downs discovers in bureaucracies generally a 'Law of Increasing Conservatism" wherein "there is an inherent pressure upon the vast majority of officials to become conservers in the long run." He explains that "as an official acquires more and more power, income, prestige and influence over policy, the probability rises that changes in the status quo will reduce his stock of these 'goods' instead of increasing it." [66] Thus he fights to save what he has won.

Peter Drucker, an economist and critic of modern government, worries about the loss of manageability.

There is no government today that can still claim control of its bureaucracy and of its various agencies. Government agencies are all becoming autonomous, ends in themselves, and directed by their own desire for power, their own rationale, their own narrow vision.[67]

Drucker also comments brilliantly on the disintegration of cities following massive immigrations:

No city in history has ever been able to absorb an influx of such magnitude as the American cities have had to absorb since the end of World War II. Whereas it happened in the past, there was the same collapse of family, community and local government—in the cities of England in the late eighteenth century when the Irish came in; in the cities of North America around 1840, again . . . the Irish; in Europe . . . the Czechs . . . into the Vienna of the Hapsburgs. The influx of almost two million rural Negroes and Puerto Ricans into New York City alone in less than a fifteen year period exceeded any of these earlier migrations. It is unprecedented in the history of cities.[68]

He then discusses whether decentralization of government or "reprivitization," letting business actually manage an activity, would—as in the World Bank or COMSAT—better perform the needed tasks. This argument for urban education would suggest financing "alternative schools" run by community development corporations or private agencies.

What does this mean for the professional educator? While it offers new careers for the very young and for minority educators, it threatens the man who has climbed near the top of a city school system bureaucracy. It explains the severe anxiety and defensiveness felt by educators, especially in New York City, when blacks and white liberals sought to change a system which did not respond sufficiently to the needs of poor newcomers for basic literacy and employable skills.

Gittell suggests that the earlier reform of city school systems was too successful:

The enormous emphasis on professionalism has greatly undermined the role of the lay citizenry in the policy process. A major element in the alienation of large segments of the city population is the great reliance on professionals that is integral to the reform ethos. This is not to suggest that reform in the 1970's will include an absolute rejection of professionalism but rather to hope its role will be tempered.[69]

Gittell wants professionals to relinquish control to communities and warns that administrative reforms may offer only temporary relief if the public feels excluded.

Kenneth Clark takes the position that programs of social change require a "coalition of professionals and the poor" since "the poor themselves have so far not been able to plan, sustain, and bring to a positive conclusion effective programs for social change." He calls for "concerned, committed and independent professionals to develop machinery and organization which would mobilize the power of intelligence and concern on behalf of the poor," training the latter to confront public officials realistically and serving the poor as they would serve themselves.[70]

Professionals will continue to play a major role, whether in "reprivitization" or "decentralization." But, as Downs suggests, the sharing of power will be quite painful for a generation of professionals selected by the rating systems assembled by boards of examiners. The history of bureaucracies, and of the examiner system in New York City, demonstrates the great difficulty in persuading "mandarins" in any nation to relinquish power or open the gates to those who have not learned an intricate code of rules and procedures. All the debate about decentralization, control, and accountability suggests that once again the cities need to respond to the very immediate needs of the newcomers and allow them access to decisions themselves.

Can the big-city school superintendent help to make the system respond? Some outsiders can, but rarely will an insider escape the entrapment of a life-long career in a school bureaucracy. There are exceptions, Manch of Buffalo and Drachler of Detroit, where an insider identified with the minority group sufficiently to advocate their cause over a sustained period of time despite severe questioning and criticism from board members. No one ever said the city school superintendency was an easy role. Nor is it necessarily the best vantage point for asserting the aspirations of the poor of any race. Therefore, community boards or school councils may be indispensable features of city school systems.

If professionals within a large-scale bureaucracy cannot respond, then professionals in community-controlled schools or alternative schools will, at least if they can, offer some indication of greater success. Naturally they must insist on some safeguards to their professionalism and that of their co-workers, but the mechanism must allow for some new sources of professionals and aides. Federal policies and those of several of the great-city teacher unions reflect an awareness that new career patterns must allow for the recruitment and training of minority-group professionals as rapidly as possible. The federal effort includes the career opportunity program under the Educational Professionals Development Act. The city teacher unions most willing to recruit new professionals and trainees included Detroit, Washington, D.C., and New York City since the 1968 strike.

THE NEW URBAN POLITICS
OF EDUCATION: A SUMMARY

The old politics of education was played in an arena in which the ward bosses used the school system as a hiring hall for custodians and even for teachers and principals. Jobs and contracts were redistributed to the new immigrant masses. Disclosure of this phenomenon usually galvanized a coalition of the old elites, the businessmen and others of substance, into action. It was the function of journalists to discover and publicize the extent of the problem. It was the function of universities to assist in surveying the damage, occasionally providing a board member and more often to train a new breed of mobile professionals to give scandal-free executive leadership to the schools.

Reform movements made structural change one of the very high priorities in the last thirty years of the nineteenth century, especially in destroying the ward base of school-patronage politics. The size of central boards was sharply reduced so that good-government leaders could hold the seats once captured. Concurrently, the school superintendency as a full-time executive director of the professional staff was strengthened. But in many cities the business, custodial, and secretarial staffs remained under separate management—even into the 1960's. Boards finally centralized even the business functions after superintendency candidates in Chicago and Cleveland demanded that all staff must be coordinated by the superintendent's office.

Reform carries a price. Lowi's study of New York found that, "the reform principle of insulating the bureaucracies from the parties has become so strongly operative that it has created a separate political force in the community. The departmental bureaucracies are not neutral, they are only independent." [71]

The phenomenon of political independence not only from parties but from mayors and even from school boards creates the new politics of urban education. The new tension arises in part out of an aroused militancy on the part of teachers and other staff groups, a militancy displayed by Chicago teachers early in the century but muted during the depression and revived during the 1960's. The other source of tension is the civil rights movement and the struggle of blacks, Puerto Ricans, and Mexican–Americans to secure the educational programs and positions previously won by immigrant groups. Pressures for community control reflect the kind of knowledge once held by ward bosses that decentralized power is more manageable and more immediately utilized than city-wide power, whether over curriculum or jobs.

This time the journalists, many professionals, and university professors to a great extent support the community leaders in their efforts to regain some control over schoolmen. Even some of the traditional good-government reformers agree that professionals have become too aloof, too unresponsive, and that the remedy is machinery to make educators "accountable" for their effectiveness.

The new politics reflects a more general concern for democratization in large-scale organizations and a search for a meaningful kind of participation in a society which has lost the kind of intimacy and community that men need to feel accepted and effective. The more radical social welfare professionals recognize both the need for client control of services and the wall of impersonality erected by the independent professionals.

The fight against a bureaucratized profession has taken on many of the characteristics and drive of the civil rights movement. On the other hand, community control of schools in the late 1960's was by some black leaders given higher priority than the less attainable goal of school integration, which required the acquiescence of large groups of white citizens in cities and even in suburbs. Some intellectuals still hope that both integration and decentralization might be achieved, although the Detroit experience casts genuine doubt on that possibility.

Teacher unions opposed community control when they felt they could not moderate its effect, as in New York City, where teacher and supervisors feared the very worst in terms of loss of community acceptance, jobs, and even life. In Detroit and Washington, D.C. the teacher unions with substantial black membership and strong ties to the community saw less to fear in community control as long as they could protect teacher tenure and transfer rights. Other cities, with less minority strength, offered administrative decentralization to reduce the pressures for community control. The other response, not necessarily sufficient, was to expand minority-group representation on the board itself.

Robert Bendiner calls community control a "desperate throwback" to the provincialism of the preceding century. Desperate it is, for the advocates of community control despair of "the system" giving them the kind of services and access to resources needed to educate their children. Nor have the high walls of civil service and professional rating systems allowed their adults a chance to work in the schools; some of the walls tumble now that boards realize the kind of colonialism the protective examination systems spawn.

The decentralized and community control boards in fact do run a risk of patronage as newly arrived ethnic groups acquire the chance to handle funds and make personnel appointments. Some of the poverty program scandals of the late 1960's indicate that this is a hidden cost of community participation, and a development usually offensive to those who already have arrived and to those elites to whom any corruption is unconscionable. Thus, one can predict a period of experimentation with community control followed by a series of scandals. The inevitable reform will very likely include "recentralization" of some personnel functions and adoption of tighter financial accounting procedures.

THE FUTURE OF CITY SCHOOL BOARDS

Will school boards exist in large cities in the year 2000? A now obscure writer on city management thirty years ago complained that students of school boards usually raised questions about the methods of selection, length of terms, pay, etc., and that, "Occasionally someone dares to question the advisability of their existence as presently constituted." He certainly dared, and in vivid terms:

In general, the urban school board is one of those instruments of torturous propensities which, beaming with an unbecoming and reflected wisdom, wanders in a twilight zone between civil grandeur and political connivance. Undoubtedly, some future public appraisal, beyond the board's discernment, will snuff it out.[72]

A better polemicist than prophet, perhaps, the author nevertheless articulates the tensions so visible in the chronicle of fourteen city school boards, the struggle between the high-minded and the job-minded. The former deny a politics of education and risk alienation of the new masses. The latter deny the purposes of education and risk alienation of the civil elites and their allies. But might boards disappear from sight entirely?

Myron Lieberman sees little use for school boards or for local control of schools which, he said in 1960, "should be limited to peripheral and ceremonial functions of education." To bring education into the mainstream of American life he urged a drive for a national policy parallel to those of industry, finance, labor relations, and communications. Local control he labeled a corpse, at least intellectually, and advised those who want to revolutionize education to direct their energy as follows:

. . . for short-run, relatively minor but more immediate improvements, concentrate upon local school board elections; for long-range major improvements, concentrate upon the State and National election of education-minded legislators and executives who have the power to shape the context and limits of local action.[73]

Educational decisions of the 1950's and 1960's confirm some of Lieberman's contentions. An education-minded governor like Terry Sanford of North Carolina did more for education in that state than could thousands of individual school board members. And the Congress, not school boards, took the necessary action in the 1960's to invest heavily in a new science and mathematics curriculum, to establish elementary school libraries for millions of children, to finance bilingual programs for the Spanish-speaking, and many other improvements. Federal authorities have not eliminated racial segregation nor eliminated the effects of poverty and malnutrition through the schools, but their leadership has in general been more inspiring than those of most city school boards. The latter tend to react more than to initiate reforms, with a few spectacular exceptions.

Another educational scholar looked at the new emphasis on states as a vehicle for federal revenues and for educational policy and predicted, "As a consequence, the local school board's importance will decline. By 1980, these may be mere ceremonial bodies—a vestigial remnant of past government, roughly equal to what the county superintendent's office is in some states." [74]

These epitaphs for local school boards cannot be ignored. Many decisions about education quite clearly will or already do involve other levels of government:

1. The states have long supervised teacher education and certification, thus guarding entrance into the teaching profession and, although the qualifications and mode of training will change, the states are unlikely to yield all power to the communities at any point.
2. The most rapidly growing taxes are those levied by the federal government, especially the several income taxes. The pressures on local and state tax bases are so great that the sharing of revenues will very likely increase through the 1970's but with the state as the immediate recipient and distributor to constituent agencies including school systems.
3. The inevitable path to racial integration is that of metropolitanism, although more frequently a voluntary and heavily subsidized federation than one achieved through a popular groundswell of voter enthusiasm. In other words, suburban school districts will not in large numbers surrender their alleged autonomy but might accept grants, as do several dozen communities in the Boston, Hartford, and Rochester areas, to participate in programs to reduce racial imbalance in the central cities.
4. Teacher organizations will want to negotiate "where the

money is," and increasingly that will be at the state level, similar to Canadian provinces and most of the European nations, indeed the world. Not only money but considerations of negotiating time and educational equity will force the negotiation of state-wide contracts with appropriate differentials for teaching certain specialty subjects or in difficult or remote areas.

At the same time, the pressure for adequate performance measures and teacher "accountability" will increase. So difficult is the task of measuring the accomplishment of objectives and evaluating the cost benefit ratios of alternative proposals that few local boards—certainly very few community school boards—will solve the productivity problem in any real economic sense. This requires massive research on the scale of the Coleman Report or medical research on cancer or heart disease (the educational malady has often been termed "academic retardation," which even sounds quasi-medical.)

But outraged central-city parents will not accept exhortations patiently to support more research and development of measures. They want redress of grievances now, especially those who feel their children are treated in a patronizing fashion. Where these parents are numerous, the insulation of teachers from the community will not last. Nor can a city school board continue to legislate a uniform curriculum and standard formulae of staff assistance to cope with the diversity of the city. Not even the supposedly docile European immigrant groups accepted such a regimen.

1. The most frustrated and alienated parents will enthusiastically support any of the several tuition voucher plans. Vouchers will incidentally keep alive a number of private and church-related schools which otherwise may close. The so-called competition, ironically, may force these schools to change curriculum, guidance, or personnel practices much more than the public schools for which "alternative schools" have never posed much of a threat; public schools are usually content to lose their most vocal critics.

2. If a voucher plan is accepted, it will siphon off much of the pressure behind community control and decentraliza-

tion. The most vigorous critics will not accept administrative decentralization anyway, settling for nothing less than control over funds, facilities, firings, and other prerogatives that neither the board nor teacher groups will yield. Thus, the community control movement will churn on either until the city school board responds more flexibly (e.g., by allowing curriculum experimentation; hiring of black personnel in larger numbers, etc.) or until the alternative schools receive either direct state aid or tuition vouchers.

Only at their peril will city school boards deny the diversity of their city, the ethnic and racial groups and their children. What local boards can do best is to reconsider many of their policies and establish quasi-judicial procedures to protect the rights of pupils, teachers, principals, and parents in any age of high conflict between parties.

States can improve the lost of urban education by taking these steps:

1. The financing of urban education at the state level at which level teacher salaries would be set and additional funds allocated for special urban education programs.
2. The adoption of regional (metropolitan, multi-county, or multi-community) planning and administration of certain services, especially occupational education, special education, television instruction, teacher re-training, and system evaluation, and of programs to overcome racial imbalance in schools.
3. The requirement that city-wide boards work closely with other municipal and social service agencies and that school departments serve adults as well as children. They would become "human resource development" agencies in the sense that the mission would be not simply to educate children ages 6–16, but to provide continuing education for all ages in coordination with public health, manpower, cultural, and recreational agencies.
4. The provision for parent participation and parent–teacher–student discussions at the level of each school as well as in clusters of schools in a natural community or section of a city. Such participation shall in-

clude the right to review the budget, staffing patterns, new programs and personnel, and to request additional resources of central or state authorities. Local school councils or boards would be selected not in general elections but in elections of parents, of the faculty, and at the secondary level of the students.

5. The appointment of a school ombudsman to investigate complaints about unsatisfactory school administration, ineffective or inappropriate education, and other problems identified by councils or individuals and not resolved through the usual channels. An alternative would be the creation of community dispute settlement boards or panels to hear complaints and pronounce remedies.

6. The improvement of urban teacher and administrator training programs, including insistence on periodic retraining in the problems of the poor or of new ethnic or racial groups as they appear.

7. The mandating of appropriate evaluation and management tools to make the schools accountable not only financially but educationally through the presentation of factual information on which skills, facts, and values have been learned by individuals in a school.

Should boards be appointive or elective? It does not appear to make much difference except in the willingness to hire outside superintendents. Whether appointive or elective it seems sensible to provide for some at-large and some sectional or district members to provide representation to each section of the city.

Bendiner correctly observes that city school boards cannot by themselves cope with the conflict overload now assigned to them. But he and others cannot simplify the issues by saying "metropolitanism" is the answer nor is "community control" by itself satisfactory. Conflicts should be resolved at the level at which resources are available to settle disputes. Thus, most money matters will come to be decided at the federal, state, and regional levels. On the other hand, citizens ought to be able to present budget requests, review the criteria for selecting a new principal, and evaluate the program and operations of the school at the local level. Local boards may indeed wither away in time, but popular sentiment will demand continued involvement of laymen at all levels in the discussion of programs which shape the lives of children.

Boards for a century have borne the brunt of criticism, from the humorist Mark Twain, furious at the banning of *Huckleberry Finn* from New York City schools, to the most recent spokesmen for a forgotten minority.[75] The marvel is that boards enjoyed such remarkable stability even through turbulent times, and that the potential influence of school superintendents continued to rise. City school systems can, in fact, survive, but only by granting to pupils, parents, and professionals new ways to participate in policy decisions which most immediately concern their destinies.

NOTES

1. The bibliography of urban school protest starts with Nat Hentoff, *Our Children Are Dying* (New York: Viking, 1966), and Jonathan Kozol, *Death at an Early Age* (Boston: Houghton Mifflin, 1967), and includes Herbert Kohl's *36 Children* (New York: New American Library, 1967), and the books of John Holt, Paul Goodman, and Patricia Sexton. It culminated in Charles Silberman's *Crisis in the Classroom* (New York: Random House, 1970), which transmitted much of the same criticism to a broader audience.

2. Zwerdling's statement at the July 1, 1969, annual meeting of the Detroit board embraced the need for "solid and total reform." He reminded the citizenry, "I am an advocate of increased community control" but asked that the Kerner Report warnings of two societies be heeded through legislation linking Martin Luther King High School and the Grosse Point school district.

3. See Raphael O. Nystrand and Luvern L. Cunningham, "Federated Urban School Systems Comprising the Centralization-Decentralization Issue" in Frank W. Lutz (ed.), *Toward Improved Urban Education* (Worthington, Ohio: Charles A. Jones, 1970).

4. New York City teachers in 1961 were the first to win the right to exclusive representation for collective bargaining purposes. The integration and community control controversies were hot very early in New York City. Many of the major civil rights tactics, of course, were pioneered in the South. Exceptions are numerous: Chicago had a union quite early in the century and Buffalo a severe teacher strike in 1947. But in the 1960's the shock waves from New York City tended to ripple out to engulf other cities as well.

5. Vernon S. Vavrina, "The History of Public Education in the City of Baltimore, 1829–1956," unpublished Ph.D. dissertation (Washington, D.C.: The Catholic University of America, 1958).

6. Robert L. Crain *et al.*, *The Politics of School Desegregation* (Chicago: Aldine, 1968), pp. 78–79. See also Marilyn Gittell and T. Edward Hollander, *Six Urban Schools* (New York: Praeger, 1968), pp. 179–180, and Robert Bendiner, *The Politics of Schools* (New York: Harper & Row, 1969), pp. 140–145 for discussions of the Baltimore board.

7. Bendiner, *op. cit.*, p. 145.

8. New York State Department of Education, *Buffalo Public Schools in the Mid-Twentieth Century, Report of a Survey of the Public Schools of the City of Buffalo* (Albany: The University of the State of New York, 1951), p. 379.

9. *Ibid.*, p. 373.

10. Descriptions of the Buffalo board can be found in Crain *et al.*, *op. cit.*, pp. 59–71, and Bendiner, *op. cit.*, pp. 147–154.

11. Crain *et al.*, *op. cit.*, pp. 59–71.

12. Bendiner, *op. cit.*, p. 150.

13. Joseph Pois, *The School Board Crisis: A Chicago Case Study* (Chicago: Educational Methods, 1964).

14. See James Q. Wilson, *The Amateur Democrat* (Chicago: The University of Chicago Press, 1962). Two major surveys of Chicago schools ignored the board structure and stressed school integration and various changes in programs and organizations; both were chaired by University of Chicago professors, one by Hauser and one by Havighurst.

15. Peter Binzen, "How to Pick a School Board," *Saturday Review*, vol. XLVIII, no. 16 (April 17, 1965), p. 73.

16. William R. Odell, *Educational Survey Report for the Philadelphia Board of Public Education* (Philadelphia: The Board of Education, February 1, 1965), p. 16.

17. *Ibid.*, p. 367.

18. *Report of the Select Commission to Study the Pittsburgh School Board.* (Pittsburgh: Chatham College, 1969).

19. Binzen, *op. cit.*, pp. 72–73.

20. Crain *et al.*, *op. cit.* pp. 81–94, especially 92–94.

21. Tom Wicker, "Melting Pot Astir," The New York *Times*, November 4, 1971, p. 47.

22. See editorials in the *Boston Globe*, November 24, 1944 and the *Boston Herald*, January 13, 1945.

23. Martin Meyerson and Edward C. Banfield, "What Price Public Schools?" One in a series of articles commissioned by the New England Merchants National Bank in the *Boston Globe*, week of January 18, 1963.

24. Joseph M. Cronin and Richard M. Hailer, *Organizing an Urban School System For Diversity* (Boston: The Massachusetts Advisory Council on Education, 1970).

25. *Ibid.*, p. 20.

26. Mark C. Schinnerer, interview with author, July 1964.

27. National Commission on Professional Rights and Responsibilities, *Cleveland Ohio: When a Board of Education Fails to Fulfill Its Responsibilities, Report of an Investigation* (Washington, D.C.: The National Education Association, June 1964), p. 24. When I visited Cleveland in July 1964, and talked informally with teacher union and teacher association representatives familiar with past campaigns, all agreed that endorsement by the Cleveland labor council and the Democratic party were powerful assets to a candidate in the 1960's.

28. Gittell and Hollander, *op. cit.*, pp. 151–152.

29. Act no. 244, Public Acts of 1969, State of Michigan.

30. William R. Grant, "Community Control vs. School Integration: The Case of Detroit," *The Public Interest,* no. 24 (Summer 1971), p. 79.

31. National Commission for the Defense of Democracy through Education, *Investigation Reports Abridgments* (Washington, D.C.: The National Education Association, 1960). See "Houston, Texas, December, 1954," including a chronology of events following the Houston investigation, pp. 48–59.

32. Vincent A. Ostrom, "School Board Politics: An Analysis of Non-Partisanship in the Los Angeles City Board of Education," unpublished Master's thesis, (Los Angeles: The University of California at Los Angeles, October 1945), p. 138.

33. Vincent A. Ostrom, "Education and Politics," *Social Forces Influencing American Education,* National Society for the Study of Education, Part II (Chicago: The University of Chicago Press, 1961), p. 35.

34. Donald J. McCarty, "Motives for Seeking School Board Membership," unpublished Ph.D. dissertation (Chicago: The University of Chicago, 1959), p. 78.

35. Binzen, *op. cit.*, pp. 83 and 84.

36. Binzen, *ibid.*, p. 84.

37. Crain *et al.*, *op. cit.*, pp. 14 and 191.

38. Marilyn Gittell, *Participants and Participation* (New York: Center for Urban Education, 1967), p. 158.

39. Gittell and Hollander, *op. cit.*, p. 164.

40. *Ibid.*, p. 89.

41. Theodore J. Lowi, *At the Pleasure of the Mayor* (New York: The Free Press, 1964).

42. The classic contemporary statement of residual ethnic identities in a major U.S. city is found in Nathan Glazer and Daniel P. Moynihan, *Beyond the Melting Pot* (Cambridge, Massachusetts: Harvard University Press and The M.I.T. Press, 1964).

43. .Crain *et al., op. cit.,* pp. 194 and 356–365.

44. Dwight H. Newell, "Relationships Between State Legal Provisions and School–Community Interest," Ed.D. dissertation (Stanford, California: Stanford University School of Education, 1961).

45. H. Thomas James, James A. Kelly, and Walter Garms, *Determinants of Educational Expenditures in Large Cities of the United States* (Stanford, California: Stanford University School of Education, 1966).

46. Charles R. Adrian, "A Typology for Nonpartisan Elections," *Western Political Quarterly,* vol. XII (June 1959), pp. 452 ff.

47. Don Martindale, "The Theory of the City," preface to Max Weber's *The City,* (New York: Collier Books, 1962), p. 22.

48. Edward Banfield, *Big City Politics: A Comparative Guide to the Political Systems of Nine American Cities* (New York: Random House, 1965), pp. 7–11.

49. James Morris, *The Great Port* (New York: Harcourt Brace Jovanovich, 1969), pp. 183, 206, 181.

50. Lincoln Steffens, *The Autobiography of Lincoln Steffens* (New York: Harcourt Brace Jovanovich, 1931), p. 403.

51. Peter Schrag, *Village School Downtown* (Boston: Beacon Press, 1967), pp. 147–153.

52. Bendiner, *op. cit.,* p. 226.

53. *Suburbia* (Boston: Houghton Mifflin, 1959), p. 65.

54. *Ibid.,* p. 82.

55. *Ibid.,* p. 300.

56. Basil G. Zimmer and Amos H. Hawley, *Metropolitan Area Schools: Resistance to District Reorganization* (Beverly Hills: Sage Publications, 1968).

57. Jean Gottman, *Megalopolis* (Cambridge, Massachusetts: The M.I.T. Press, 1961).

58. Gottman does not denounce "special districts" which he feels have coordinated certain special activities in a helpful way, but he points out that the megalopolis has really "muddled through" its difficulties. He sees in the future an evaluation toward "new, nebulous, and perhaps colloidal forms." *Ibid.,* pp. 758–761.

59. *The End of Liberalism* (New York: Norton, 1969), p. 306.

60. See the arguments of Murray Weidenbaum, Assistant Secretary of the Treasury for Economic Policy and Walter Heller, former economic advisor to John F. Kennedy, interviewed by J. M. Cronin in the November 1969 issues of the *Phi Delta Kappan,* vol. no. XXVI.

61. Milton Friedman, *Capitalism and Freedom* (Chicago: The University of Chicago Press, 1962), p. 92.

62. Theodore R. Sizer and Phillip Whitten, "A Poor Children's Bill of Rights," *Psychology Today,* vol 2, no. 3 (August 1968), pp. 59–63.

63. Paul Goodman, "Mini-Schools: A Prescription for the Reading Problem," *The New York Review of Books,* January 4, 1968.

64. Christopher S. Jencks, "Private Schools For Black Children," *New York Times Magazine,* November 3, 1968, p. 29.

65. For a response to these criticisms see Christopher S. Jencks and Judith Areen, "Education Vouchers: A Proposal for Diversity and Choice," *Teachers College Record,* vol. 72, no. 3 (February 1971).

66. Anthony Downs, *Inside Bureaucracy* (Boston: Little, Brown, 1967), p. 99.

67. Peter Drucker, *The Age of Discontinuity* (New York; Harper & Row, 1968), p. 220.

68. *Ibid.,* p. 227.

69. Maurice R. Berube and Marilyn Gittell, *Confrontation at Ocean Hill–Brownsville* (New York: Praeger, 1969), p. 331.

70. Kenneth B. Clark and Jeannette Hopkins, *A Relevant War Against Poverty* (New York: Harper & Row, 1968), p. 254.

71. Lowi, *op. cit.,* p. 207.

72. Henry G. Hodges, *City Management* (New York: F. S. Crofts, 1939), pp. 680–681.

73. Myron Lieberman, *The Future of Public Education,* (Chicago: The University of Chicago Press, 1960), p. 283.

74. Laurence Iannaccone, "The Future of State Politics of Education," Chapter IV in Frank W. Lutz and Joseph J. Azzarelli (eds.), *Struggle for Power in Education* (New York: The Center for Applied Research in Education, 1966), p. 65.

75. Twain placed in the mouth of Puddin'head Wilson the invective, "First God made idiots. That was for practice. Then he made school boards." He could not understand the reluctance of boards to authorize for classroom use his *Huckleberry Finn,* a volume in which a racial epithet appeared so often.

INDEX